GRANT IAN THRALL

LAND USE AND URBAN FORM

The consumption theory of land rent

Methuen
New York and London

First published in 1987 by
Methuen, Inc.
29 West 35th Street, New York NY 10001

Published in Great Britain by
Methuen & Co. Ltd
11 New Fetter Lane, London EC4P 4EE

Printed in Great Britain at the University Press, Cambridge

Library of Congress Cataloging in Publication Data

Thrall, Grant Ian.
  Land use and urban form.
  Bibliography: p.
  Includes index.
  1. Land use, Urban – Mathematical models.   2. Space in economics – Mathematical models.   3. Rent (Economic theory)   I. Title.
  HD108.4.T47   1987   333.77′13   87–1678

ISBN 0 416 35540 4

British Library Cataloguing in Publication Data

Thrall, Grant Ian
  Land use and urban form: the Consumption theory of land rent.
  1. Land use, Urban   2. Land
  I. Title
 ·333.77   HD111

ISBN 0 416 35540 4

To my parents

WILLIAM HERMAN THRALL
CAROLYN MAY BROWN THRALL

This book is a direct consequence of their decision to migrate in 1947 from Columbus, Ohio, to San Gabriel, California. I could not have had a better laboratory to learn the importance of urban space than post World War II Los Angeles.

Contents

List of figures

List of tables

Preface

Personal background to the book

This book presents a geometry of urban land rent and rationale for why cities acquire their particular spatial form. I call the method the Consumption Theory of Land Rent (CTLR).

I first started working on the foundations of the geometric method presented in this book while I was a graduate student at Ohio State University, and continued to work on it, off and on, for more than a decade. As a student I made what I then thought to be a minor move following completion of my MA degree from the Department of Economics and relocated across the corridor of Hagerty Hall to complete a Ph.D. from the Department of Geography. Indeed, it was my intrigue with space that drew me, and has kept me, within the discipline of geography. This is important to the reader, in that the CTLR analysis is differentiated from microeconomic consumer behavior theory by way of the geographers' emphasis upon space; the central theme of this book and the CTLR methodology is upon how certain things determine land use and affect the spatial form of the city.

Between 1975 and 1978 I presented a series of lectures on mathematical land rent theory in the Departments of Geography and Economics at McMaster University in Canada. At that time I presented the CTLR alongside the contemporary calculus-based mathematical land rent literature, first demonstrating the CTLR solution followed by the solution in calculus. I presented a course based exclusively on the CTLR paradigm between 1978 and 1983 in the Departments of Geography and Economics, where I then had a joint appointment, at the State University of New York at Buffalo, and beginning in 1984 at the University of Florida.

In 1980, under the prompting of one of my mentors from my years as a graduate student, Reginald Golledge, I rather belatedly published the foundations of the CTLR in the first volume of his journal, *Urban Geography*; without his encouragement that article and consequently this book would not have been written. Subsequent to that first article in *Urban Geography*, I published a succession of CTLR formulations with the dual purpose of demonstrating the power of the paradigm, and also to provide solutions that had not yet been done in the general mathematical land rent theory. Many of the chapters in this book are based upon those articles – Chapters 2, 3, 4, 5, and 6: *Urban Geography* (1980, 1982); Chapters 9, 10, and 11: *Professional Geographer* (1981); Chapter 13: *Papers of the Regional Science Association* (1982); Chapter 9 and part of Chapter 14: *Canadian Geographer* (1982); and Chapter 12: *Political Geography Quarterly* (1983). The analysis of Chapter 8 is based upon my work in *Professional Geographer* (1979, 1981).

At the same time, this book is more than an essay about journal articles I have written. Though the analysis dates to lectures I gave at SUNY-Buffalo, no part of Chapter 7 has been published elsewhere, and much of Chapters 4 and 14 are being published for the first time; space restrictions in the case of journal articles are typically more severe than in books thereby requiring cuts, usually at the expense of explanation. A not insignificant benefit of the CTLR presented here for the first time in book form is that while the articles were written to stand independent of one another, the paradigm of the CTLR can be seen holistically from the sum of its constituent parts. Moreover, the CTLR is presented, again for the first time, in a new format.

The presentation is divided into both *direct* and *indirect* effects. Direct effects include the impact upon the system resulting from the change in some external component of the model while holding land rent constant; indirect effects isolate the subsequent effect that adjustments in land rent have upon the system. The direct effects are first derived which explains the behavior of the system down to a small last step, where the results of the open, closed, and planned cities can be derived. The benefit of the direct and indirect vehicle is that instead of open, closed, and planned cities appearing as entities independent from one another, they are clearly seen as slight though important variations of one another.

I have found the CTLR geometry to have four general advantages over the calculus formulations. First, the CTLR is a paradigm whose use presents a firm explanation of the underlying forces for the behavior of the system. In contrast, the calculus often reduces the problem to one of statement of the problem followed by solution; the mechanics of calculus as typically deployed by all the mathematical land rent literature is with a lack of explanation as to why the solution is as it is.

Second, many problems that have been stated in the calculus-based mathematical land rent theories become, due to their complexity, intractable and often unsolvable without alluding to numerical methods of solution (Thrall, 1979a); though not entirely without rewards, such approaches lack both generality and again forsake explanation as to why the system behaves as it does. Regardless of its simplicity, the CTLR is here demonstrated to be able to solve and explain many problems that are finally intractable using alternative approaches.

Third, the CTLR is accessible. The major theorems of mathematical land rent theory, heretofor only understandable by those with advanced training in mathematics and microeconomics, can be understood by means of the CTLR by persons whose analytic training has not extended beyond what would be expected of an entering college student. This has been accomplished without loss of rigor of the logic.

Fourth, while all the before-mentioned advantages may be value laden, this last point most certainly rests upon one's own aesthetics of research. While I recognize that not all problems in mathematical land rent theory can be solved using the CTLR, I find that when the CTLR can be used it gives me more pleasure than an equivalent solution using the calculus. My reasons are simple. Given that a problem can be stated and solved under two para-digmatical approaches, one mathematically complex versus one elegantly simple, and given that the solutions of both are compatible, I prefer the ele-gantly simple approach. For those problems that can be solved using the CTLR, I can make an even stronger and more utilitarian point that the paradigm of the CTLR should be used instead of the calculus solution because of its elegant simplicity. Our various disciplines cannot survive by limiting the important contributions to be understood only by extreme specialists in the literature. Rather, for these endeavors to continue to receive the resources from universities, and respect from the professional environ-ments, then the accomplishments must be made accessible (including to undergraduates). The CTLR is then demonstrated here to be both an effective research and pedagogical vehicle.

Content of the book

Following a brief introduction in Chapter 1, the foundations of the CTLR model are presented in Chapters 2 and 3. This includes an elementary over-view of microeconomic consumer behavior theory, the notion of spatial equilibrium in the context of the CTLR, determination of urban radius, definition of open and closed cities, and the interaction of production and consumption sectors.

The idea of direct and indirect effects in the comparative static analysis of changing household income is introduced in Chapter 4, which includes an analysis of the conditions that will lead to dominance of the inner core of cities by the wealthy or by the poor, the contribution of rising incomes to suburbanization, and the importance of income differentials and mix to migration.

Chapters 5–7 are devoted to an examination of transportation: the effect upon urban spatial structure from changing cost of transportation holding all other parameters constant, then allowing both income and transportation cost to change. These analyses assume an isotropic transportation surface;

however, in Chapter 7 this assumption is relaxed to include a limited access network analogous to a light rail rapid transit system or limited access highway.

Chapters 8–11 collectively look at the role and subsequent impact of government taxation upon the geography of the city. Specifically, the effects upon urban space from sales, property, and income taxes are derived. This analysis is followed in Chapters 12 and 13 by the derivation of the linkage between urban space and government activities.

The government provides constraints in the form of planning, analysed in Chapter 12, and in the form of the provision of goods, analysed in Chapter 13. The public goods can either be uniformly distributed or conform to positive or negative externalities. These chapters are two of the more complex and possibly more important analyses of the book. Many phenomena can be reduced to arguments conforming to externalities, including some of the components of the spatial effect of racial prejudice.

Chapter 14 demonstrates how a housing rent function can be derived, where housing is composed of a combination of capital and land. This is done for completeness. In the last chapter, the Postscript, I discuss the utility and application of the CTLR, and argue for what I believe should be an appropriate balance of research (and when I have used this material in the classroom the students have been requested to read the Postscript immediately after the Preface). It is my goal that the CTLR be available at one's fingertips, like the supply and demand curve, so that one can quickly and accurately analyze problems demonstrated in this book and that may be encountered in the future.

I would like to express my gratitude to Tammy Virana, who was responsible for quickly transforming my squiggles into publication-quality figures. The diplomacy of Mary Ann Kernan, my editor at Methuen, in London, was exactly the right balance of necessary patience and pressure throughout the lengthy period of writing this book. But most important to the completion of the volume is my wife, Susan Elshaw Thrall, of the Computer Science Program of the Department of Business, Lake City College; she has been my most constructive critic, and exercised a wonderful patience in reading and commenting on the entire manuscript.

References

Thrall (1979a, 1979b, 1979c, 1979d, 1980a, 1980b, 1981a, 1981b, 1982a, 1982b, 1982c, 1983a, 1983b).

PART I

Foundations of the Consumption Theory of Land Rent (CTLR)

1

Introduction

1.1 Introduction

The Consumption Theory of Land Rent (CTLR) is a model of an ideal urban landscape. It is ideal not in the sense that it is the best place to live, rather the CTLR is an idea of an urban landscape. This ideal environment is less complicated and more uniform than the "real" places that you and I inhabit. At the same time, it should not be mistaken for a nonvaluable landscape because it lacks those complexities that make each of our own environments unique and memorable. There are four reasons why an understanding of the abstract or ideal landscape should precede the direct description of particular places.

First, whose environment should be described: yours, mine, someone else's? The CTLR describes features that are common to all urban landscapes regardless of where they are. The cost of such abstraction is the loss of the particular.

Second, the noise of the real world often distracts us, so that we do not see what is important and instead focus upon the trivial. The challenge of the mapmaker or cartographer can provide a good analogy to this. A map is an abstraction of reality; maps depict ideal landscapes. Much of this book is concerned with the creation of maps of ideal urban landscapes. To the traveler wishing to go from place A to B, the location of fire hydrants is unimportant. The inclusion of such detail on the map may clutter the map to the extent that the map becomes of little use to the traveler. But to the fireman or insurance actuary, the location of fire hydrants is of great importance. The cartographer decides which features on the real landscape to abstract out of the map, and which to include. The decision of the cartographer is based upon what from past experience and even guesswork is likely to be important to the map user at that time. Critiques of the finished map may argue that certain real-world features be restored to the ideal landscape of the map. On a map that is well designed, this should present no great difficulty; the general surface or map template will not change.

Similarly, the CTLR ideal landscape initially is simple; the simplicity makes it easy to understand for the person first encountering its ideal landscape. Afterwards, layer by layer, greater real-world complexities are to be added to the simple landscape. The final CTLR landscape can be, like our real-world landscape, quite complex. The fundamental processes responsible for the creation of the complex landscapes will then be understood.

Third, *I hold as a basic tenet that the processes that can be attributed to creating the spatial structure of each place are the same*. These processes will be analyzed in this book. Therefore, the reader who completes this book will understand the basic processes behind the creation of the urban landscape. *The weighting of the components of the processes may differ between places, but the fundamental underlying processes are the same and can be described*. The CTLR describes the underlying process. *By understanding the fundamental processes that account for the urban form of all places, the reason why a particular place has its unique form can be explained*. The CTLR model can explain and predict what the outcome will be if the individual weights of the underlying components that make up the process are changed. For example, what will happen to the urban landscape if a light rail rapid transit system is installed? A model that can explain and predict can be used to plan.

Fourth, the ideal CTLR environment is as close to a laboratory setting society should or is likely to let us get to experimentation with the landscape. The CTLR is a tool that can be used to predict what the outcome will be if certain events occur or various policies are implemented. The credibility of the CTLR model is strengthened as the environment changes in a manner corresponding to what is predicted by the CTLR. Moreover, if planners consider that a certain outcome is desirable, then the CTLR model can be used to determine what policies can be instituted to obtain these results, and what the indirect and often unintended consequences of the policy are likely to be.

1.2   Mathematical land rent theory versus the CTLR

The following discussion is provided to contrast the CTLR with the work of others in mathematical land rent theory. The reader without a knowledge of calculus or advanced microeconomics may pass over the following material and proceed to Chapter 2; it is not necessary to understand the material in the remainder of the chapter to understand the CTLR. Readers with a background in calculus and advanced microeconomics are, in addition to this section referred to the introductions to the calculus approach to land rent theory by Mills and MacKinnon (1973), Anas and Dendrinos (1976), Richardson (1977), Henderson (1977), and Dendrinos with Mullally (1985).

1.2.1 The commercial sector

There is no question, at least in the mind of this spatial theorist, that the monumental work of Johann Heinrich Von Thünen (1821) presaged by nearly a century and a half the developments of modern mathematical land rent theory.

Von Thünen's arguments began by assuming a plane devoid of all features save for a central market. There were two important actors: landusers and landowners. The criteria to the landowner was to maximize the return from the land. The landuser who received the right to produce on the land was the one who was willing and able to pay the highest rent.

The landuser's decision as to how much to bid for the right to use the land was based upon the following considerations. First, how much was the market price of the good. Second, what was the cost of producing the good. Included in the cost of production was a requirement that the landuser receive a certain minimum wage, like an opportunity cost; otherwise there would be no reason to farm the land. Land was assumed to be equally fertile; however, differing technologies could be employed in the production of the crops depending upon where the firm was relative to the city center. Third, the most important to us, once the crop was harvested, it had to be transported to market. If all land was everywhere equally fertile, then the rent bid to produce a particular crop using a specific technology would differ only between locations by the amount it cost the landuser to get the good to market and thereby receive revenues from the sale.

To sum up, in Von Thünun's model, rent can be thought of as total revenues from selling the product at the market less the cost of producing the harvest and less the cost of transporting the produce to the market. Rent curves are formed about the central market, the rate of descent of each rent function depending upon the cost of transporting the good to market; the absolute magnitude of the bid rent depending upon the cost of production, the market price, the crop yield, and the freight rate. The end-result was that Von Thünen's model produced a theoretical landscape of concentric land use patterns about the central market; the most intensive land use occurs near to the market, gradually becoming more extensive with increasing distance from the city center. Walter Isard (1956) used Von Thünen's model as an analog to describe concentric patterns of land use about the city center, with land rent and intensity declining with increasing distance from the city center.

The nature of the Von Thünen model properly limited it to the production sector: landowners and landusers sought to maximize returns at each location. Not all land uses in the city can be considered to be strictly production oriented.

1.2.2   The household sector

The limitations of applying the Von Thünen model to the urban landscape began to be overcome with the contribution of William Alonso (1964) (in writing his Ph.D. dissertation under the direction of Walter Isard at the University of Pennsylvania). Alonso's landscape was akin to that of Von Thünen, in that the city lay on a plain devoid of man-made features; the city had one center. Transportation was possible in every direction from every point in the city. Bidding for land took place in a perfect market system; the right to inhabit the land was given to the highest bidder. Households maximized their welfare u, which was composed of quantity of land q, an aggregation of all other goods referred to as the composite good z, and distance from the city center s; in symbolic terms, the household sought to:

$$\text{maximize } u = u[z,q,s], \tag{1.1}$$
$$\text{w.r.t. } z,q \quad \text{(the notation w.r.t. symbolizes ''with respect to'')}$$

subject to:

$$y - pz - rq - T[s] = w = 0. \tag{1.2}$$

The term $T[s]$ represents the cost of transportation. Partial derivatives of the Lagrangian $(u - \lambda w)$ with respect to z, q, and λ were set equal to 0. The resulting equations were used to derive the slope of the bid-rent function:

$$dr/ds = (p/q)(u_s/u_z) - (1/q)(dT[s]/ds). \tag{1.3}$$

In equation (1.3), $u_s = \partial u/\partial s$ and $u_z = \partial u/\partial z$. Since leisure time is lost as a result of commuting, $u_s < 0$. It must, then, be true that $\partial r/\partial s < 0$ since all other terms are positive in equation (1.3). Reminiscent of the earlier work of Von Thünen, part of the driving mechanism for the decay of land rent over space is the increasing cost of transportation as distance from the city center increases, namely $T_s > 0$. Unlike Von Thünen, however, is the behavioral mechanism of $u_s < 0$.

Alonso was able to demonstrate that urban land rent declined with increasing distance from the central business district (CBD). The major limitation to extending Alonso's seminal model was that it was formulated in only a partial equilibrium setting. The land rent gradient cannot be derived from equations (1.1) and (1.2) since the conditions for equilibrium between locations were not clearly specified.

The first successful spatial equilibrium model was published by Richard Muth (1969) (at the Department of Economics at the University of Chicago). Muth's model began with a formulation that, with two exceptions, was similar to that of equations (1.1) and (1.2); a minor difference was that the household did not consume land, but housing x with price v. More important, location was explicitly defined to be a choice variable for the household. Muth's model can be stated simply as:

$$\text{Maximize } u = u[z,x,s],$$
$$\text{w.r.t. } z,x,s \qquad\qquad (1.4)$$

subject to:

$$y - pz - vx - T[s] = w = 0. \qquad\qquad (1.5)$$

Using equations (1.4) and (1.5), the first partial derivatives of the resulting Lagrangian function (Muth, 1969, p. 22) $L = (u - \lambda w)$ are set to 0:

$$\partial L/\partial z = u_z - \lambda \rho = 0 \qquad\qquad (1.6)$$

and:

$$\partial L/\partial x = u_x - \lambda v = 0 \qquad\qquad (1.7)$$

and:

$$\partial L/\partial s = -\lambda(xv_s + T_s) = 0 \qquad\qquad (1.8)$$

and:

$$\partial L/\partial \lambda = y - pz - vx - T[s] = 0. \qquad\qquad (1.9)$$

Equation (1.9) merely states that the household spends the entire budget. Equations (1.6) and (1.7) represent the standard microeconomic (partial) equilibrium conditions that the marginal utility per dollar spent is the same on all commodities. The geographic or spatial equilibrium condition comes from equation (1.8).

Implicit in equation (1.8) is that $u_s = 0$. That is, in spatial equilibrium, welfare does not change over space. Moreover, equation (1.8) can be rearranged as:

$$-xv_s = T_s \quad \text{or } v_s = -(1/x)T_s. \qquad\qquad (1.10)$$

Equation (1.10) states that in equilibrium "the household's net savings on the purchase of a given quantity of housing and transport costs which would result from a very short move – either toward or away from the CBD – would be equal to zero. Stated differently, the household is unable to increase its real income by any change of location" (Muth 1969, p. 22). Muth assumed that the urban radius occurred where the population density reached a certain minimum level. Since conditions for urban radius were specified, as well as conditions for economic and geographic equilibrium, then Muth's model is closed allowing equations (1.6)–(1.9) to be solved simultaneously for spatial equilibrium land rent.

Following the publication of Muth's book (1969), Emilio Casetti (1971) (from the Department of Geography at Ohio State University) published a similar spatial equilibrium solution. Like Alonso, Casetti stated the problem as:

$$\text{Maximize } u = u[z,q,s], \qquad\qquad (1.11)$$
$$\text{w.r.t. } z,q$$

subject to:

$$y - pz - rq - ks = w = 0 \qquad (1.12)$$

where transportation costs are linear, namely k per unit distance s from the city center. Partial derivatives of the Lagrangian function $(u - \lambda w)$ with respect to z, q, and λ are set equal to 0. The resulting equations are solved simultaneously for the demand for z and q in terms of income, location, and prices. These demand functions are then used to derive the indirect utility function $u[y,p,r,s]$; Casetti states that when the system is in *spatial equilibrium* no household can be better off by relocating. To operationalize this condition for spatial equilibrium mathematically, he set the indirect utility function equal to a constant $\bar{\bar{u}}$:

$$u[z\{s,p\},q\{s,r\}] = \bar{\bar{u}}. \qquad (1.13)$$

Function (1.13) can then be rearranged to solve for spatial equilibrium land rent in terms of $\bar{\bar{u}}$ and s.

Robert Solow (1972) subsequently published a formulation quite similar to that of Casetti's except that instead of setting the indirect utility function $u[y,p,r,s] = $ constant, he, like Muth, set the derivative of utility equal to zero: $du[y,p,r,s]/ds = 0 = $ constant.

There are slight differences in the mechanics whereby spatial equilibrium is attained between the formulations of Muth, Casetti, and Solow (hereafter, MCS models); yet the results of each approach are consistent with one another. The reason for the consistency of results is that, in each instance, the meaning of each of the partial equilibrium conditions is the same: microeconomic consumer behavior dictates that in equilibrium the value of the marginal utility of each good be the same, and geographic equilibrium requires that welfare of all households with the same income and taste preferences will be the same regardless of location.

So, too, the CTLR is a method of solution differing significantly from the procedures used in the MCS models. At the same time, the meaning of spatial equilibrium in the CTLR is fundamentally the same as in the MCS models, and the CTLR satisfies the partial equilibrium conditions required of the microeconomic consumer behavior theory as well. Hence, the solutions of the CTLR should be compatible with that of the MCS models. The MCS models require a uniform set of theorems, necessitated by their similar use of calculus, without which they could not have been developed or extended; the CTLR based upon the mathematics of geometry requires its *own* principles in order for the model to have been developed and extended to a variety of settings including the evaluation of a planned city which does not necessarily rely upon the notion of spatial equilibrium. In the remainder of this book, I present the necessary principles – and many of their implications – of the CTLR.

1.3 Conclusion

The following chapters present a geometry of urban land rent and rationale for why cities acquire their particular spatial form. I call the general method the Consumption Theory of Land Rent, or CTLR.

The CTLR geometric method has several advantages over calculus-based mathematical land rent theory. These advantages include that the CTLR paradigm provides an explanation of the underlying forces for the behavior of the system. Many problems stated in the calculus-based mathematical land rent theories become intractable and often unsolvable. The CTLR is accessible. Finally, using the criteria of Occam's razor, I believe that when the CTLR can be used, it should be used instead of artificially complex settings.

The CTLR is a paradigm that serves to describe an ideal urban landscape. It is designed to provide generalities about all urban landscapes. The landscapes that can be described and explained can be quite complex and provide significant insights to our real-world landscapes. The methods of solution differ radically between CTLR and MCS models. But the results of the CTLR and MCS classes of models will be consistent because of the similarities between consumer and spatial equilibrium conditions.

References

Alonso (1964)
Anas and Dendrinos (1976)
Berry *et al.* (1963)
Bourne (1971)
Brunn and Williams (1983)
Casetti (1971)
Clark (1982)
Dendrinos, with Mullally (1985)
Henderson (1977)
Isard (1956, 1975)
King and Golledge (1978) pp. 213–37
Lounsbury *et al.* (1981)
Mayer and Hayes (1983)
Mills (1972)
Mills and MacKinnon (1973)
Mumford (1961)
Muth (1969)
Newling (1966)
Pirenne (1925)
Richardson (1977)
Solow (1972)
Thrall (1980a)
Von Thünen (1821)
Wilson (1974)

2

Foundations

2.1 Introduction

In this chapter the foundations of the Consumption Theory of Land Rent (CTLR) are presented. The chapter concerns the mechanics and methodology of the general model. The general method presented here is used throughout the remainder of the book. Chapter 3 adds several specification issues to the general method. Each chapter thereafter is concerned with adding a specific important complexity to the basic model. The CTLR model is not however limited to the complexities that will be dealt with in this book. Rather, each chapter addresses what may be a frequently encountered parameter change. In this sense these chapters can serve as illustration as to how to evaluate other phenomena that arise and challenge us in the future.

2.2 The basic landscape

The landscape upon which our ideal city is located is as follows. It is a featureless plain. The plain extends into the distance in all directions. There are no roadways or rivers, it is devoid of all features built by nature and humankind. Such a surface is referred to as isotropic. The landscape is perfectly malleable, that is the spatial distribution of people and composition of land use can change instantaneously. There are two categories of land use: residential and nonurban. The landscape is inhabited by people.

The people that live on the landscape are identical in every way. They may form into households; all households are of the same size n. The n-person households may then be of size 1-person, 2-person, and so on. The households each have the same income and the same taste preferences. The households all receive income from employment that is located at the central geometric point known as the central business district (CBD); all shopping is done by the households at the CBD.

The households make decisions concerning the mix of goods that they will consume. The household can make a decision about only two goods: quantity of land to consume, and quantity to consume of all other goods collectively referred to as the composite good. With the exception of land and transportation, the composite good is a conglomerate of all other goods, and includes expenditures on housing capital. The households can also choose to relocate.

The household has perfect information about each location in the city: the price of goods there, the transportation cost there, and the quality of the environment including population density there. At each location, the household is presented with a market price for land, the market price for composite good, and the market price for transportation to and from the CBD for work and shopping. Faced with these market prices, the households are rational in the sense that they will choose at each location that combination of composite good and land that provides the greatest satisfaction of their preferences while at the same time limiting expenditures so as to not exceed their limited income.

2.3 The spatial welfare surface

The households are distributed in some fashion across the residential landscape. At each location, the individual household can obtain some magnitude of happiness by being able to satisfy to varying degrees its collection of preferences. Since in all other respects the households are identical, this magnitude of happiness or level of attainable welfare u is dependent only upon location. To the household, the desirability of a location is based solely

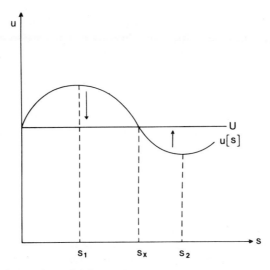

Figure 2.1 The unfolding of household welfare over space (after Thrall, 1980a)

upon the level of welfare that can be obtained there. Because households prefer higher levels of welfare to lower levels, they are attracted to the more desirable locations. The more desirable locations receive an inflow of persons thereby raising density of persons there: less desirable locations lose people to the more desirable locations thereby having a decrease in population density. An illustration of such a welfare surface is presented in Figure 2.1.

In the figure, the increase in demand for locating at s_1 will bid up the land rent there; the higher population density and higher land rent at s_1 will decrease the desirability for locating there. The decrease in demand to locate at s_2 will result in a decline in the market value of land there; the new lower population densities and lower land rent at s_2 will translate into an increase in the desirability for locating at s_2. Households continue to relocate upon the residential landscape until population density and land rent adjust, so that no household can obtain a level of welfare higher than can be obtained at their present location. Variation across space in the level of obtainable welfare is thereby minimized. This may be succinctly stated in the following proposition.

Proposition 2.1   The state of spatial equilibrium is attained when all households with the same income and taste preferences have the same level of welfare.

The ideal spatial equilibrium welfare surface that proposition 2.1 defines is represented by U in Figure 2.1.

If households do not have perfect information and have costs of relocation, the welfare surface can then deviate from the spatial equilibrium U by some level before there is sufficient motivation to relocate. Say a household will tolerate W_L less welfare than is the spatial equilibrium before a decision is made to relocate, and that a location must have higher welfare of W_H before households have an incentive to relocate there. Then the spatial equilibrium level of welfare U can be said to lie within a welfare band with the range $U + W_H$ and $U - W_L$. The spatial equilibrium welfare band is represented in Figure 2.2. Without significant loss of real-world applicability or generality, the analysis in this book will assume that $W_H = W_L = 0$. The values can be made to be nonzero at any point in the analysis if it is desired to evaluate the implications of a spatial equilibrium welfare band.

2.4   The households' decision process

The households must decide upon the mix of goods that will result in providing them the highest obtainable welfare that can be achieved at the particular location. Prices presented to the individual household are not within their individual control, but are the consequence of the collective actions of the households. The household chooses between the quantity of

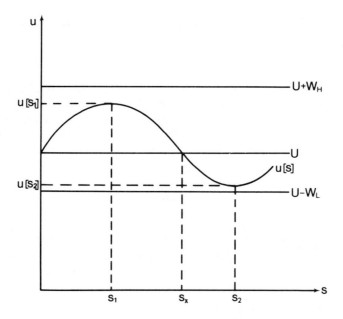

Figure 2.2 Spatial equilibrium welfare band

land q whose per unit price is r, and composite good z with price p. The total expenditures on land, rq, and on composite good, pz, must not exceed the household's disposable income y^*. Without significant loss of generality, and with the benefit of making the subsequent analysis much more tractable, savings can be restricted to be 0; hence, expenditures must equal income.

Thus, the households will choose that combination of goods that results in their greatest possible individual level of welfare, while at the same time not have expenditures exceed their limited income. Two forces, therefore, must be balanced: the restriction that expenditures must not exceed income, and welfare must be maximized. These two components to the households' decision process, first, will be described individually in more detail, and then combined.

2.4.1 The budget constraint

Disposable income at distance s from the CBD is that amount of income remaining after transportation expenditures have been accounted for; disposable income is then the difference between transportation costs k per unit distance s from the CBD and gross household income y. A linear transportation cost function will generally be assumed; hence, total transportation costs are ks. Disposable income y^* can then be written:

$$y^* = y - ks. \tag{2.1}$$

And since expenditures on land and composite good must equal disposable income, we can write:

$$y - ks = pz + rq. \tag{2.2}$$

Equation (2.2) is the households' budget constraint. Because the CTLR uses the mechanics of geometry, it is necessary to graph the budget constraint on a grid that includes on the axes the two goods z and q. To accomplish this, two important relations from equation (2.2) are useful. These are the intercept on the composite good axis or ordinate:

$$z = (y - ks)/p \quad \text{(given } q = 0) \tag{2.3}$$

and the intercept on the quantity of land axis or abscissa:

$$q = (y - ks)/r \quad \text{(given } z = 0). \tag{2.4}$$

Equations (2.3) and (2.4) are the quantity of either z or q that the household can afford to consume if the entire disposable income is devoted to one of those two products. Also equation (2.2) can be rearranged to be in the familiar form:

$$z = (y - ks)/p - (r/p)q. \tag{2.5}$$

The budget line in equation (2.5) is a straight line with intercepts as given in equations (2.3) and (2.4), and whose slope is the ratio of land rent to composite good price. The budget constraint can be graphed as in Figure 2.3.

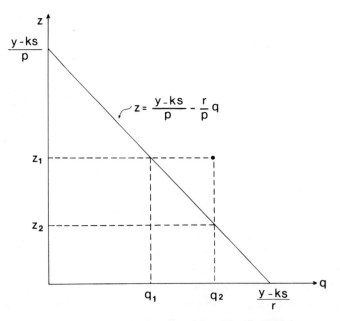

Figure 2.3   The budget line (after Thrall, 1980a)

A household can afford to consume any combination of z and q within the area bounded by the budget line. If the household were to consume $z_2 q_1$, then the household would have savings equal to the distance between the interior point and the budget line. Since we have restricted savings to be 0, the household then is restricted to consume combinations of goods identified by the budget line.

The household may not consume goods above the budget line because a combination of goods like $z_1 q_2$ results in expenditures exceeding the limited income of the household. To consume this combination of goods, the household must borrow; without significant loss of generality, borrowing will not be allowed. However, in a subsequent chapter mortgage interest rates will be introduced into the model (Chapter 9).

The zero savings restriction and the zero borrowing restriction limit the choice of goods that the household may consume as to that combination of goods identified by the budget line. The household, for example, may consume z_1 units of composite good and q_1 units of land, or z_2 and q_2, or any other combination of goods whose coordinates lie on the budget line. The budget line identifies an infinite number of combinations of composite good and land that the household can afford to consume; however, only one combination of z and q will both yield to the household the greatest satisfaction of preferences while simultaneously satisfying the budget constraint.

2.4.2   The utility frontier

A utility or indifference curve (Figure 2.4) maps out the combination of two goods between which the household is indifferent. All bundles of goods that provide the household the same level of utility lie on the same indifference curve. The shape of an indifference curve is dictated by the rate at which the household is willing to trade off one good for the other. In Figure 2.4, along indifference curve $u[s_2]$ the household will be equally happy consuming either z_1 and q_1, or z_2 and q_2. Since more of a good is preferred to less, z_1 and q_3 on indifference curve $u[s_x]$ is preferred to any combination of goods traced out by lower indifference curves such as $u[s_2]$. The household receives more of at least one good the further from the origin is the indifference curve; hence, the household receives greater welfare the higher or further from the origin is the indifference curve. Moreover, utility curves are assumed to be everywhere dense, meaning that any combination of z and q can be identified as lying on a unique indifference curve.

Utility curves are typically drawn such that they are bowed toward the origin. This convexity conforms to the "law" of diminishing marginal utility (Figure 2.5), and we will illustrate this by example. Consider the combination $z_2 q_2$; the household is consuming a relatively large amount of z and small amount of q. Because q is scarce, a large amount of z must be obtained by the household to compensate for a further reduction in q, say, from q_2 to q_1. At

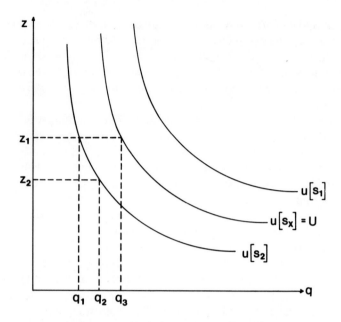

Figure 2.4   Utility frontier (after Thrall, 1980a)

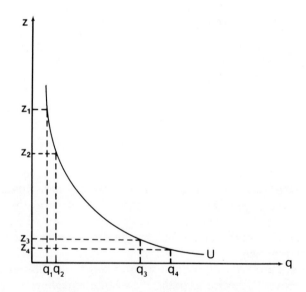

Figure 2.5   Diminishing marginal utility

the other extreme, if the household is consuming z_4q_4, it would be willing to trade a relatively large amount of q, $q_4 - q_3$, to obtain an additional small amount of z, $z_3 - z_4$, since in this case z is relatively scarce. Hence, each tail of the utility curve becomes more closely aligned with the axis as points are identified along the utility curve away from the origin.

Utility curves are generally assumed not to intersect. Consider the logical problems that are encountered if utility curves were to intersect as in Figure 2.6. In zone I, U_2 is preferred to U_1 since combinations of goods on U_2 offer more of at least one good as compared to combinations on U_1. However, U_1 is preferred to U_2 in zone III. A utility curve cannot be both inferior and superior to another utility curve. Furthermore, at zone II, U_1 and U_2 share a bundle of goods thereby implying that the household is indifferent to U_1 and U_2. A utility curve cannot be inferior, superior, and equivalent to another utility curve.

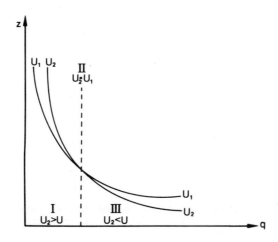

Figure 2.6 Utility curves do not intersect

2.4.3 The equilibrium solution

By superimposing the budget line in Figure 2.3 onto the utility frontier in Figure 2.4, the level of welfare that the household can afford to obtain can be determined (Figure 2.7). Moreover, the precise combination of goods that the household will consume will be identified. The utility curve tangent to the budget line will identify the obtainable level of welfare for the household; at the point of tangency, the particular combination of the two goods that generates the highest level of utility subject to satisfying the budget constraint is identified.

Consider the budget line in Figure 2.7, and the combination of goods z_1q_1.

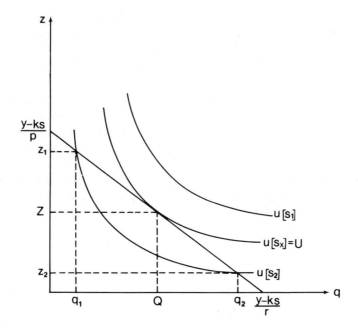

Figure 2.7   Equilibrium consumption of goods

By the household reducing the consumption of z, more q may be obtained thereby placing the household on increasingly higher utility curves. Utility curves are everywhere dense; hence, every combination of z and q is on a unique utility curve. Similarly, if the household is consuming $z_2 q_2$, by reducing q and increasing z the household may move to a higher utility curve. The household would prefer to consume any combination of goods on utility curve $u[s_1]$, though it cannot afford to do so. The highest utility curve that the household can afford is U. To obtain utility U, the household must consume the unique bundle of goods composed of ZQ. This, then, is the equilibrium mix of goods that the household will consume.

2.5   Rent, the unknown price

Terms whose values are known somehow from outside of the system, such as income, are referred to as *exogenous*. Terms whose values are to be derived within the system, such as Z and Q, are referred to as *endogenous*. The review of the consumer behavior theory in the previous sections of this chapter treated the prices p, r, and k as all exogenous in the standard fashion of microeconomics; given the prices and income, the level of welfare that the household can obtain is determined. However, the CTLR generally treats the price of land r as unknown; land rent is endogenous. Here, and in equation (2.1), the CTLR becomes geographic.

The equilibrium between budget constraint and household welfare has been evaluated. To close the system and derive the price of land, the equilibrium of the household in space must be determined. Refer back to Figure 2.1 and the condition for spatial equilibrium. The spatial equilibrium condition depicted in Figure 2.1 is required to obtain a solution for spatial equilibrium land rent, and subsequently the spatial equilibrium quantities of land and composite good consumed at a given distance s from the CBD. The geography of the system allows for two polar cases in the solution of spatial equilibrium land rent. One case, known as the *open city*, considers household welfare to be exogenous; this also determines the spatial equilibrium number of households that inhabit the city. The second case, known as the *closed city*, derives spatial equilibrium land rent and level of household welfare compatible with an exogenously given number of households. For the present we will focus only upon the first or open city case, where household welfare is exogenous.

Let U in Figure 2.8 equal the exogenously given spatial equilibrium level of welfare U. The spatial behavior of U is as depicted in Figure 2.1. Say the household is located at distance s_1 from the CBD. The spatial equilibrium land rent at location s_1 can then be derived. At distance s_1 from the CBD, the disposable income ($y^* = y - ks_1$) is a constant. Since income and the composite good price p are also constants, then the point where the budget line intersects the vertical axis is determined as in Figure 2.8 for all households at distance s_1 from the CBD. The only term in the intercepts that can change in Figure 2.8 and thereby generate tangency between the indifference curve U and the budget line is the rent per unit of land r.

A market value of land at distance s_1 equal to r' will result in the budget line labeled AA which lies everywhere to the left of U. The level of welfare that this budget line allows is less than that required by the proposition for spatial equilibrium: all households with the same income and taste preferences have the same level of welfare. A smaller value of land rent equal to r'' will swing the budget line like a pendulum to the right, twice intersecting U; since budget line AC partly lies to the right of U, a level of welfare greater than the spatial equilibrium level can be attained. To satisfy the condition of spatial equilibrium, rent at distance s_1 must equal $R[s_1]$. Throughout this book endogenous terms that are capitalized will represent spatial equilibrium values; square brackets represent functional relationships.

The spatial equilibrium quantity of composite good consumed $Z[s_1]$ and the spatial equilibrium quantity of land consumed $Q[s_1]$ are identified by the tangency between the utility curve U and the budget line (Figure 2.8). The total spatial equilibrium expenditure on land by each household at distance s_1 from the CBD is then calculated by the product $R[s_1]Q[s_1]$. The total spatial equilibrium expenditure on composite good is the product $pZ[s_1]$.

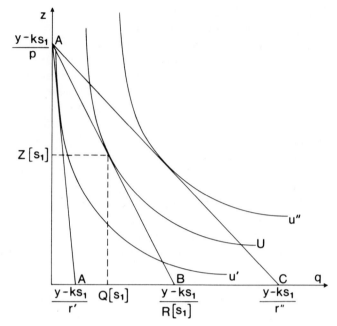

Figure 2.8   CTLR solution for spatial equilibrium land rent (after Thrall, 1980a)

Although the discussion of the closed city will be left for a subsequent chapter, one can determine the effect that different levels of welfare have upon several endogenous spatial equilibrium variables. In Figure 2.9, if spatial equilibrium welfare were equal to U, the household at s_1 would consume $Q[s_1]$ quantity of land at price $R[s_1]$. If spatial equilibrium welfare were to become less than U, say U', the households' spatial equilibrium land consumption would be reduced to $Q[s_1]'$; spatial equilibrium land rent would increase to $R'[s_1]$. $R'[s_1]$ must be greater than $R[s_1]$ since the intercepts of the budget line have the same numerator, namely, the disposable income ($y - ks_1$), and the intercept on the quantity of land axis generated by U' is less than that generated by U. Conversely, the greater the level of households' welfare, the greater will be the consumption of land and the lower will be the price per unit of land, all other things being equal. This result may be stated in the following principle.

Principle 2.1   Relatively higher household welfare is associated with greater consumption of land, and lower rent per unit of land, all other things being equal.

Compare the spatial equilibrium land rent between two locations, s_1 and s_2. Let s_1 be closer to the CBD than s_2. It will be demonstrated that land rents decline as distance from the CBD increases.

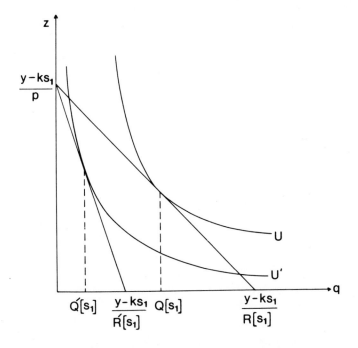

Figure 2.9 Spatial equilibrium land rent and household welfare (after
Thrall, 1980a)

Households located at distance s_2 from the CBD have a lower disposable
income than do households at distance s_1 since transportation expenditures
for households more remote from the CBD are greater than households with
greater proximity to the CBD, namely:

$$ks_2 > ks_1. \tag{2.6}$$

Hence, the terms in the numerator of the intercepts for the budget line for
locations s_1 and s_2 are unequal:

$$y - ks_1 > y - ks_2. \tag{2.7}$$

To demonstrate that it is not possible for land rent to be the same at both
locations s_1 and s_2 in this setting, it is shown what would happen if land rent
were restricted to be the same at both locations. Set land rent for s_1 and s_2 both
equal to a constant amount, say, $R[s_1]$. With the denominators for the intercepts on the horizontal axis set equal to the same value,

$$(y - ks_1)/R[s_1] > (y - ks_2)/R[s_1] \tag{2.8}$$

it is easy to prove that inequalities (2.8) and (2.7) are equivalent. Therefore,
the intercepts of the composite good axis and the quantity of land axis will be
greater at distance s_1 than at distance s_2, as shown in Figure 2.10. Further-

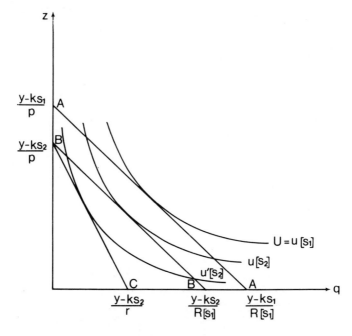

Figure 2.10 Land rent is neither constant nor increasing with
increasing distance from the city center (after Thrall,
1980a)

more, recall from equation (2.5) that the slope of the budget line is the ratio of
land rent to composite good price. Since both prices are presently held
constant, budget lines AA and BB must be parallel.

When households located at s_2 are restricted to paying the same rent as
households at s_1, s_2 households face budget line BB and are thereby reduced
to welfare $u[s_2]$ which is less than the spatial equilibrium U afforded by s_1
households with budget line AA. Therefore, land rent cannot be everywhere
the same.

Using the same diagram (Figure 2.10), consider whether land rent at s_2 can
be greater than at s_1. Let $r > R[s_1]$. The budget line then shifts obliquely
further to the left to BC thereby reducing welfare to $u'[s_2]$. Hence, land rent
at more remote locations cannot be greater than land rent at locations more
proximate to the CBD under these conditions.

Now that it has been established that land rent at more remote locations
cannot either equal or be greater than land rent at locations more proximate
to the CBD, consider next the remaining case of whether more remote
locations have lower land rents (Figure 2.11). Initially hold land rent constant
as we move from s_1 to s_2. The budget line shifts parallel downward and to the
left to BB, which is tangent to a lower level of welfare than is AA. By reducing

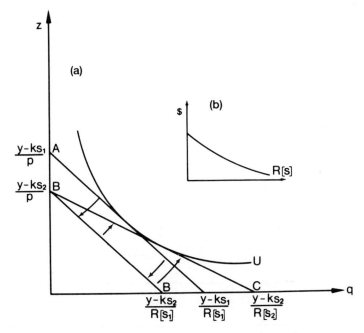

Figure 2.11 Spatial equilibrium land rent decreases as distance
between the city center and the land site increases (after
Thrall, 1980a)

spatial equilibrium land rent from $R[s_1]$ to $R[s_2]$, households at s_2 can obtain
the spatial equilibrium level of welfare. Hence, land rent decreases as
distance from the CBD increases.

Figure 2.12 repeats the analysis of Figure 2.11 but for three evenly spaced
locations $s_1 < s_2 < s_3$, where $s_2 - s_1 = s_3 - s_2$. Spatial equilibrium consumption of land and composite good can be contrasted among the three locations.

Several significant implications from the CTLR can now be stated about
urban spatial structure. First, since $R[s_1] > R[s_2]$, then land rents decline as
distance from the CBD increases. Second, since $Q[s_2] > Q[s_1]$, then consumption of land increases with increasing distance from the CBD (Figure
2.12). Third, since $Z[s_1] > Z[s_2]$, composite good consumption decreases as
distance from the CBD increases. These three results can be stated as the
following principles:

Principle 2.2   Land rent adjusts thereby compensating households from
locating in places that have relatively inferior access to central locations.
In general, rent per unit of land decreases with a reduction in access to the
central location, all other things being equal.

Principle 2.3   The consumption of land is inversely related to the households' access to the central location.

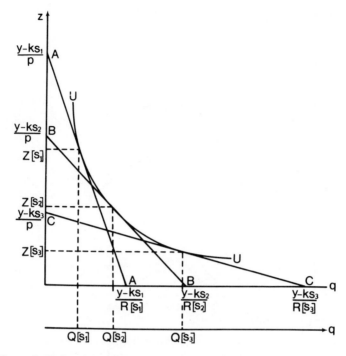

Figure 2.12 Spatial equilibrium land rent, land consumption, and composite good consumption for three example locations (after Thrall, 1980a)

Principle 2.4   The consumption of the composite good is directly related to the households' proximity to the central location.

Consumption of land and population density are inverse functions of each other; consequently, because of principle 2.3, population density is expected to be the greatest at the CBD, declining with increasing distance from the CBD. Hence, a corollary to principle 2.3 describes the expected unfolding across space of population density:

Principle 2.5   Population density increases directly in proportion to increases in proximity to the central location.

By inspection of Figure 2.12, the budget line for households on annulus of distance *s* from the CBD is demonstrated to become lower and less steep with increasing distance from the city center. This can be stated in the following principle, which will be regularly drawn upon throughout this book:

Principle 2.6   The budget lines of households become lower and flatter as proximity between their location and the CBD diminishes.

Finally, by inspection of Figure 2.12, and as a direct implication of the "law of diminishing marginal utility" and principle 2.6, each additional increment in distance from the CBD will result in a smaller reduction in Z and a larger increase in Q. The manner in which Z and Q unfold over space is dependent upon the shape of U and the rate of change over space of disposable income. Moreover, as the greater is the consumption of land on any annulus, the less can be the population density, then the following two principles can be stated:

Principle 2.7 The spatial equilibrium quantity of land consumed increases at an increasing rate, and hence population density decreases at a decreasing rate with increasing distance from the city center.

Principle 2.8 The spatial equilibrium consumption of composite good consumed decreases at a decreasing rate with increasing distance from the city center.

The simultaneous unfolding across space of the spatial equilibrium welfare surface, consumption of land and composite good is shown in Figure 2.13.

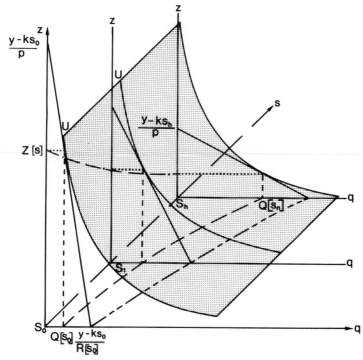

Figure 2.13 Unfolding across space of spatial equilibrium welfare
surface, land, and composite good consumption using the
CTLR methodology (after Thrall, 1980a)

2.6   Conclusion

In this chapter the foundations for the Consumption Theory of Land Rent (CTLR) have been presented. Unlike the microeconomic analysis where all prices are exogenous to the analysis, the geographic CTLR derives endogenously the price of land by way of introducing the geographic condition for spatial equilibrium. Households will change locations when the difference in the level of welfare between two locations is sufficient to make it worth their while; the movement of households affects land values and population density. In general, less desirable locations lose population and have lower land rents; more desirable locations gain population and have higher land rents. Spatial equilibrium prevails when no household has an incentive to relocate in order to obtain a higher level of welfare.

Because of transportation costs, households at more remote locations have lower disposable incomes than households at locations more proximate to the central business district. To compensate for this reduction in disposable income, land rents are less and consequently households can afford to consume more land. Households adjust to the higher land rents near to the city center by consuming less land and instead purchasing more composite good than households at more remote locations. An important implication of the CTLR is that since land consumption is directly proportional to distance from the city center, and since population density and land consumption are inverse functions of each other, population density declines at a decreasing rate with increasing distance from the city center.

References

Thrall (1980a, 1980b, 1981a)

Further specification of the CTLR model

3.1 Introduction

This chapter contains a discussion of two important basic definitional problems of the ideal city: first, the ability of the population to in- or out-migrate; and second, the forces that determine the breaking-point between urban and nonurban regions. Each definitional issue will be evaluated in turn.

3.2 The urban fringe

What delineates the radial extent of the city: government organizational boundaries? Zoning ordinances? The equality of urban and nonurban rents? Where people live? Where people live and recreate? Or do the economic hinterlands determine the boundaries of the city? Each definition, to various extents, is regularly employed in research and practical application.

For example, one method that has been used by the United States Census is to define Standard Metropolitan Statistical Areas (SMSAs) as extending from the central city out to radius s where the population density $D[s]$ no longer exceeds a critical cut-off limit, such as 2000 persons per square mile. For other purposes the Census Bureau uses the definition of a Standard Economic Area (SEA), defined as the range over which persons regularly commute to the central city. These definitions may be satisfactory for descriptive purposes; however, the normative theoretical analysis requires definitions more precise than these rules-of-thumb so as not to lead to ambiguity in the subsequent analysis. Our goal is to explain *why* the radial extent of the city is as it is rather than use the urban fringe "as it is" for some subsequent purpose.

For our purposes the way in which the urban fringe is delineated can follow one of these definitions (Thrall, 1979a):

Definition 3.1 Interactive. Land is classified as urban where the urban land rent is greater than or equal to the cost of converting nonurban land to urban land utilization.

Definition 3.2   Radially constrained. The radial extent of the city is determined exogenously by a central planning authority or by a collusion of monopolistic landowners.

Definition 3.3   Solitary. Indirect geographic determinants cause the population density to behave in some unspecified manner: the city is defined to occur where population density exceeds a specified number of persons per square mile.

Each of the three definitions will be discussed, in turn, and their implications will be made clear throughout the remainder of the book.

3.2.1   The interactive city

The range of the interactive city (Figure 3.1) depends upon the interaction between the urban land economy and the nonurban economy. There are three general land use categories: urban, transition, and nonurban. Nonurban may be agriculture. The urban region extends to radius h where spatial equilibrium land rent $R[h]$ is equal to the cost of converting nonurban land to urban utilization $\delta[h]$.

The cost of conversion is equal to the sum of nonurban land rent ρ and various overhead costs; the nonurban land use may be agricultural. Overhead costs include compensation for the nonurban landowner to replace immobile agricultural capital such as barns and fruit trees, and the normal market price

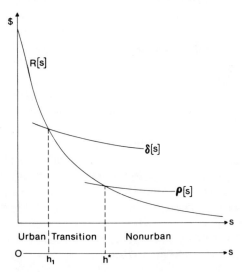

Figure 3.1   Derivation of urban limits for an interactive city (after Thrall, 1980a)

for agricultural land. Agricultural land rent may be a minor component in the cost of conversion. Generally more important than nonurban land rent are the overhead cost of infrastructure capital required for the land to be used as urban, such as the cost of laying streets and installing sewers, and electricity and water lines. Overhead costs also include normal speculative earnings of the developers.

The zone between h_1 and h^* (Figure 3.1) is transitional in the sense that urban land rent is greater than nonurban land rent, though not by enough to lead to immediate development. Land speculation in this zone is likely. The transition zone can be further partitioned into subcategories such as that zone where urban land rent is greater than the cost of the sum of the compensation to agriculture and speculators' earnings. In the absence of regulations concerning improvements in infrastructure, development in such a region is possible. In the United States, this may include low-density housing developments often with unpaved roads, water wells and underground septic systems. Often in the United States this zone of transition leads urban development to the extent that the infrastructures of highways and other public goods are installed after the zone is largely developed. The transition zone may include high-, median-, or low-income housing; in the southern part of the United States, low-income housing is often accommodated in this zone through the use of house trailers. In less developed countries, the transition zone may include squatter housing.

In this book, when an interactive city is assumed, the breaking-point between urban and nonurban is defined to be on that annulus h about the city center where $R[h] = \delta[h]$. Between the central business district (CBD) and h persons are willing and able to pay the cost of converting nonurban land to urban land use; hence, the land here will be urban. This is equivalent to requiring that infrastructure be in place prior to development and that the cost of the infrastructure is paid by the new residents at the urban margins. Beyond annulus h, since households are not willing to pay the cost of conversion, and even though the urban land rent is greater than nonurban land rent in some regions beyond h, land use here is assumed to be nonurban.

3.2.2 The radially constrained city

The boundary between the radially constrained city and the nonurban environment occurs on an annulus h about the CBD that is determined by a city planner or collusion of landowners. The annulus may be chosen to attain some objective such as prohibiting encroachment of the urban area into agricultural areas, or to maximize the returns to the landowners. The objective is to constrain the urban area to lie within a boundary less than would be generated by a freely operating market.

The effect of radially constraining a city will be fully developed in Chapter 12 (on planning). As an illustrative example, let h_2 represent the urban radius

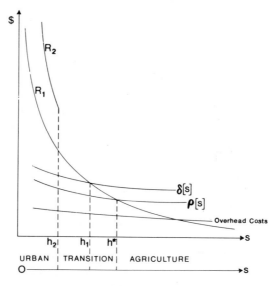

Figure 3.2 Derivation of urban limits for a radially
constrained city (after Thrall, 1980a)

set either by city planners or conspiratory landowners who have colluded in
some manner to control fringe land use development (Figure 3.2). Assume
that the city is constrained to have the same total urban population regardless
of whether the urban boundary is at h_1 or h_2. The city is perfectly malleable.
Say that the initial urban fringe was established as for an interactive city on
annulus h_1. The area of the interactive city is πh_1^2, while that for the radially
constrained city is πh_2^2. Since $\pi h_1^2 > \pi h_2^2$, the population of the radially
constrained city is squeezed into an area smaller than in the interactive
city; population density must then be greater in the radially constrained
city.

Population density and land consumption are inverses of each other. High
population density is coincident with high land rent and lower levels of household welfare, as can be verified from Figure 2.9. Radially constraining the
city will, therefore, increase land rent from $R_1[s]$ to $R_2[s]$ thereby reducing
household welfare. Within this setting, a "planned" radially constrained city
generates a spatial setting whose inhabitants have a lower level of welfare
than those in an "unplanned" interactive city. The justification for city planning rests upon the existence of a market unable to make corrective action for
externalities and interdependencies of households' welfare. We will discuss
this issue further in Chapters 12 and 13.

3.2.3   The solitary city

The radial extent of the solitary city is classified to extend over some region in a manner that by some rule-of-thumb is considered useful, such as 2000 persons per square mile. I use the term ''solitary'' because the radial extent of such a city does not depend upon either another economy external to the city, such as agriculture, nor does it depend upon the existence of a second sector, such as through local government planners, that can delineate the radial extent of the city. The solitary city is in isolation from other sectors of the economy.

The use of the solitary city definition can lead to improper conclusions about the urban area if, say, an inappropriate value for population density is chosen. For illustration, let h_3 (Figure 3.3) be that radius where population density is equal to 2000 persons per square mile. The zone between the CBD and h_3 has been labeled I since it is both defined to be and is within the urban area. Zone II, on the other hand, can justifiably be considered as part of the urban area, though it is not defined to be urban. If population density is added up at every distance and direction about the CBD, then the sum should equal total urban population. The transition zone and nonurban zone have been drawn with a population density that reflects the discussion of Figure 3.1 in section 3.2.1 on interactive cities. However, since the summation for the solitary city extends only to h_3, persons in zone II are not included in the population-counting analysis. The solitary city can thereby result in an underestimate of urban population. Moreover, for most purposes the solitary city lacks explanatory power.

3.3   Population or welfare

A city whose total population is an exogenously given constant is referred to as a *closed city*. A closed city was assumed in the discussion of the radially constrained city of section 3.2.2. In that discussion, the radius of the city and the manner in which it is determined was demonstrated to influence household welfare. The counterpoint to the closed city, where population is free to enter and exit the city, is referred to as an *open city*.

The ideal city can be brought closer to reality by defining it to have degrees of openness. Cities occur on a continuum between the two polar cases of open and closed, their position being determined by the willingness and ability of the population to in- and outmigrate. Whether a city is defined to be open or closed is as important to subsequent implications as how the radial extent of the city is determined.

In Figure 2.9, the spatial equilibrium quantity of land consumption was demonstrated to be a function of household welfare and, in Figure 2.12, to be a function of distance. Also, by definition, the inverse of land consumption

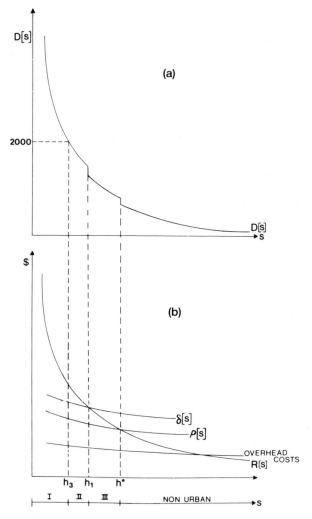

Figure 3.3 Derivation of urban limits for a solitary city (after Thrall, 1980a)

$Q[s]$ is population density $D[s]$. For illustration, if each household at distance s from the CBD consumes a half-acre, there are two households per acre.

Given that quantity of land consumed is directly proportional to distance from the CBD and spatial equilibrium welfare U, then assuming n-person households we can write:

$$D[s,U] = n/(Q[s,U]). \qquad (3.1)$$

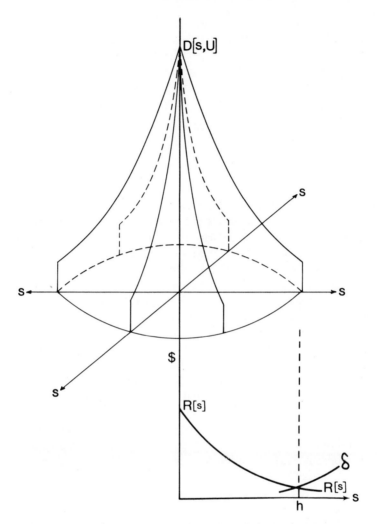

Figure 3.4 The population density cone (after Thrall, 1980a)

If population density is summed between the city center and urban radius h, the result is the total urban population P. In other words, total urban population is the volume of a population density cone. A projection of the population density cone for the ideal city is given in Figure 3.4. The higher the density gradient, or the further out along the density gradient one adds, the larger will be total population. Hence, spatial equilibrium total urban population is directly proportional to the radius of the city and inversely proportional to the spatial equilibrium welfare, namely:

$$P = P[h,U]. \tag{3.2}$$

Given that the urban fringe is determined by one of the three methods discussed in section 3.2, equation (3.2) can be reduced to two terms, P and U. In the closed city, P is exogenously specified allowing the endogenous variable $U[P]$ to be determined. In the open city, U is determined exogenously and we solve instead for the endogenous variable $P[U]$. We can now state the definitions for the two polar ideal cities:

Definition 3.4   The ideal *closed city* has an exogenous population and endogenous household welfare, namely $U[P]$.

Definition 3.5   The ideal *open city* has an endogenous total population and exogenous spatial equilibrium welfare, namely $P[U]$.

For illustration, reconsider the example of the radially constrained city in Figure 3.2; however, now define the city to be open. Households located beyond h_2 cannot relocate to within the new urban boundary as before because doing so would increase land rents there. An increase in land rents would decrease household welfare. Since welfare in the open city cannot change, and since there is no mechanism to compensate households who reside between the city center and h_2 for an increase in land rents, households between h_2 and h_1 must relocate to another region. Simply, such households are assumed to vanish from the diagram.

An alternative to viewing households as "vanishing" from the landscape is to draw the picture in a comparative static manner for two "sister cities" on the landscape: one city has an urban radius determined interactively, while the second city is radially constrained. If both cities are open, then the only difference between the sister cities is that the one that is radially constrained will have a smaller population and naturally a smaller urban radius. Discussion of cities from the standpoint of before and after the change will be used throughout this book interchangeably with the comparison between the two cities analogy.

To recap from Chapter 2, and from the above discussion, we can state in tandem the following two principles that result from the same problem but assuming the polar cases of open and closed cities. Given that the radius of the closed-interactive city is greater than the closed radially constrained city:

Principle 3.1   The spatial equilibrium welfare of a household in a closed radially constrained city will be less than the welfare of a household in a closed-interactive city.

Principle 3.2   The population of an open radially constrained city will be less than an otherwise equivalent open-interactive city.

This illustrates the importance of clearly specifying the model. (See also Table 3.1.) Different assumptions about the ideal city can give rise to significantly different implications. Recognition of this is critical when interpreting the real world in light of the implications of the Consumption Theory

Table 3.1 Listing of endogenous and exogenous variables for open- and closed-interactive cities

Open-interactive city		Closed-interactive city	
Endogenous	*Exogenous*	*Endogenous*	*Exogenous*
$Z[s]$	y	$Z[s]$	y
$Q[s]$	p	$Q[s]$	p
$D[s]$	k	$D[s]$	k
$R[s]$	δ	$R[s]$	δ
h	ρ	h	ρ
P	U	U	P

of Land Rent (CTLR). The closed model may best conform to economies that are highly developed economically, whereas the open setting may best correspond to regions in early stages of development, or late stages of economic decline. Depending upon the resistance to migration, cities can be located on a continuum between the polar open and closed cases. To interpret correctly the implications of the CTLR, one must consider where on the continuum the case-study city resides.

3.4   Conclusion

The purpose of this chapter has been to introduce two fundamental issues required for the proper specification of the CTLR model: the determination of the location of the delineation between urban and nonurban regions, and the decision as to whether welfare or population is to be endogenous, given the exogenous value of the other term.

For the purposes of this book the urban radius can be determined in any of three pure forms: interactive, radially constrained, and solitary. The interactive city has the boundary defined as the intersection between urban land rent and the cost of conversion of nonurban land to urban land utilization. Agricultural land rent may represent only a small component of the cost of conversion. A radially constrained city has its radius specified exogenously; in practice, this can be because of local planning ordinances or because land at the urban margins is withheld from the market. An island city may be radially constrained by nature. The radial extent of the solitary city is defined to be at that location where population density no longer exceeds, say, 2000 persons per square mile. In this book, generally an interactive city will be assumed; a departure from this will be Chapter 12 where city planning is evaluated.

In an open city, spatial equilibrium population is derived as a consequence of other factors, including exogenously given household welfare. In a closed city, the relative level of spatial equilibrium welfare is determined as a consequence of other factors, including population being an exogenously given constant. Table 3.1 has summarized what is endogenous and exogenous for the two polar open-interactive city and closed-interactive city cases. It is important to recognize that although the polar cases are valuable for arriving at the geometric solutions, cities exist on a continuum between open and closed, that is cities have degrees of openness.

References

Thrall (1979a, 1980a, 1982b)
Wheaton (1974)

4

Income

4.1 Introduction

Since the early 1950s the nominal median income of both black and white households in the United States has risen exponentially (Figure 4.1). The median income of black households has remained at about one-half of the level of white household median income.

In the United States, the poor of the larger cities frequently inhabit the inner core, while the more wealthy reside at the urban margins. In Canada, the United Kingdom and Europe, and South America, the rich often inhabit

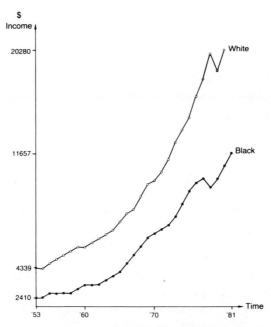

Figure 4.1   Median family income for black and white four-person households in the United States (after Thrall, 1980a)

what is considered the more desirable central core, while the poor live at the residual urban margins. Under what conditions does the Consumption Theory of Land Rent (CTLR) describe the different observed spatial distributions of households by income? An understanding of this can contribute to our intuition, as well as generate testable hypotheses as to why rich and poor people live where they do.

This chapter focuses upon three issues that concern the distribution of households by income. The first question analyzes what happens if household income increases. This question translates into an explanation as to why persons of different incomes live where they do. The second question deals with how an exogenous change in a parameter of the system can be transmitted spatially from one income group to the other. The third question concerns the pull that income (and its subsequent effect upon urban spatial structure) has upon human migration. Which of two ideal cities, one that is homogeneous and the other heterogeneous in income, will generate the higher level of welfare for its inhabitants?

The solution to these three questions requires, first, the determination of the *direct effect* upon the budget line and utility curve resulting from a change in some exogenous parameter such as income:

Definition 4.1   Direct effects are the consequence of a change in an exogenous parameter while holding spatial equilibrium land rent equal to its initial value.

Direct effects are the same for open and closed cities. Following the analysis of the direct effects, the *indirect effects* are analyzed:

Definition 4.2   Indirect effects are the endogenous changes that are the result of the system regaining spatial equilibrium once it has been propelled into a state of spatial disequilibrium.

Indirect effects are endogenous changes that are mainly the result of adjustments in spatial equilibrium land rents; the indirect effects are specific to the definitions of open and closed cities.

4.2   Direct effects of a change in household income

What influence does a change in income have upon urban spatial structure? For this problem, assume that income decreases from y to y'.

The first step in determining the direct effect of a decrease in income is to solve for the direction of the change in the budget line: does it move outwards from the origin, inwards toward the origin, or remain the same? If the budget line changes, is the shift parallel or oblique?

Recall from equation 2.4 the intercept $(y - ks)/r[s]$ on the abscissa (*x*-axis) or quantity of land axis. What is the direct change in the intercept resulting from a decrease in income? This can be phrased:

$$(y' - ks)/R[s] <?> (y - ks)/R[s] \text{ for } 0 < s < h. \qquad (4.1)$$

The term $<?>$ here (and hereafter) will denote that the direction of the inequality is unknown; upon solving for the direction of inequality (4.1) any or all of the three terms $<$, $>$, or $=$ may substitute for $<?>$. Multiplying equation (4.1) through by $R[s]$ and adding ks to both sides of the remaining expression results in:

$$y' <?> y \text{ for } 0 < s < h. \qquad (4.2)$$

Since it is known by assumption that $y' < y$, then the direction of the inequality in both (4.1) and (4.2) must be $<$; that is inequality (4.1) may be rewritten as:

$$(y' - ks)/R[s] < (y - ks)/R[s] \text{ for } 0 < s < h. \qquad (4.3)$$

A decrease in income results in a decrease in the intercepts on the abscissa.

Recall equation (2.3), the intercept $(y - ks)/p$ on the ordinate (*y*-axis) or quantity of composite good axis. What is the direct change in the intercept resulting from a decrease in income? This can be written:

$$(y' - ks)/p <?> (y - ks)/p \text{ for } 0 < s < h. \qquad (4.4)$$

By multiplying inequality (4.3) through by p, and adding ks to both sides of the subsequent expression, one is left with the same expression as in inequality (4.2). Hence, the sign of inequality (4.4) must also be $<$.

It is not actually necessary to inspect for direct effects that shift the intercepts of the budget lines on the abscissa in this example because by inspection it is seen that the income term y is not present in the expression for the slope of the budget line $- (r/p)$; since the slope is not directly affected by the change in the parameter y, the shift in the budget line is parallel. Therefore, a decrease in income results in a parallel and inward shift of the budget line.

The second step in determining the direct change in the budget line is to determine if the change in the budget line for households is everywhere the same, or is the change larger or smaller for households on annuli at increasing distance from the central business district (CBD)?

Let households on three annuli about the CBD, $s_1 < s_x < s_2$, have budget constraints respectively *AA*, *BB*, and *CC*. It was shown in principle 2.6 that the budget lines for households become lower and less steep with increasing distance from the CBD. Therefore, intercepts on the ordinate are arranged $A > B > C$, and for the intercepts on the abscissa $A < B < C$ (Figure 4.2).

The problem is to determine the relative magnitude of the shift in the budget constraints between locations. This is accomplished by comparing the change in intercepts between pairs of locations, say, s_1 and s_x, and then s_x and s_2.

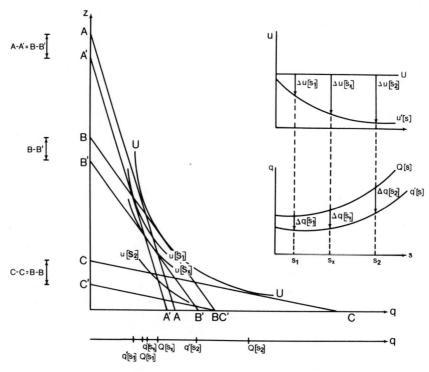

Figure 4.2   Direct effects from a decrease in household income

On the ordinate, determine whether the change in intercepts for budget lines for households on annulus s_x is $>$, $=$, or $<$ the change in the intercepts for the budget line for households on s_1. In other words, on the ordinate, is . . .?

$$A - A' <?> B - B' \tag{4.5}$$

Substitution of the appropriate equations for the intercepts as required in inequality (4.5) results in:

$$(y - ks_1)/p - (y' - ks_1)/p <?> (y - ks_x)/p - (y' - ks_x)/p. \tag{4.6}$$

Multiplying equation (4.6) through by p, taking the terms out of the braces, and rearranging the resulting expression leaves:

$$y - y' = y - y' \text{ or } 0 = 0. \tag{4.7}$$

The analysis of inequality (4.5) demonstrates that the solution of $<?>$ is $=$, meaning that the shifts in the intercepts on the ordinate of the budget lines are equal for annuli s_1 and s_x. The same can easily be shown for any other pair of locations such as s_x and s_2.

The results of the preceding analysis can be stated in the following principle:

Principle 4.1 On the direct effect of a spatially uniform change in household income: regardless of the household's location, each budget line will move parallel by the same amount, and move in the same direction as the change in income.

It has therefore been proven that if income decreases, the budget line shifts parallel, downward and to the left (Figure 4.2), and that the change in intercept on the ordinate is the same regardless of household location. This is represented by the budget lines shifting from AA to $A'A'$, BB to $B'B'$, and CC to $C'C'$ in Figure 4.2 for households respectively at $s_1 < s_x < s_2$, and where on the ordinate $A - A' = B - B' = C - C'$.

Because the change in the budget line intercept on the ordinate is the same for all locations, and because the slope of the budget line $-(R[s]/p)$ becomes flatter with increasing distance from the CBD, the reduction in income can be seen in Figure 4.2 to reduce household welfare more, the greater the distance the household is located from the CBD, and demonstrating that the direct effect of a reduction in income leaves the welfare surface for locations $s_1 < s_x < s_2$ as $u[s_1] > u[s_x] > u[s_2]$ (Figure 4.2).

This direct effect upon household welfare can be stated in the following principle:

Principle 4.2 On the direct effect of a spatially uniform change in household income: the change in household welfare is directly proportional to the change in income and directly proportional to the distance the household is located from the CBD.

The incidence of the change in income upon household welfare is not spatially neutral.

The direct effects upon consumption resulting from a decrease in income can be seen in Figure 4.2. Household consumption of land is reduced in direct proportion to distance from the CBD; this can be stated in the following principle:

Principle 4.3 On the direct effect of a spatially uniform change in household income: the change in household consumption of land is directly proportional to the change in income and directly proportional to the distance the household is located from the CBD.

The necessary indirect effects required for the system to return to a state of spatial equilibrium depend upon whether the city is open or closed.

4.3   Indirect effects from a reduction in income in an open-interactive city

4.3.1   A reduction in income

The restriction that households in an open city remain on an unchanging spatial equilibrium level of welfare is violated since $u[s] < U$ in Figure 4.2; the system must internally compensate for the decrease in income in order to regain spatial equilibrium. The compensation is not expected to be spatially uniform because, as demonstrated in principles 4.2 and 4.3, the incidence of a change in income is not spatially uniform. At any given distance s, all terms in the intercepts of the budget lines except land rent are exogenous; $R[s]$ is endogenous. With the change in income, $R[s]$ no longer satisfies spatial equilibrium conditions. A decrease in land rent will swing the budget constraints obliquely to again be tangent to the initial U.

The indirect effects are those changes that occur after the change in an exogenous parameter, and after land rent adjusts to return the system to spatial equilibrium. Some of the indirect effects of a reduction in y can be read from Figure 4.3.

For clarification, a repeat of the scenario for location s_x is as follows: the direct effect of the reduction in income is to shift budget line BB from being tangent to U to $B'B'$, everywhere below U. Land rents must decrease at s_x by an amount sufficient for $B'B'$ to again shift, this time obliquely, to $B'B''$ and regain tangency to U; effects attributable to this second shift in the budget line are referred to as indirect. Similarly, indirect effects are for budget lines $A'A'$ and $C'C'$ for locations s_1 and s_2 to obliquely shift to the right respectively to $A'A''$ and $C'C''$, tangent to U.

The repeat of the quantity of land axis (Figure 4.3(a)) carries over from Figure 4.2 the initial spatial equilibrium quantity of land consumed and the values attributable to the direct effects; these values can be contrasted to the new spatial equilibrium values that result from the indirect effects. Figure 4.3(b) summarizes these results. The direct effect upon land $\Delta Q^\wedge[s]$ from a reduction in income is for land consumption to decrease by $Q[s] - q'[s]$, namely:

$$\Delta Q^\wedge[s] = Q[s] - q'[s]. \tag{4.8}$$

The indirect effect of the reduction in land rents upon land consumption $\Delta Q^-[s]$ following a decrease in income is:

$$\Delta Q^-[s] = Q'[s] - q'[s]. \tag{4.9}$$

Equation (4.9) is the compensation in land consumption necessary for the household to regain spatial equilibrium welfare U. The change in land consumption that is revealed to occur at s attributable to the change in y is

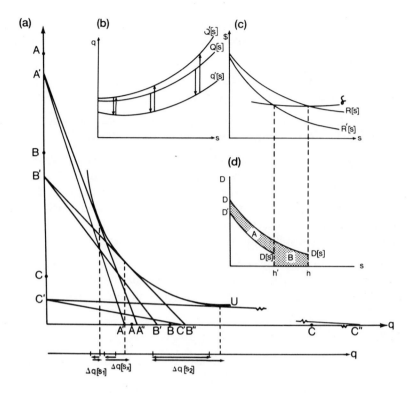

Figure 4.3 Indirect effects in an open-interactive city from a decrease in household income

from $Q[s]$ to $Q'[s]$. In other words, the *revealed change* in land consumption is the difference between indirect and direct effects:

$$\Delta Q^-[s] - \Delta Q^\wedge[s] = Q'[s] - Q[s]. \qquad (4.10)$$

Because the revealed effects in equation (4.10) are positive, households increase land consumption, thereby requiring a negative revealed effect upon population density. Further revealed effects are summarized in Figures 4.3(c) and (d). The now less wealthy city is not able to extend to radius h because land rents with the lower income are not sufficient to cover the cost of conversion there. Population must then 'vanish' from zone B in Figure 4.3(d); this is referred to as the *radius effect*. Because population density is less within the remaining zone of the city, then the less wealthy city has a population less within the inner zone by the shaded area marked A; this is referred to as the *density effect* (Thrall, 1982b):

Definition 4.3   Revealed effects are the difference between the indirect and direct effects that are attributable to some change in system definition or parameter.

Definition 4.4   The *radius effect* is the revealed change in population attributable to a change in the radial extent of the city.

Definition 4.5   The *density effect* is the revealed change in population attributable to a shift in the population density gradient.

In other words, between two ideal cities whose parameters are identical in every respect except income, then the population of the city with the lower income will be less than that of the city with the greater income. The difference in population is equal to the summation of radius and density effects as illustrated in zones A + B in Figure 4.3(d).

These results can be stated in the following principle:

Principle 4.4   Between two open cities whose households obtain identical welfare, the city whose inhabitants have the greater income will also have the greater population density, land rent, urban radius, and total population.

A corollary to principle 4.4 can also be given:

Principle 4.5   Between two open cities where households of one city have greater incomes than households of the other city, the welfare of both cities can still be the same if the poorer city has lower population density and land rent, smaller urban radius, and less total population.

Consider the following definition:

Definition 4.6   A ''large'' city has greater population density and land rent, larger total population, and generally greater radial extent than a ''small'' city.

Using definition 4.4, a corollary to principle 4.5 can be stated:

Principle 4.6   For the welfare of households in a ''large'' city to be the same as households in a ''small'' city the households of the large city must have a greater income than households in the small city.

The above principles address comparisons between open cities. Further analysis is required to answer the following question: if the open city contains households not all of the same income, then will the households partition themselves in space in some regular and identifiable manner?

4.3.2   *The open-interactive case: location of rich and poor*

Let the households of the open city be partitioned into two income groups.

Call households with the relatively higher income y_R rich, and those with the relatively lower income y_P poor. Let the welfare of the rich be greater than that for the poor; therefore:

$$U_R > U_P \tag{4.11}$$

and:

$$y_R > y_P. \tag{4.12}$$

The setting identified by equations (4.11) and (4.12) is portrayed in Figure 4.4. Initially assume that households of each income inhabit the city. To inhabit the city, the households must reside somewhere. Because of this, if one income group can be shown to reside at the CBD, then if the other group is to be represented in the city, it must reside at the urban margins. At later stages of the analysis one income group may everywhere outbid the other income group, thereby excluding the group that was outbid from the city.

At the CBD distance s is equal to 0. The numerator of each intercept in the budget line for households at the CBD then reduces to the income of the respective rich or poor household group.

Figure 4.4 reveals the possibility of two cases. In both cases, the intercept of the budget line for poor on the ordinate is less than that for rich, since both groups pay the same composite good price p and disposable income is greater for rich than it is for poor at the CBD. However, on the abscissa, in the first case the poor households' intercept is greater than that for the rich households, while the converse is true for the second case.

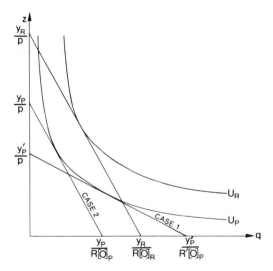

Figure 4.4 Derivation of the relative location of rich and poor households in an open-interactive city (after Thrall, 1980a)

A setting with a substantial income differential is represented in the first case (Figure 4.4), so that:

$$y'_P/R'[0]_P > y_R/R[0]_R. \tag{4.13}$$

Inequality (4.13) can be rearranged as:

$$y'_P/y_R > R'_P/R_R \text{ for } s = 0. \tag{4.14}$$

Since in equation (4.12) it has been assumed that income for poor is less than income for rich, then we can write:

$$1 > y'_P/y_R. \tag{4.15}$$

Using inequalities (4.14) and (4.15):

$$1 > y'_P/y_R > R'_P/R_R \text{ for } s = 0. \tag{4.16}$$

Rearranging inequality (4.16), we have:

$$R_R/R'_P > 1 \text{ for } s = 0. \tag{4.17}$$

or:

$$R_R > R'_P \text{ for } s = 0. \tag{4.18}$$

Because of the analysis for equation (4.18), the following principle can be stated:

Principle 4.7 When there is substantial income or welfare inequality, the rich will reside at the city center. If the poor are to live in the city, they will reside at the urban margins.

This result will hold even as the difference in income separating the two population groups diminishes so long as the welfare difference between the two groups also proportionately diminishes. Therefore, rich reside in the inner city if there is relatively great income inequality and great welfare inequality, or small income inequality and small welfare inequality so long as inequality (4.13) remains true.

In the second case (Figure 4.4), there is small income inequality, but the same welfare inequality as in the first case. Let the poor have income y_P instead of y'_P, so that $y_P > y'_P$. The sign in inequality (4.13) switches, namely:

$$y_P/R_P < y_R/R_R \text{ for } s = 0. \tag{4.19}$$

Following the same methodology as in inequalities (4.13)–(4.18), we have:

$$R_R <?> R_P \text{ for } s = 0. \tag{4.20}$$

The second case does not have a definite solution to the relative location of rich and poor. It can lead to three solutions: (a) the rich are not willing to outbid the poor for the right to reside near to the city center, thereby leaving the rich to live at the urban margins; (b) the poor bid the same as the rich leading to a solution where both income groups are spatially integrated at the inner core of the city; or (c) the rich outbid the poor for the right to inhabit the inner core of the city. These results can be stated in the following principle:

> *Principle 4.8* If the income inequality is small and welfare inequality large, then neighborhoods that are heterogeneous in income are possible as are homogeneous neighborhoods with either poor or rich at the city center.

What are the incentives for one population group to outbid the other population group for the right to inhabit the inner core of the city? The relative size of the income groups can be a contributing factor. Say that the poor inhabit the inner core of the city. If the population size of poor households is large as compared to rich households, then a large circular urban-core poor population would be surrounded by a thin ribbon of rich households at the urban periphery. Households in this ribbon may not achieve benefits of spatial proximity to others of similar income. Costs of spatial dispersion may be reduced by agglomerating. This suggests the following proposition:

> *Proposition 4.1* Let there be nontrivial benefits to population agglomerating by income. If the ratio of rich households to poor households is small, the rich will agglomerate at a central location such as (but not necessarily), the urban core. If the ratio is large, the rich will reside at the urban margins. A tipping-point should then exist, and if so, where the changeover takes place can be calculated.

The location of the tipping-points, their stability, and verification of proposition 4.1 must be determined by empirical research.

4.4 Indirect effects of a change in income in the closed-interactive city

4.4.1 A change in income

There is no restriction as in the open city that the closed city system will return to welfare U. Instead a change in an exogenous parameter of a closed city may lead to a new spatial equilibrium level of welfare. The resulting welfare may be greater than, equal to, or less than the initial spatial equilibrium welfare. How is the new spatial equilibrium welfare derived? Consider the following proposition:

> *Proposition 4.2* Somewhere on the closed city landscape direct effects are sufficient for households there to be in spatial equilibrium.

Recall in the general discussion of utility curves and budget constraints that utility curves are everywhere dense; every combination of z and q can be located on some utility curve. Similarly, given that disposable incomes and prices are continuous, there are an infinite number of budget lines, a subset of these budget lines that will be tangent to either U and U', where U and U' are parallel to each other and U' is the new spatial equilibrium level of welfare. The problem, then, is to solve for the value of s_x for the appropriate budget line initially tangent to U and whose direct effects make it tangent to U'.

It is sufficient to know that s_x can be somewhere, either within or outside the city. Following a change in one of the exogenous parameters of the system, the budget line becomes tangent to $u[s_x]$. There is no restriction that the budget line of only one location will satisfy the requirements for s_x or that any household would reside on annulus s_x. The utility curve $u[s_x]$ is constrained to be parallel to U. Because the budget line for households at s_x is tangent to what "coincidently" becomes the new spatial equilibrium level of welfare, no subsequent indirect effects that result from a change in land rent are required for the households at s_x to be in spatial equilibrium; hence, $R'[s_x] = R[s_x]$.

The relative spatial location of s_x can be derived following specification of the problem under study. The solution for the location of s_x following a decrease in income will be demonstrated by example.

Let there be three annuli about the CBD s_1, s_x and s_2, where:

$$s_1 < s_x < s_2. \tag{4.21}$$

Households on annuli s_1, s_x, and s_2 have budget constraints denoted respectively *AA*, *BB*, and *CC*. By principle 2.6, budget lines become lower and flatter with increasing distance from the city center. Figure 4.2 illustrates the direct effects of a decrease in y, while Figure 4.5 portrays the subsequent indirect effects.

The household (Figure 4.5) on annulus s_x has a decrease in income from y to y'; the budget line shifts from *BB* to *B'B'*. The budget line is tangent to $u[s_x]$. Because $u[s_x]$ is equal to the spatial equilibrium level of welfare for households with income y', direct effects suffice there for the system to be in spatial equilibrium; no adjustment in the spatial equilibrium land rent is necessary at s_x.

Following some perturbation to the system such as a change in income, somewhere no indirect effects are required to reestablish spatial equilibrium at that location. Proposition 4.1 is then restated as the following principle:

Principle 4.9   On unknown annulus s_x, where $s_x <?> h$, direct effects are sufficient to identify the change in spatial equilibrium welfare.

Also the result that U' is less than U is worth stating in the following principle:

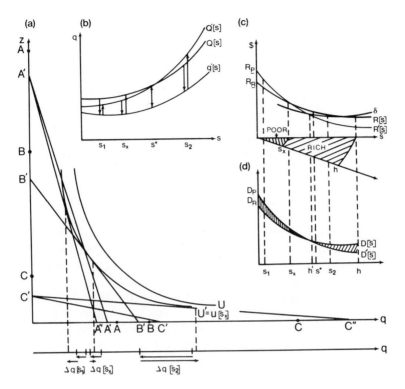

Figure 4.5 Indirect effects in a closed-interactive city from a decrease in household income

Principle 4.10 The spatial equilibrium level of welfare in a closed city is directly related to the income of the households, all other things being equal.

Are the direct effects also sufficient to shift budget lines at s_1 and s_2 to be tangent to $u[s_x] = U'$?

The answer can be found by inspecting Figure 4.2, where it is demonstrated that $u[s_1] > u[s_x] > u[s_2]$. Households at s_2 must be compensated in some manner to bring their welfare up to that which can be obtained at locations interior to it including s_x, while negative compensation or a penalty is necessary for households at s_1 to reduce their welfare to U'. To receive the higher levels of welfare, households move into the inner core of the city from locations further from the CBD than s_x. Land rent interior to annulus s_x increases. Land rent in the urban margins beyond s_x decreases.

Specifically, households will inmigrate to s_1 thereby leading to indirect effects in the budget line; through the adjustment in spatial equilibrium land rent at s_1, the budget line swings obliquely from $A'A'$ to $A'A''$. The shift to the left is accomplished by an increase in spatial equilibrium land rent from

$R[s_1]$ to $R'[s_1]$. It can be demonstrated by inspection of Figure 4.5(a) that there is a revealed decrease in spatial equilibrium quantity of land consumed at both s_1 and s_x, with the proportionate change at s_1 larger than at s_x.

The same scenario is followed for the change in the budget line at s_2, following a decrease in y to y'. The direct change in the budget line at s_2 is the same as for s_x; namely, C − C′ = B − B′ on the ordinate. In this case, the direct shift in the budget line reduces household welfare at s_2 to be a value less than the new spatial equilibrium level. Households outmigrate, thereby reducing land rents. Because of the decline in land rent, the budget line at s_2 then swings outward from $C'C'$ to $C'C''$ which is tangent to the new spatial equilibrium level of welfare U'.

Commensurate with an outmigration of households at s_2, population density decreases. The fewer remaining households at s_2 partition the land between themselves thereby leaving each with a greater quantity of land. However, at s_x land consumption decreases. It must be, then, that if space is smooth and continuous, consumption of land does not change at some location between s_x and s_2, say s^*, where $s_x < s^* < s_2$.

The closed city includes, by definition, the restriction that total population be the same before and after any change in an exogenous parameter of the system. The lower income restricts the radius of the city to be smaller by $h - h'$; the number of persons within the "lost" urban margins must be accommodated within the remaining urban core. Hence, the number of persons identified by $D[s]$ between h' and h will account for the difference between $D'[s] - D[s]$ for $0 < = s < = h'$.

From inspection of Figure 4.5(c) and (d), we can state the following three principles:

Principle 4.11   Land rent in the closed city is directly proportional to income at the urban margins and inversely proportional to income at the urban core.

Principle 4.12   The greater the income of households in a closed city, the less steep will be the rent gradient.

Principle 4.13   The greater the income of households in a closed city, the less steep will be the population density gradient.

The resulting changes in the spatial structure of the city following a reduction in income from y to y', depicted in Figure 4.5(b)–(d) are summarized by location in Table 4.1. Population density and land rent both increase at the CBD and decrease at the urban margins; however, it is interesting to note that the breaking-points are not the same between where the old density and rent gradients intersect with their respective new gradients.

Table 4.1 demonstrates that a spatially uniform change in a parameter of the system, in this case income, translates into a remarkable variation in the way the change affects land consumption and the price of land depending

Table 4.1 Locational effects of a reduction in household income in a closed-interactive city

Line	Location	Direction in change of variable		
		$R[s]$	$Q[s]$	$D[s]$
1	$0 < = s < s_x$	+	−	+
2	s_x	0	−	+
3	$s_x < s < s^*$	−	−	+
4	s^*	−	0	0
5	$s^* < s < h$	−	+	−

upon *relative spatial location*. It is tempting to interpret land within the aspatial nomenclature as being a normal good with price and quantity varying inversely with each other (in lines 1 and 5); and an inferior good, perhaps a Giffin good (in line 3), because price and quantity consumed change in the same direction. However, in addition to changes in income, price, and quantity, there remains the additional component that because of the geography of the system, households have different disposable incomes while, at the same time, having the geographic restriction that they everywhere attain the same welfare surface.

4.4.2 The closed-interactive case: location of rich and poor

Let there be two income groups, rich and poor. The rich have income $y_R = y$ with welfare $U_R = U$, and the poor have income $y_P = y'$ with welfare $U_P = U'$, as in Figure 4.5.

The population density of the poor will then equal the $D_P = D'[s]$ function, and the population density of the rich will equal the $D_R = D[s]$ function (Figure 4.5(d)). The respective income groups will inhabit that sector of the city where they are willing and able to outbid the other population group for the right to use that space. Hence, the rich will possess the urban margins between s_x and h, while the poor will live in the inner core of the city between the CBD and s_x.

Because the breaking-points between rent gradients do not coincide with the breaking-points for the density gradients, there will be a sudden change in density at s_x. Since the total population of the closed city is constrained to be constant, regardless of being partitioned into rich and poor households, the number of persons identified either by D_P $[0< =s< =h']$ or $D_R[0< =s< =h]$ must equal the number of persons identified by the discontinuous function $D[D_P[0< =s< =s_x], D_R[s_x<s< =h]]$. At the same time, the relative levels of welfare, U_R and U_P, identify the relative population size of rich and poor.

4.5   Consumption and production theories combined

The second question in this chapter concerns how an exogenous change in a parameter of the system can be transmitted spatially from one income group to another.

Recall that from principle 4.12 the greater the income, the less steep is the households' rent gradient; conversely, the less the households' income, the more steep will be the rent gradient. The interaction of such rent gradients gives rise about the CBD to circular bands containing households with increasingly greater income as distance from the CBD increases (Figure 4.5(c)). As in the previous analysis, let the two income groups be rich and poor. Note that here rich people pay less per square foot for the use of land than poor people. The inner core of the city will be inhabited by poor people, while the urban margins will contain rich people.

Further distinguish landusers as to whether they use land as the result of a consumption decision (CTLR) or as a result of a production decision. An in-depth analysis of the Production Theory of Land Rent (PTLR) is beyond the scope of this book; however, the reader is encouraged to review the classic work by Von Thünen (1821), briefly mentioned earlier in section 1.2.1 of this book. Let $L[s]$ represent Von Thünen's rent gradient for central city commercial activities. It is assumed that business benefits from central locations, so that the rent business is willing to pay will be greater than that for households at the CBD, and steeply decline with loss of proximity to the CBD.

The ideal city now has spatial dimensions for the CBD in contrast to the more usual point coordinate. Immediately adjacent to the commercial center of the city are located the poor households, with the rich households some distance from the CBD. Assume that the city is interactive. An illustration of the spatial structure for the ideal city implied by these assumptions is as in Figure 4.6.

Say some exogenous force causes an increase in the rent function for the commercial sector. It is assumed that this business prosperity is not passed into increasing household income.

4.5.1   Revealed effects of an increase in production rent in an open city

First, consider an open city (Figure 4.6). An increase in $L[s]$ to $L'[s]$ yields an increase in the radius of the CBD from s_1 to s'_1. The population of the city is less by the number of poor households previously resident between s_1 and s'_1. The rich being insulated by the poor from expansion of the commercial sector receive no other subsequent effects. The closed city requires somewhat more complex analysis.

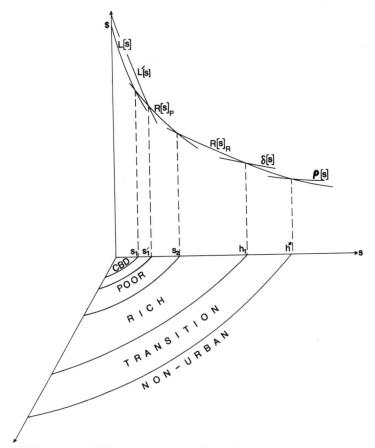

Figure 4.6 Combining the production (PTLR) and consumption (CTLR) theories of land rent (after Thrall, 1980a)

4.5.2 *Revealed effects of an increase in production rent in a closed city*

For the closed case (Figure 4.7), contrast the two commercial rent gradients, $L[s]$ from a local center or "low-order city," and $L[s]$ from a "high-order city" $L[s] < L'[s]$ (for discussion of city order see King, 1984). The proportion of the land area inhabited by poor people in the city with the higher commercial rent is reduced. The higher commercial rent affords an increase in the land area devoted to commercial land use, thereby limiting poor persons to a smaller area which translates into an increase in population density of poor people. A corollary of principle 2.1 (p. 20) is that the greater the population density, the higher will be the land rent, and the lower will be the spatial equilibrium level of welfare. Rent for the poor, therefore, increases from $R[s]_P$ to $R'[s]_P$ and U_P decreases to U'_P.

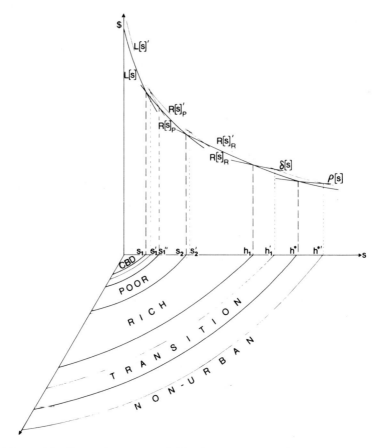

Figure 4.7   Inner city commercial land rent changes and their effect
upon the household sector (after Thrall, 1980a)

Because of the higher commercial rent, the poor rent gradient is for some
distance greater than the rich rent gradient beyond the previous breaking-
point at s_2. As the poor move outward from the CBD there is a decrease in the
volume of land previously inhabited by rich households; the rich have an
increase in population density and subsequently an increase in land rent from
$R[s]_R$ to $R'[s]_R$. The breaking-point between rich and poor becomes s_2.

The urban radius grows from h_1 to h'_1. The zone of transition increases
from h^* to $h^{*'}$. Rich now have greater population density and greater land
rents, and many have greater transportation costs than existed prior to the
increase in $L[s]$. The higher commercial rent has led to a decrease in the
spatial equilibrium welfare of rich to U'_R. The implications of the above
analysis can be stated in the following principle:

Principle 4.14   If higher-order cities have greater production rents than lower-order cities, and if the level of welfare between high- and low-order cities is to be the same, then households in higher-order cities must receive some form of compensation, such as greater incomes, than their counterparts in lower-order cities all other things being equal.

Say that the expansion of the business sector results in an increase in households' income. Because welfare and income have been shown to be directly related (principle 4.12), the following planning recommendation can be stated:

Principle 4.15 If households receive compensation that is akin to an increased income by an amount that (more than) balances the decrease in welfare attributable to the higher population density and land rents, then

(i) households should be indifferent to (prefer) commercial expansion.

(ii) In the absence of compensatory payments, households will be worse off following commercial expansion, all other things being equal.

Income is one form of compensation; public goods and externalities as presented in Chapter 13 can also provide compensation.

4.6 Migration

The third and last question of this chapter concerns the income mix of a city: given several cities with the same total population P, will a city that is heterogeneous in income distribution generate welfare levels greater than, equal to, or less than those that may be obtained for any income group in a homogeneous city? This question can be translated into a strategy of household migration:

Which, between two cities, would a household choose to migrate to if one city was composed of inhabitants identical in income to itself, versus another city whose inhabitants had incomes different than the migrating household?

The question is formalized in the following manner. Let there be three closed cities. The first city has a poor population of P_{P1} and a rich population of P_{R1}, with respective welfare levels of U_{P1} and U_{R1}. The second city is composed entirely of P_{P2} poor households, with welfare level U_{P2}, and the third city has P_{R3} households with welfare U_{R3}; thus:

$$P_{P1} + P_{R1} = P \text{ for } P_{P1}, P_{R1} > 0 \tag{4.22}$$

and:

$$P_{P2} = P \tag{4.23}$$

and:

$$P_{R3} = P. \tag{4.24}$$

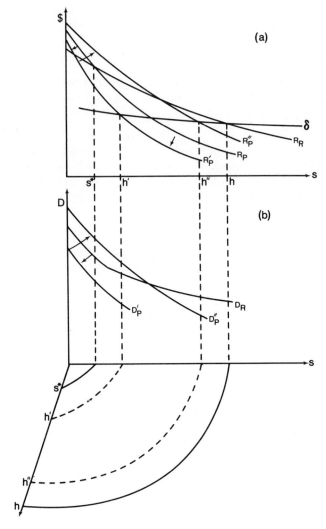

Figure 4.8   CTLR proof that households' welfare is greater in cities
composed of households with incomes different than themselves
(after Thrall, 1980a)

In the discussion of equation (3.1), it was demonstrated that population
density and land consumption are the inverse of each other and, in the
discussion of Figure 3.4, that total urban population and population density
are directly related, all other things being equal. Recall also principle 2.1, that
land rent and population density are inversely related to household welfare;
in summary:

$$\uparrow P \rightarrow \uparrow D \rightarrow \uparrow R \rightarrow \downarrow U. \qquad (4.25)$$

Let the first city be composed of rich and poor households with rent gradients R_P and R_R (Figure 4.5(c)), and population density D_P and D_R (Figure 4.5(d)). These relationships are redrawn in Figure 4.8(a) and (b). Poor households reside interior to s^*, and rich reside between s^* and h.

To evaluate the relative level of poor households' welfare between cities 1 and 2, first eliminate the rich households in city 1, they will be replaced by poor households. The rich rent gradient vanishes. Competition from rich for land between s^* and h is eliminated. The rent gradient for the poor is greater than the cost of conversion for some distance beyond s^*. Because of the greater area of land now attainable by poor, the population density will decrease between 0 and s^* as poor relocate beyond s^*. The new density function for the poor is D'_P, commensurate with rent gradient R'_P. Because total population is now less, poor households temporarily have a higher level of welfare.

To conform to equation (4.23), increase the poor population. The density gradient of the poor D'_P must shift outward to D''_P. This new function D''_P is greater than the original D_P function, since the number of poor people accommodated over the range $s^* - h'$ is less than the volume of rich under the D_R function that needs to be replaced. As the poor "fill up" the city, and their density increases, the rent gradient shifts from R'_P to R''_P. Poor households' population density and rent gradients are now greater than before the substitution of poor for rich. The poor households' welfare, therefore, results in a net decline.

The welfare of the rich households between cities 1 and 3 can be evaluated in the same manner. Since the total population size is held constant, rich households in the third city (equation (4.24)) will have a lower level of welfare; in other words,

$$\uparrow P_R \rightarrow \uparrow D_R \rightarrow \uparrow R_R \rightarrow \downarrow U_R. \qquad (4.26)$$

The argument in expression (4.26) can be stated in the following principle.

Principle 4.16 In a closed city, the household can attain a higher level of welfare the fewer the number of households with the same income.

Welfare for both rich households and poor households increases in a closed city as a result of the metamorphosis from a homogeneous to a heterogeneous city. This can be interpreted that households are better off the less competition they have for space from individuals with the same income. If rent gradients from a particular income sector do not overwhelm that of other income groups, then where one has a choice, one should choose the heterogeneous over the homogeneous city. This can be stated in the following principle:

Principle 4.17 In a set of closed cities whose parameters are identical except for composition of household income, the household can attain a higher level of welfare by migrating to a heterogeneous city with the least number of households with the same income.

For illustration, say that management all receive the same income, and all blue-collar workers have the same income, but management income is greater than blue-collar income. Management would be able to attain a higher level of welfare residing in a town dominated by blue-collar workers, and a lower level of welfare in a town whose inhabitants are largely management. If all other things were equal, especially barring externalities (Chapter 13), by this reasoning managements' welfare in Toledo, Ohio, would be higher than their counterparts' welfare in Santa Barbara, California.

4.7   Conclusion

In this chapter three general issues concerning household income have been analyzed. First, what happens if household income increases? The general result for an open city is that land rents and population density increase as a compensating penalty. For a closed city, as incomes increase, land rents and population density become lower and flatter. Extend the question to evaluate where households of differing income reside. In the closed city, the poor reside in the inner core surrounded by the rich. The open city is more complex: where both income and welfare differentials are at the extreme positions as being either very large or very small, then the rich reside at the city center, leaving the poor at the urban margins; however, if income differentials are large and the welfare differential small, there is no unique spatial solution: rich or poor, or both, could reside in the inner city.

Second, the CTLR has been combined with a Production Theory of Land Rent setting. As exogenous parameters affected the production sector, the effect is spatially transmitted to the household sector. In the open city, the burden of the increase in land rents falls entirely upon the households residing immediately adjacent to the city center and their numbers decrease by an amount necessary to eliminate any indirect effects. In the closed city, the burden is shared between each of the different groups of households; land rents increase and welfare decreases for each income group.

Third, the effect of income distribution and its pull upon migration has been examined. It was determined that households would be better off the fewer are the numbers of households with the same income; this is because households with the same income compete for the same space, thereby driving down each other's welfare. The households would be better off in cities composed of richer and poorer households competing for other locations.

References

Clark (1986)
King (1984)
Pines (1975)
Rogers (1985)
Thrall (1979a, 1982b, 1985)
Von Thünen (1821)
Yellin (1974)

PART II

Transportation Systems

Transportation cost

5.1 Introduction

The effect that changing transportation cost has upon the spatial structure of the ideal city is the topic of this chapter.

The two decades following 1950 were for most western countries the period of greatest suburbanization. In the United States, the post World War II era was also noted for nominally inexpensive gasoline prices and the introduction

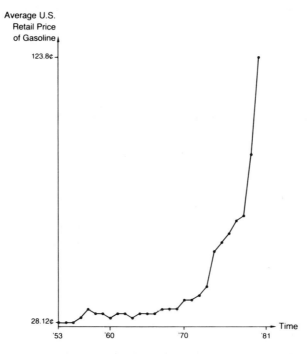

Figure 5.1 Average retail price in the United States of a gallon of regular gasoline in a full service station, 1953–81 (after Thrall, 1982c)

of the interstate highway system. The interstate highways that transected cities, followed by the construction of outer belts, allowed quick commuting from the central city to distant suburbia. A commuter who could drive 50 miles an hour, and was willing to allocate one half-hour each way to work, could live 25 miles from work. Moreover, at say $0.30 per gallon, with an automobile receiving 10 miles per gallon, it would cost only $1.50 for the round trip to work, not considering the depreciation and maintenance of the automobile.

Between 1953 and 1966, the price of regular gasoline at a full service station was relatively constant. The price of gasoline began to increase in 1967. Increases were substantial following the 1974 Arab oil embargo against the United States. The figure reveals, however, that the price increase actually began about four years before the embargo, around 1970. The nominal price of gasoline in the United States increased by 347 percent between 1970 and 1981. However, in the mid-1980s the price of gasoline remained relatively constant, and at the time of writing this book appears at least in the short term to be on the decline. Gasoline prices in 1985 for various locations about the world are given in Table 5.1. With nominally high-priced gasoline since the mid-1970s, will the attraction to the suburbs diminish?

Table 5.1   World prices for regular gasoline at a self-service station in the United States (gallons in US dollars for first quarter of 1985)

	$		$
USA average	1.18·	Stockholm	1.86
Sydney	1.33	Brussels	1.88
Toronto	1.34	Paris	2.04
Frankfurt	1.59	Dublin	2.29
Geneva	1.61	Tokyo	2.41
London	1.73		

Source: International Petroleum Annual (see also *International Energy Annual*).

This chapter evaluates what is the effect upon urban spatial structure following a change in the transportation cost component k of the households' budget constraint. The change in k is assumed to be spatially uniform. The spatial invariance in the transportation surface will be relaxed in Chapter 7 with the introduction of a low-cost transportation cost network containing nodes of access and egress.

5.2   Direct effects of an increase in transportation cost

In the analysis, it is assumed that transportation cost increases. Because the Consumption Theory of Land Rent (CTLR) is a smooth, continuous

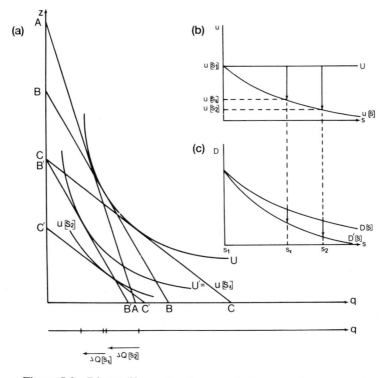

Figure 5.2 Direct effects of an increase in the cost of transportation (after Thrall, 1982c)

geometry, the effect of a decrease in transportation cost is the opposite of an increase in transportation cost.

Let there be three annuli from the central business district (CBD) designated by s_1, s_x, and s_2, where $s_1 < s_x < s_2$. Let the spatial equilibrium welfare initially be U. Households face budget constraint AA at s_1, BB at s_x, and CC at s_2.

An increase in transportation cost k results in a decrease in the numerator of the intercepts of the households' budget line in equations (2.3) and (2.4) (see p. 14). The intercepts of the budget line decrease with an increase in k since the direct effects are evaluated holding land rent constant in the denominator of the abscissa. The k term is not present in the slope $-(r/p)$, thus the budget line's shift is parallel. An increase in k to k' decreases disposable income at any given distance s from the CBD, thereby shifting the budget constraint for households at s parallel and downward to the left.

Next determine if an increase in k results in intercepts decreasing by the same amount at all locations, that is determine if:

$$A - A' <?> B - B' <?> C - C'. \tag{5.1}$$

Determine the relative change for $A - A'$ and $B - B'$ on the ordinate.

$$(y - ks_1)/p - (y - k's_1)/p <?>$$
$$(y - ks_x)/p - (y - k's_x)/p. \tag{5.2}$$

Multiplying equation (5.2) through by p, and rearranging the resulting expression, leaves:

$$s_1(k' - k) <?> s_x(k' - k). \tag{5.3}$$

Because $k' > k$, dividing both sides by $(k' - k)$ will not change the direction of the inequality; this operation results in:

$$s_1 <?> s_x. \tag{5.4}$$

Because s_1 is less than s_x, the direction of inequalities (5.1)–(5.4) is $<$. Therefore, the decrease in intercepts is greater the further the household is located from the CBD. This result reaffirms our intuition because the further the household is located from the CBD the greater will be that household's transportation expenditures. At the CBD an increase in transportation cost does not directly affect the household's budget line since for $s = 0$ transportation costs are not a component of disposable income; as in equation (4.10), disposable income at $s = 0$ is $y*[0] = y - k0 = y$.

The change in the intercept of the budget constraint on the abscissa can also be shown to be directly proportional to distance:

$$(y - ks_1)/R[s_1] - (y - k's_1)/R[s_1] <?>$$
$$(y - ks_x)/R[s_x] - (y - k's_x)/R[s_x]. \tag{5.5}$$

Rearranging equation (5.5) leaves:

$$s_1(k' - k)/R[s_1] <?> s_x(k' - k)/R[s_x]. \tag{5.6}$$

Dividing both sides by $(k' - k)$, and rearranging the remaining terms, leaves:

$$R[s_x]/R[s_1] <?> s_x/s_1 \text{ (for } k' > k). \tag{5.7}$$

From principle 2.2 (p. 23), we know land rent decreases with increasing distance from the CBD, hence:

$$R[s_x]/R[s_1] < 1. \tag{5.8}$$

Because $s_x/s_1 > 1$, we can then interpret the sign of inequality (5.7) as:

$$R[s_x]/R[s_1] < 1.0 < s_x/s_1 \text{ (for } k' > k). \tag{5.9}$$

The direction of the sign of inequality (5.5) is the same as equation (5.9): $<$. Therefore, for a change in k, the change in the intercepts on the abscissa is greater the further from the CBD that the household is located.

One need only have derived the change in either ordinate or abscissa intercept because for direct effects the slope of the budget line is independent of k. The same analysis can be repeated with the same results for any pair of locations, including s_x and s_2. The above results can be summarized by the following principle:

Principle 5.1 Direct effects of a change in transportation cost: the change in budget line is inversely related to a change in transportation cost; the magnitude of the change is greater the further the household is located from the CBD.

Principle 5.1 is used to complete the geometric analysis. Let s_1 be at the CBD. Since $s_1 = 0$, the budget line AA then does not change following an increase in k; there are no direct effects upon the welfare of households at s_1 (Figure 5.2).

The budget line at s_x shifts parallel, downward, and to the left, from BB to $B'B'$. The restriction is satisfied that $B - B' > A - A'$ since $A - A' = 0$ and $B - B' > 0$. Direct effects at s_x reduce households' welfare to $u[s_x] < U$.

The budget line at s_2 also shifts parallel, downward, and to the left, from CC to $C'C'$. By principle 5.1, the shift in the budget line at s_2 must be greater than that at s_x. The restriction that $C' - C' > B - B'$ has been accommodated in Figure 5.2 in the following manner. For location s_2, $C - C'$ was drawn to equal $B - B'$; the important feature to read from the relative change in budget lines is that $u[s_2] < u[s_x]$. Had $C - C'$ been drawn by any amount greater than $B - B'$, this result would remain the same. Hence, for any $C - C' > = B - B'$, $u[s_2] < u[s_x]$.

The results of the direct effects, derived in Figure 5.2(a) and summarized in Figure 5.2(b) and (c), can be stated in the following principle:

Principle 5.2 Direct effects of a change in transportation cost: the change in household welfare is inverse to a change in transportation cost. The further the household is located from the city center, the greater will be the change in welfare.

The next two sections of this chapter evaluate the indirect effects of an increase in transportation cost for open and closed cities.

5.3 Indirect effects of a change in transportation cost in an open city

In the open city, welfare is constrained to remain at U. Only at $s_1 = 0$ does a budget line remain tangent to U following an increase in k. Hence, only at the city center will there be no indirect effects attributable to a change in transportation costs. For every location other than $s = 0$, land rents must decrease to accommodate the necessary swing of the budget constraints obliquely to the right to become again tangent to U. This is shown in Figure 5.3. Because the decrease in welfare was greater, the further the household is

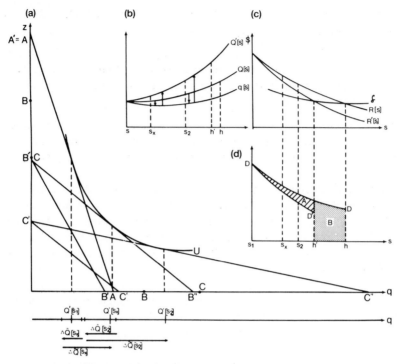

Figure 5.3　Indirect effects of an increase in the cost of transportation in an open-interactive city (after Thrall, 1982c)

located from the CBD, then the compensation through changing land rents must be greater for the relatively more remote locations.

Households at $s_1 < s_x < s_2$ initially had budget lines respectively AA, BB, and CC. The direct effect of the increase in k was to shift the budget lines parallel and downward to $A'A'$, $B'B'$, and $C'C'$. Because of principle 5.1, $A - A' < B - B' < C - C'$, namely the magnitude of the decrease is greater the further that the household is located from the CBD. Quantity of land consumed was initially $Q[s]$ (Figure 5.3(b)) and decreased to $q'[s]$; but for $s = 0$, $q'[0] = Q[0]$.

The indirect effects act as compensation to households for the increase in k. Land rents decrease from $R[s]$ to $R'[s]$ (Figure 5.3(c)); but for $s = 0$, $R'[0] = R[0]$. The decrease in land rents can be demonstrated to be greater the further that the household is located from the CBD by inspecting the shift in the intercepts on the abscissa: $(A'-A'') < (B'-B'') < (C'-C'')$ (Figure 5.3(a)). Land consumption becomes $Q'[s]$ (Figure 5.3(b)), resulting in a shift from population density gradient DD to DD' (Figure 5.3(d)).

Since spatial equilibrium population is the summation of population density between the CBD and urban fringe, population must then be less because of the decline in the population density. The total population of the city prior to the increase in k was equal to the volume identified by the rotation about the CBD of *DDh*. The total spatial equilibrium population following an increase in k is identified by *DD'h'*. The population that is not accommodated in the city because of the higher transportation cost is given by the volume of the shaded area *DDh–DD'h'*. The area labeled *B* represents the loss of population attributable to the radius effect, while the area labeled *A* represents the loss of population attributable to the density effect.

What, then, characterizes two places that except for transportation costs are otherwise identical? The place with the lower transportation costs will have higher land rent and greater population density, and the range over which persons will commute will be greater. It is also interesting to note that the population density and land rent gradients in the lower transportation cost city will have a shallower distance decay than in the higher transportation cost city which has a relatively steep distance decay function.

5.4 Indirect effects of a change in transportation cost in a closed city

The spatial effects of an increase in transportation cost in a closed-interactive city will not be the same as that for an open city. In Figure 5.4, budget lines *AA*, *BB*, and *CC* are carried over from the analysis of the direct effect of a change in k. Following an increase in k, the budget lines drop parallel to *A'A'*, *B'B'*, and *C'C'*, as discussed in section 5.2. By principle 5.2, the direct effects incidence of an increase in k is not spatially uniform; rather households at the urban margins receive a greater reduction in welfare than households located at the CBD. Using principle 4.9, direct effects are sufficient for households at s_x to be in spatial equilibrium. Budget constraint *B'B'* for location s_x is tangent to $U' = u[s_x]$. No indirect effects associated with a change in spatial equilibrium land rent effects are required at s_x. Indirect effects can be traced for all other locations relative to s_x.

Budget line $A'A' = AA$ intersects U', thereby allowing those households a greater level of welfare than households located further from the CBD than s_1. Immigration of households to s_1 increases land rents. The budget constraint at s_1 consequently shifts obliquely to the left from $A'A'$ to $A'A''$.

At $s = s_2$, for $s_2 > s_x$, direct effects result in budget constraint *C'C'* lying below U'. In compensation, the indirect effects reduce land rents, thereby shifting budget constraints to the right to bring households' welfare at those locations up to the new spatial equilibrium level.

Land consumption decreases at s_1 and s_x, and increases at s_2 (Figure 5.4(b)). Assuming that space is smooth and continuous, some location $s*$ between s_x and s_2 must have no change in land consumption. It can be demonstrated that

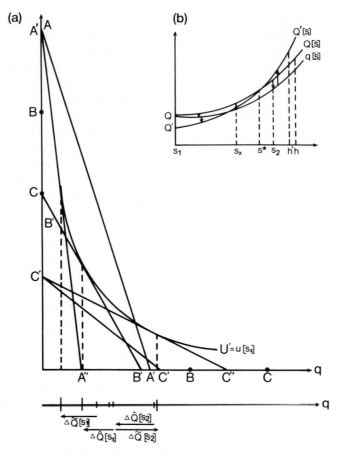

Figure 5.4   Indirect effects of an increase in the cost of transportation
in a closed-interactive city (after Thrall, 1982c)

there is a location which generates budget lines, so that plumblines drawn at
the point of tangency between initial budget line and U, and final budget line
and U', fall upon the same point on the abscissa (Thrall, 1982c, p. 129).
Population density increases within the inner core of the city between 0 and
s^*, and decreases at the urban margins beyond s^*, where $s^* > s_x$ (Figure
5.4(d)).

The rotation about the CBD of the shaded area to the right of s^* (Figure
5.4(d)) represents the total number of households that have relocated. The
rotation about the CBD of the shaded area to the left of s^* represents the
number of households that have inmigrated to the urban core. Because total
population is constant in the closed city, the shaded area to the right of s^*
must equal the shaded area to the left of s^*.

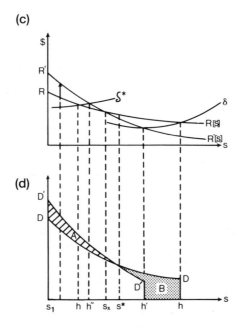

Figure 5.4 *continued*

Using δ as the cost of conversion in Figure 5.4(c) results in an urban radius seen to decrease from *h* to *h'* following an increase in *k*. Compare this result to one where the cost of conversion is instead δ*. The use of δ* is logically incompatible with the CTLR system (Figure 5.4(c)). For cost of conversion δ*, neither s_x nor $s*$ can be observed on the landscape. Rather, urban radius increases from *h* to *h"* and population density increases between 0 and *h"*, thereby increasing total population because of radius and density effects; this result is in violation of the definition of a closed city where population is assumed to be constant. This demonstrates that $s_x < h$ and $s* < h$.

Population density and land rent both increase at the CBD and decrease at the urban margins. The breaking-points where the old density and rent gradients intersect with the new gradients are not the same. This can be demonstrated by inspection of Figure 5.4(c) and (d), whose results were obtained from Figure 5.4(a). The results are summarized by location in Table 5.2.

A change in income can result in land having an increase, no change, or decrease in price, and the manner in which households respond to the change in price depends upon the households' *relative spatial location*. Therefore, even though all households are identical in income and taste preferences in this model, the change in land rent attributable to an increase in transportation cost, and in turn the response of households to changing transportation

Table 5.2 Locational effects of an increase in transportation cost in a closed-interactive city

| | Location | Direction in change of variable: | | |
		$R[s]$	$Q[s]$	$D[s]$
1	$0 \leqslant s < s_x$	+	−	+
2	s_x	0	−	+
3	$s_x < s < s^*$	−	−	+
4	s^*	−	0	0
5	$s^* < s \leqslant h$	−	+	−

cost and land rent, is spatially determined and differs between locations.

Inspection of Tables 5.2 and 4.1 reveals that for the closed city the effect of an increase in transportation cost is identical to a decrease in income. This result was obtained regardless of the fact that the intercepts of the budget lines shifted by the same amount for a change in income versus intercepts of budget lines shifting in magnitude at an increasing rate with increasing distance from the CBD for a change in transportation cost. The similarity in results for the closed city is because the shift in both sets of budget lines was parallel. However, this similarity does not carry over to open cities: a decrease in income reduced the land rent at the CBD in the open city, while an increase in transportation cost had no effect upon land rent in the open city's CBD.

5.5   Conclusion

In this chapter, an analysis has been presented of the effect of a change in transportation cost upon urban spatial structure.

For open cities, land rent and population density at the CBD are unaffected by changes in transportation costs. This is a consequence of households there having no transportation expenditures, and there being no necessity for the CBD to adjust to changes in welfare at other locations; in the open city welfare does not change. However, for remote locations, land rent and population density were shown to vary inversely with per unit distance transportation charges. The more remote the location from the central city, the greater will be the change in land rent and also population density following a change in the charge of transportation. This result is reminiscent of the analysis of a change in the cost of transportation in Von Thünen's Production Theory of Land Rent setting.

For a closed city, the effect of an increase in transportation cost is identical to a decrease in income. Clearly, the Von Thünen setting and the CTLR setting for a closed city are different. Decreases in transportation cost translate into decreases in land rent and population density at the city center, and relocation of the population to the outer margins of the city; suburban development is accommodated by an increase in land rent there. It is interesting to note that at some locations land rent increases are accompanied by increases in land consumption, while at other locations land rent increases are accompanied by decreases or no change in land consumption, thereby underscoring the intriguing complexities that result when space is included in the analysis.

References

Bruce-Briggs (1974)
Fischler (1976)
Thrall (1982c)
Wheaton (1974)

6

Transportation effort

6.1 Introduction

In explaining and anticipating the long-term effect upon urban spatial structure, one exogenous parameter has been allowed to change, while all other parameters were held constant. In this way, the pure effect that the parameter has upon the model, and hence upon urban spatial structure, can be traced in isolation of all other noise. (This method incidentally was first employed in the social sciences by Von Thünen in his seminal studies on agricultural land rent.)

In Chapter 5, transportation cost per unit distance from the central business district (CBD) increased, while all other exogenous parameters of the Consumption Theory of Land Rent (CTLR) model were held constant. The empirical argument for being concerned with the parameter of transportation cost was supported in Figure 5.1 (p. 63), where gasoline prices were near constant during the 1950s and 1960s, while the 1970s were characterized in the United States by steady increases. In Chapter 4, household income changed, while all other exogenous parameters were held constant. The diagram of median household income in the United States (Figure 4.1) (p. 37) revealed a geometric increase in median household income in the period spanning the two decades following 1950. Therefore, during the period that gasoline prices increased households also had more money to spend.

The CTLR analysis indicated that increasing transportation cost and increasing income are forces pulling the city to a great extent in opposite directions; that this is so can be seen clearly by comparing Tables 4.1 and 5.2 (pp. 51, 72). Which force dominates? Is there a solution for when two parameters change simultaneously as has actually occurred and as revealed in the empirical figures?

To answer this question, in this chapter the CTLR model will be extended to evaluate simultaneously the change in transportation costs and the change in income. The model will be structured to replicate closely the actual proportionate change in both income and transportation cost.

The proportion of income allocated to a particular expenditure is referred to as effort (Thrall, 1983a). *Transportation effort E* may be formally expressed as:

$$E = ks/y. \tag{6.1}$$

The variable E is the percentage of household's income that is required to cover transportation expenditures if that household has income y and transportation cost ks; this is encapsulated in the following definition:

Definiton 6.1   Transportation effort is the percentage of income required to obtain transportation; it is calculated as the ratio of transportation expenditures to income.

Say that total yearly gasoline consumption for households at s is 1000 gallons. Say that the price of gasoline is p_g. Equation (6.1) can then be rewritten as:

$$E = 1000(p_g/y). \tag{6.2}$$

Figure 6.1 depicts equation (6.2) using the United States average price of regular gasoline from a full service station. In the simulation, the data value for y is the United States median income for a family of four disaggregated into that for black and that for white households. Call the effort for black and white households to purchase gasoline in year t respectively $E_{B,t}$ and $E_{W,t}$.

Both $E_{B,t}$ and $E_{W,t}$ steadily decrease between 1953 and 1968. Following 1968, the ratios become relatively constant, and then increase in 1974. Effort decreases slightly for both racial groups in 1976 in spite of the substantial gasoline price increases depicted in Figure 5.1.

$E_{W,t}$ decreased between 1975 and 1978 since median white household income increased at a greater rate than did gasoline prices. However, between 1978 and 1980 $E_{W,t}$ nearly doubled; it began at least a half-decade-long decline in 1981. Even at the point of maximum effort in 1980, effort never exceeded that observed for either racial group in 1958. Hence those forces that are related to income and gasoline prices which led to the massive suburbanization of the 1950s and 1960s in the United States are still active there today.

In the following analysis, it will be determined what the effect is expected to be if between two time periods effort to acquire transportation is constant as shown in Figure 6.1, yet income has increased as shown in Figure 4.1 and transportation cost has increased as shown in Figure 5.1.

6.2   Direct effects of constant effort with increasing transportation cost and income

Effort in equation (6.1) and by definition 6.1 is the ratio of transportation

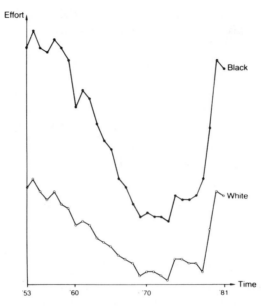

Figure 6.1　Proportion of median income required to purchase
regular gasoline (effort) in a full service station in the
United States, 1953–81 (after Thrall, 1982c)

expenditure by a household at s to the household's income. The effort ratio
can be seen in Figure 6.1 to be the same for the median household in 1981 as it
was in about 1958. This can be formalized within the context of the CTLR
model as, for the household located on annulus s, between time periods t and
$t + 1$:

$$E[s]_{t+1} = E[s]_t. \tag{6.3}$$

Using equation (6.1), in equation (6.3):

$$k_t s/y_t = k_{t+1} s/y_{t+1}. \tag{6.4}$$

By rewriting equation (6.4), income in $t + 1$ can be expressed in terms of the
level of income at time t and the ratio of transportation costs:

$$y_{t+1} = y_t(k_{t+1}/k_t) \quad \text{(for all } s\text{)}. \tag{6.5}$$

The direct effect upon household welfare attributable to an increase in
transportation cost, holding effort constant, is determined by evaluating the
change in the intercepts of the budget line. Note that though income and
transportation costs are allowed to change in proportion to each other, the
price of composite good is held constant, namely:

$$p[y_t,k_t] = p[y_{t+1},k_{t+1}] = p. \tag{6.6}$$

What effect does $y_{t+1} > y_t$ and $k_{t+1} > k_t$, while $E_{t+1} = E_t$, have upon the intercepts of the budget lines of households in the ideal city? That is evaluate the direction of the sign of the inequality of:

$$(y_t - k_t s)/p <?> (y_{t+1} - k_{t+1} s)/p. \tag{6.7}$$

Substituting equation (6.5) into equation (6.7) and rearranging:

$$(k_t - k_{t+1})(y_t - k_t s) <?> 0. \tag{6.8}$$

Unless all the households' income were to be allocated to transportation, then:

$$y_t - k_t s > 0. \tag{6.9}$$

Transportation costs have been assumed to increase between time t and $t + 1$; therefore:

$$k_t - k_{t+1} < 0. \tag{6.10}$$

The product of the positive value in equation (6.9) and the negative value in equation (6.10) yields a negative value; hence, the direction of the sign in inequality (6.7) is $<$. The interpretation of this result is that the budget line is greater in time period $t + 1$ than it was in time period t, given $y_{t+1} > y_t$, $k_{t+1} > k_t$, and $k_{t+1} s/y_{t+1} = k_t s/y_t$.

The intercept on the ordinate of the budget constraint increases when both y and k increase in proportion to each other. The same direct effect can be shown for the intercept of the budget constraint on the abscissa, holding land rent constant. Because the slope (r/p) is not directly affected by an increase in y or k, the budget constraint shifts upward and parallel to the right.

Next determine if intercepts of the budget lines everywhere shift by the same amount, or whether the magnitude of the shift is dependent upon location. That is, for the difference in intercepts on the ordinate for budget lines from locations $s_1 < s_2$, determine the direction of the sign of the inequality:

$$(y_{t+1} - k_{t+1} s_1)/p - (y_t - k_t s_1)/p <?>$$
$$(y_{t+1} - k_{t+1} s_2)/p - (y_t - k_t s_2)/p. \tag{6.11}$$

Equation (6.11) can be reduced to:

$$s_1(k_t - k_{t+1}) <?> s_2(k_t - k_{t+1}). \tag{6.12}$$

Dividing both sides of inequality (6.12) by $(k_t - k_{t+1})$ leaves:

$$s_1 < s_2. \tag{6.13}$$

Because $(k_t - k_{t+1}) < 0$, the direction of the sign of inequality (6.13) is opposite that of inequality (6.11); the direction of the sign of inequality (6.11) should, therefore, read $>$. The magnitude of the shift in the budget line is smaller the further that the household is located from the CBD. It can be

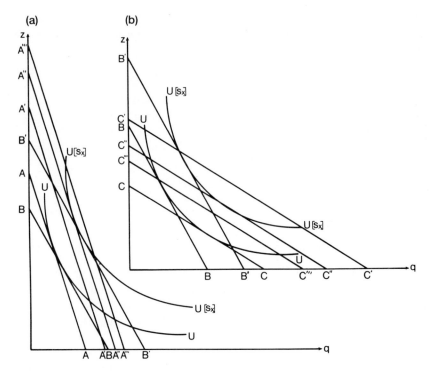

Figure 6.2   Direct effects of constant effort with increasing transportation cost
and income (after Thrall, 1982c)

shown that the greater the increase in y and k, while holding effort constant,
the larger will be the parallel shift to the right in the budget constraint. The
above results can be summarized in the following principle:

Principle 6.1   On the direct effects of constant transportation effort, and
changing income and transportation cost: the budget line will shift
parallel, directly proportional to the change in income. The change will be
less the further the household is located from the CBD.

Let *BB* represent the budget constraint for households at s_x (Figure 6.2(a)).
As k and y increase subject to effort remaining constant, the budget
constraint shifts parallel and upward to the right to $B'B'$. The direct effect is
to place the household on a higher level of welfare, $u[s_x]$. Let *AA* represent
the budget constraint for households at s_1. As we have seen from principle
6.1, the shift in budget line at s_1 must be drawn greater than that at s_x, for $s_1 <$
s_x. Line $A'A'$ has been drawn for comparison, so that $A'-A = B'-B$; the
budget line for households at s_1 must lie above $A'A'$. By inspection, the
resulting budget line for households can be below $u[s_x]$, be tangent to $u[s_x]$,
or intersect $u[s_x]$. Three cases are, therefore, possible.

The budget line for households at s_2, for $s_2 > s_x$, shifts from CC parallel and upward to the right to $C'C'$ (Figure 6.2(b)). As we have seen from principle 6.1, the shift in budget line at s_2 is required to be less than that at s_x. Line $C'C'$ has been drawn for comparison, so that $C'-C = B'-B$; the budget line for households at s_2, then, must actually be parallel but lie below $C'C'$. Such a budget line can be below $u[s_x]$, be tangent to $u[s_x]$, or intersect $u[s_x]$. Again, three cases are possible. How the three cases are evaluated, and which cases can be excluded, depends upon whether the city is open or closed.

6.3 Indirect effects in an open city of constant transportation effort, increasing transportation cost, and increasing income

Because budget lines shift parallel upward to the right, households at every location can obtain a higher level of welfare attributable to direct effects of increasing income and transportation costs, while effort remains constant. However, welfare in the open setting is constrained to remain at U.

Households are attracted to inmigrate to the city. To compensate for the increase in welfare, land rents increase from R_t to R_{t+1} (Figure 6.3(a)), shifting budget constraint BB obliquely to that of $B'B''$ which is tangent to U. Similarly, budget lines (Figure 6.2) shift from $A'A'$ to $A'A''$ and $C'C'$ to $C'C''$ (not drawn). Because of the three cases that result from the direct effects, the relative magnitude of the swings in the individual budget lines and consequently the magnitude of the relative increase in land rents cannot be determined.

However, there is no uncertainty that land rents increase. Hence, the urban fringe expands from h_t to h_{t+1} (Figure 6.3(b)). Land consumption decreases from $Q_t[s]$ to $Q_{t+1}[s]$ (Figure 6.3(a)) which, in turn, increases population density (Figure 6.3(c)). Total population increases by the summation of radius and density effects.

These results for an open-interactive city can be stated as a principle:

Principle 6.2 On the indirect effects in an open city of constant transportation effort, and changing income and transportation cost: land rents, urban radius, population density, and total population will vary directly with the tandem change in income and transportation cost.

6.4 Indirect effects in a closed city of constant transportation effort, increasing transportation cost, and increasing income

In the closed-interactive city, let BB be the budget line for households at s_x (Figure 6.4). Following principles 4.9 (p. 48) and 6.1, let the parameter change move the budget line parallel to the right from BB to $B'B'$ to become

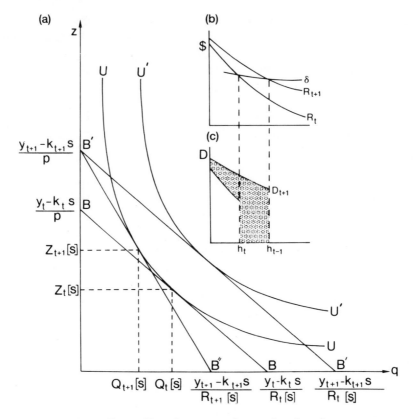

Figure 6.3   Indirect effects in an open-interactive city where
transportation effort is constant while transportation cost
and income both increase (after Thrall, 1982c)

tangent to the new spatial equilibrium level of welfare $u[s_x] = U_{t+1}$. The
remaining direct effects were described in section 6.2.

Three cases are candidates for describing the effect upon urban spatial
structure in the closed city. These are dependent upon the magnitude of the
parallel shift in budget constraints.

If budget constraint AA swings to $A'''A'''$, then land rents at s_1 will
increase as in Figure 6.4(b); land rents by principle 4.11 are constrained to
remain the same at s_x. If the budget constraint increases from AA to $A''A''$,
then no adjustment in land rent is necessary to satisfy spatial equilibrium
conditions (Figure 6.4(c)); the conditions of no change in land rent as at s_x
hold for all locations. If $A'-A$ is slightly greater than $B'-B$, then a decrease in
land rents at s_1 as indicated in Figure 6.4(d) is necessary for spatial equilibrium. Each of these three cases will be examined in turn.

First, consider the case in Figure 6.4(c). Like s_x, all locations have constant

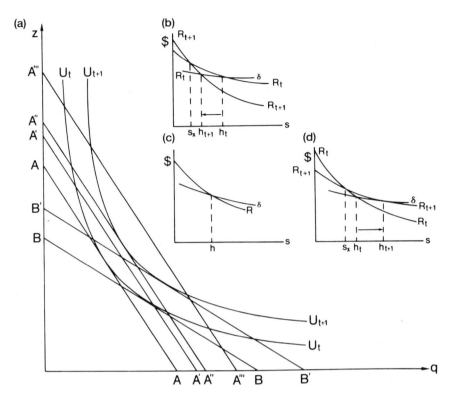

Figure 6.4 Three cases for indirect effects in a closed-interactive city where transportation effort is constant while transportation cost and income both increase (after Thrall, 1982c)

land rent. Budget lines for households at $s_1 < s_x < s_2$ are initially AA, BB, and CC (Figure 6.5). Budget constraints shift to $A''A''$, $B'B'$, and $C''C''$. Because the new budget constraints are tangent to spatial equilibrium welfare $U_{t+1} = u[s_x]$, no adjustment in land rent is necessary.

By inspection of Figure 6.5, $Q[s]_{t+1} > Q[s]_t$ at all locations. Therefore, population density everywhere decreases. Total population residing within radius h_t decreases in proportion to the shaded area between D_t–D_{t+1} for $s < h_t$ (Figure 6.5(c)). However, total population is constant in the closed city. The shaded area to the left of h_t must, then, equal the shaded area to the right of h_t. But population cannot relocate beyond h_t because urban land rents are sufficient to cover the cost of conversion only between the CBD and h_t. Therefore, the case in Figures 6.5 and 6.4(c) is not possible.

Second, evaluate the case in Figure 6.4(b). Let budget lines for households located on annulus $s_1 < s_x < s_2$ be initially AA, BB, and CC (Figure 6.6). Because of the parameter change, let budget lines move to $A'''A'''$, $B'B'$, and $C'''C'''$, where $A'''A''' > B'B' > C'''C'''$. As usual, no adjustment in land

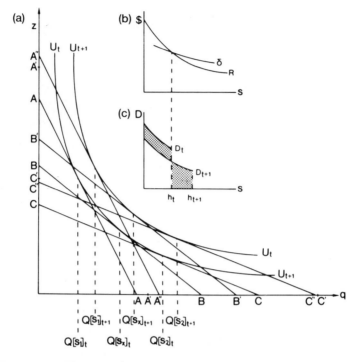

Figure 6.5   The case of constant transportation effort and
unchanging land rents in a closed-interactive city while
transportation cost and income both increase (after
Thrall, 1982c)

rent at s_x is necessary since $B'B'$ is tangent to the new spatial equilibrium level
of welfare.

By inspection of Figure 6.6, direct effects lead households at s_1 to receive a
level of welfare higher than their counterparts at s_x; $A'''A'''$ (not drawn)
intersects U_{t+1}. Land rents increase, obliquely shifting the budget constraint
to $A'''A^*$, tangent to U_{t+1}.

By inspection, direct effects lead to a level of welfare for households at s_2
that is less than their counterparts obtain at s_x. At location s_2 because $C'''C'''$
(not drawn) lies below U_{t+1}, land rents decrease, thereby obliquely shifting
the budget constraint to $C'''C^*$ tangent to U_{t+1}.

In this second case, land rents increase over the range $s < s_x$ and decrease
over the range $s > s_x$. Since population density everywhere decreases, the
radius of this closed city must increase to be consistent; s_x must, then, be
greater than h for this case to be consistent. Therefore, land rents R_t and R_{t+1}
must intersect so as to allow the cost of conversion to be positioned as with δ^*.
Within such a framework, the second case is internally consistent and therefore a possible solution.

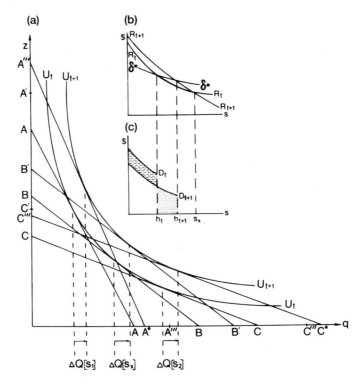

Figure 6.6   The case of constant transportation effort and increasing urban core land rents in a closed-interactive city while transportation cost and income both increase (after Thrall, 1982c)

Third, evaluate the case of Figure 6.4(d). At s_x, the parameter change results in budget constraint BB again moving to $B'B'$, tangent to U_{t+1} (Figure 6.7). Households at s_1 and s_2 have budget lines respectively AA and CC; the direct effect of the change in parameters is to move the budget lines respectively to $A'A'$ (not drawn) and $C'C'$ (not drawn); the budget line coordinates on the ordinate have been drawn, so that $(A'-A) > (B'-B) > (C'-C)$.

At s_1, $A'A'$ lies below U_{t+1}. Land rents decrease and $A'A'$ moves to $A'A''$. $A'A''$ is tangent to U_{t+1}. At s_2, $C'C'$ intersects U_{t+1}. Hence, land rents increase to move the budget line to $C'C''$, tangent to U_{t+1}.

By inspection of Figure 6.7(a), it is seen that quantity of land consumed everywhere increases. Population density must, then, also everywhere decrease (Figure 6.7(c)). Because land rent increases at the urban margins, so long as δ is in relative position to R_t and R_{t+1} as shown, then the radius of the city increases and can thereby accommodate households in the less dense

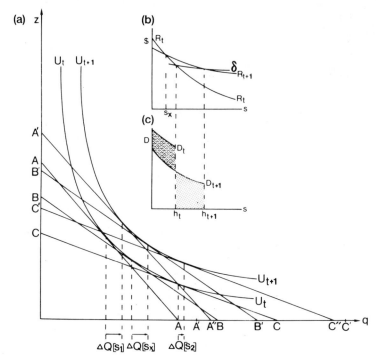

Figure 6.7   The case of constant transportation effort and decreasing urban core land rents in a closed-interactive city while transportation cost and income both increase (after Thrall, 1982c)

environment (Figure 6.7(b) and (c)). Therefore, the third case is internally consistent and possible.

To sum up, there are two possible scenarios that may occur in the closed-interactive city following an increase in income and transportation cost while effort remains constant. In one scenario, land rents everywhere increase; in another scenario, land rent decreases at the inner core of the city and increases at the urban margins. In both scenarios, population density everywhere decreases.

6.5   Conclusion

The nominal price of gasoline has increased, but then so too has household income. In fact, the proportion of median income required to purchase a given quantity of gasoline in the mid-1980s is equivalent to the same proportion that prevailed during the period of rapid suburbanization in

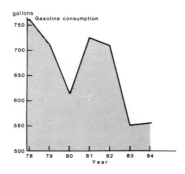

Figure 6.8 Per capita consumption of gasoline in the United States, 1978–84

western countries over twenty years earlier. It is naive in the context of empirical data to argue that nominally increasing transportation costs will have a significant effect upon urban spatial structure when, in fact, other parameters are changing that to a large extent can nullify the effect that changing transportation costs may have. Another component that has reduced the proportion of income allocated to transportation expenditures (effort) is that automobiles are being manufactured and purchased that get better mileage; this is in part responsible for the decline in per capita gasoline consumption in many developed countries, as suggested in Figure 6.8.

In the CTLR analysis, the percentage of income required to purchase transportation between two time periods is constant, while both income and transportation cost have become greater in the second time period. In the open city, both land rents and population density increase while the city radially expands; total population increases. In the closed setting, welfare increases. The city radially expands and population density decreases; land rents increase at the urban margins and can either increase or decrease in the central core of the city.

During periods of rapid increases in transportation costs, such as the 1970s, city planners have been quick to claim that the "silver lining" to an otherwise black cloud is that the higher transportation costs lead to a revitalization of the inner core of the city; indeed, increasing transportation costs have been considered by many to be the elixir of urban core redevelopment. Moreover, there are indications that the inner core of many cities is being revitalized, but so long as increases in income keep pace with increasing transportation costs, then transportation cost increase is an unlikely parameter to hold responsible for the redevelopment.

Moreover, the CTLR is a smooth mathematic: changes in a parameter will drive the system toward a particular equilibrium, while a reversal of the parameter change will return the system to its initial equilibrium. Many phenomena do not conform to a smooth, two-way mathematic; rather a reversal of a parameter may send the system toward a new and different equilibrium. The dynamics of the system depend upon which equilibrium the system is starting from. This concept is most important, I believe, when considering the effect of changing transportation costs upon slowly malleable cities. Consider this when reading Chapter 7 on low-cost transportation nodes. Decreasing transportation costs may create multiple nucleated cities, and a subsequent increase in transportation costs may actually only lead to a strengthening of the new local nodes rather than returning the system to its original single center setting.

References

Bruce–Briggs (1974)
Gordon, Richardson and Wong (1986)
Thrall (1982c, 1983a)

7
Transportation nodes

7.1 Introduction

In this chapter the assumption of the ubiquitous linear transportation cost surface is modified to include a limited access, low-cost transportation network.

What is the effect upon urban spatial structure of introducing a rapid transit system into cities no longer undergoing significant population expansion such as has been done recently in the United States in Miami, San Francisco, the District of Columbia, Pittsburgh, and Buffalo? What has been the effect upon such cities as Toronto whose post World War II growth was coincident with an efficient electric trolley-car system, and later an underground light rail rapid transit system? What has been the effect upon urban spatial structure of the London Underground, the Paris Metro, and the over 2000 miles of light rail rapid transit track for Pacific Electric's "Red Car" line, in the 1940s, in Los Angeles?

Within the Consumption Theory of Land Rent, nodes may be identified on the ideal landscape where households can access networks that allow a reduction in transportation cost from the location of the node to a central point. Once the node is reached by the household, the additional cost of accessing the city center may take on the form of a fixed flat-rate user fee, a reduction in the linear transportation cost per unit distance from the city center, or no cost at all. The introduction of nodes into the CTLR model is an analog of a central place hierarchy template being superimposed upon the ideal landscape, with each node acting as one of several high-order centers in a multinucleated city; the lower the cost of accessing the central business district, the more that node acts as a surrogate CBD (for a review of central place theory see King, 1984). The following analysis will delineate a low-cost transportation network accessible by a node.

7.2 Direct effects of introducing nodes of low transportation cost

In this example of the CTLR, let d be distance between the node and the location of the household. Let c be the transportation cost per unit distance overland "across the grain" to the node, where $c <=> k$. The households' cost of access to the node is then cd. Say that the node is located at distance $s\#$ from the CBD. The case where transportation between the node and CBD is a linear function of distance the household travels on the network will be developed first; afterwards it will be easy to adjust the analysis to include a flat-rate user fee, or fee gratis.

7.2.1   Linear transportation fees between node and CBD

Once at the node, the additional cost of transportation to the CBD is $k's\#$, where $k's\# < ks\#$. For the household located distance d along the same annulus as the node, the total transportation cost of traveling to the node and then onto the CBD is the sum of overland transportation expenditures and network transportation expenditures, namely $cd + k's\#$. Figure 7.1(b) represents the location of a node relative to several example locations and the CBD.

The budget constraint for households located on annulus $s\#$ traveling to the CBD by way of the node also located on annulus $s\#$ is:

$$y = pz[s\#,d] + r[s\#,d]q[s\#,d] + k's\# + cd. \qquad (7.1)$$

The intercepts of the budget line resulting from equation (7.1) are:

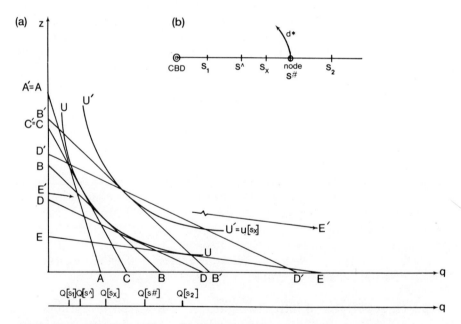

Figure 7.1   The direct effect of introducing a low-cost transportation network accessible by a single node

$$z = (y - k's^* - cd)/p \qquad (7.2)$$

and:

$$q = (y - k's^* - cd)/r. \qquad (7.3)$$

The effect upon the intercepts of the budget line from the introduction of the low transportation cost node is calculated by comparing the intercept with the node and the intercept not including the node:

$$(y - (k's^* + cd))/p <?> (y - ks^*)/p. \qquad (7.4)$$

Rearranging equation (7.4) results in:

$$(k - k')s^*/c <?> d. \qquad (7.5)$$

The interpretation of the direction of the sign of inequalities (7.4) and (7.5) takes on three cases:

$$(y - (k's^* + cd))/p > (y - ks^*)/p \quad (\text{when } d < d^*) \qquad (7.6)$$

$$(y - (k's^* + cd))/p = (y - ks^*)/p \quad (\text{when } d = d^*) \qquad (7.7)$$

$$(y - (k's^* + cd))/p < (y - ks^*)/p \quad (\text{when } d > d^*). \qquad (7.8)$$

The direction of the inequality sign in equation (7.4) can be derived and interpreted by determining the value of d, say, d^*, where the left and right sides of the inequality are equal as in equation (7.7). The interpretation is that d^* is the distance away from the node where the household will be indifferent between traveling directly to the CBD or to the node and then onto the CBD. For values of d greater than d^* (inequality (7.8)), it would cost the household more to travel by way of the node then onto the CBD than it would to travel directly to the CBD. For values of d less than d^* (inequality (7.6)), the household would be left with a greater disposable income by traveling by way of the node to the CBD.

At distance d^* along annulus s^*, the household is indifferent between traveling by way of the node or directly to the CBD. Solve equation (7.7) for d^*:

$$d^* = (k - k')(s^*/c). \qquad (7.9)$$

As k' or c decrease, or as k or s^* increase (equation (7.9)), the greater is the distance that the household is willing to travel to the node and then onto the CBD. The results of equations (7.1)–(7.9) can be stated in the following principle:

Principle 7.1   On the direct effect of introducing a low-cost transportation network accessible by a node:
  (i) The closer the household is to the node along the same annulus, and

the further the node is located from the CBD, the greater will be the increase in budget line attributable to the node.

(ii) A breaking-point may exist beyond which households will not benefit from the introduction of the node.

Say the household is located on a ray passing from the CBD through the node; also that household's transportation costs will be the overland cost along the ray to the node, $k(|s - s^*|)$, and then onto the CBD, $k's^*$, for $s < = > s^*$. The household's budget constraint will appear:

$$y = pz[s, s^*] + r[s, s^*]q[s, s^*] + k(|s - s^*|) + k's^*. \quad (7.10)$$

How does the introduction of the low transportation cost node affect households with budget constraint as in equation (7.10)? The change in intercepts on the ordinate will be:

$$(y - (k(|s - s^*|) - k's^*))/p <?> (y - ks)/p. \quad (7.11)$$

Rearranging unknown inequality (7.11) results in:

$$ks - k(|s - s^*|) - k's^* <?> 0. \quad (7.12)$$

Evaluation of inequality (7.12) requires consideration of three cases, where : (i) the household is located beyond the node, namely $s > s^*$; (ii) the household is located closer to the CBD than the node, namely $s < s^*$; and (iii) the household is located at the nodal site, namely $s = s^*$.

First, consider the case for the household located at $s > s^*$. Equation (7.12) can be rewritten as:

$$ks - ks + ks^* - k's^* <?> 0 \quad (7.13)$$

or

$$s^*(k - k') > 0 \text{ for } k > k'. \quad (7.14)$$

Because $s^* > 0$, and $(k - k') > 0$, then the left side of inequality (7.14) is greater than 0. The direction of the sign of the inequality in equation (7.11) is then also $>$. Hence, the direct effect of the introduction of the node at s^* for households located beyond s^* is to increase their budget line, the direct effect of which is to increase their welfare. The budget constraint in equation (7.10) for households located at $s > s^*$ may be rearranged as:

$$y' = y + s^*(k - k') = pz[s] + r[s]q[s] + ks. \quad (7.15)$$

In equation (7.15), the effect of the node can be seen to be identical to a lump-sum increase in income by the amount $s^*(k - k')$ (see Chapter 4). The further from the CBD is s^*, or the greater is the reduction in transportation cost by way of node versus overland, the greater will be the lump-sum income effect. This result may be stated in the following principle:

Principle 7.2   For households located on a ray extending through the

CBD and the low-cost transportation node, beyond the node, the direct effect of introducing a low-cost transportation network accessible by way of the single node:

(i) For households located beyond the node, the further from the CBD the node is located, and the greater the reduction in transportation cost attributable to the node, the greater will be the shift in households' budget line and increase in welfare.

(ii) The introduction of the node has the same effect as a lump-sum increase in income.

Second, evaluate the case where the household is located on a ray between the CBD and the node, namely $s < s^*$. To reach the node, the household must travel away from the CBD. Once the node is reached, the household's initial travels will be retraced but at a lower per unit cost, and thence onto the CBD. In this scenario, equation (7.12) becomes:

$$ks - ks^* + ks - k's^* <?> 0 \qquad (7.16)$$

or

$$s <?> (k'/k + 1)(s^*/2). \qquad (7.17)$$

The interpretation of inequality (7.17) is as follows. Define that location on the ray transecting the CBD and the node where the household is indifferent between traveling by way of the node or directly to the CBD as $s^\wedge$; that is,

$$s^\wedge = (k'/k + 1)(s^*/2) \quad \text{for} \quad s^\wedge < s^*. \qquad (7.18)$$

If the household is located at $s > s^\wedge$, then the household will by commuting by way of the node have a higher disposable income and, therefore, higher budget line and greater welfare from the direct effect of the introduction of the node. For $s < s^\wedge$, the household would not directly benefit from the node and, therefore, would not commute by way of the node; transportation costs would be minimized by traveling directly to the CBD. At $s = s^\wedge$, households would be indifferent between traveling by way of the node or not. The results of equations (7.16)–(7.18) can be summarized by the following principle:

Principle 7.3 On the direct effect of introducing a low-cost transportation network accessible by a single node:

(i) For households located between the node and the CBD, the closer to the CBD the household is located, the less will be the direct increase in the households' budget line.

(ii) A breaking-point may exist between the node and CBD where households interior to the breaking point will not travel by way of the node to the CBD.

Third, the effect upon the intercepts of the budget lines for households located at the node is easily evaluated by defining $s = s^*$ in equation (7.17). The resulting inequality:

$$s <?> (k'/k + 1)(s/2) \tag{7.19}$$

reduces to:

$$k <?> k'. \tag{7.20}$$

When the transport network costs less to use than commuting to the CBD by overland route, $k > k'$. The direct effect of introducing a node at the location of the households is then to shift the budget line upward and parallel to the right identical to a reduction in transportation as discussed in Chapter 5. This can be summarized by principle 7.4:

> *Principle 7.4* For households located at the node, the direct effect of introducing a low-cost transportation node is the same as a reduction in the cost of transportation.

Consider the sample distribution of places along a ray extending from the CBD through the node. Annuli $s_1 < s^\wedge < s^* < s_2$, and annulus s_x, are represented in Figure 7.1(b), with budget lines for households on these annuli respectively AA, CC, DD, EE, and BB in Figure 7.1(a).

Does the introduction of the node shift the budget lines for households located at the intersection of s^* and the ray by an amount greater than, equal to, or less than shifts in budget lines at other locations, such as at the intersection of the ray and annulus s_x and s_2, for $s_x < s_2$?

Compare, first, the relative shifts in ordinate budget line intercepts between locations s^* and s_x. In other words, is $B' - B <?> D' - D$. Substitution of the appropriate expressions into the intercepts results in:

$$(y - k(s^* - s_x) - k's^*)/p - (y - ks_x)/p <?>$$
$$(y - k's^*)/p - (y - ks^*)/p. \tag{7.21}$$

Inequality (7.20) can be reduced to:

$$s_x <?> s^*. \tag{7.22}$$

When $s_x < s^*$, then the direction of the sign of inequality (7.21) is $<$. Therefore, the budget line for households shifts more if the household is located at the node as compared to being located between the node and the CBD.

Next compare the relative shifts in ordinate budget line intercepts between locations s^* and s_2, for $s_2 > s^*$. In other words, is $E' - E <?> D' - D$. Substitution of the appropriate expressions into the intercepts results in:

$$(y - k(s_2 - s^*) - k's^*)/p - (y - ks_2)/p <?>$$
$$(y - k's^*)/p - (y - ks^*)/p. \tag{7.23}$$

Inequality (7.23) can be reduced to $0 = 0$. Therefore, the direction of the sign of inequality (7.23) is $=$. In other words, the intercepts of the budget constraints for households located directly beyond the node will shift by exactly the same amount as at the node.

The results of the discussion relating to inequalities (7.20)–(7.23) can be summed up in the following principle:

Principle 7.5 On the direct effect of introducing a low-cost transportation network accessible by a single node:

(i) Budget lines will increase more at the node than at locations between the node and the CBD.

(ii) Budget lines will increase by the same amount for households located directly beyond the node as at the node.

7.2.2 Alternative pricing schemes: flat rate and gratis

Consider the alternative pricing scheme of a flat-rate user fee T imposed regardless of nodal location. The budget constraint for households traveling to the CBD by way of node located distance d from the household is:

$$y = pz[s] + r[s]q[s] + T + cd. \tag{7.24}$$

The same analysis as that for the reduced transportation cost network in equations (7.1)–(7.20) holds except that the breaking-point where the household, on the same annulus as the node, becomes indifferent between traveling by way of the node to the CBD or directly to the CBD is calculated as:

$$d* = (ks* - T)/c. \tag{7.25}$$

As T or c decreases, or k or $s*$ increases, the greater will be the distance the household commutes to the CBD by way of the node. Also, for the household located directly between the CBD and the node, the breaking-point at which the household is indifferent between using the node versus commuting directly to the CBD is:

$$s^\wedge = (T/k + s*)/2. \tag{7.26}$$

And the direct effects to the household located directly beyond where the node is introduced will be to increase the budget line so long as $ks* > T$.

If the flat-rate fee for using the transportation network is set to 0, namely the network charge becomes gratis, equations (7.25) and (7.26) reduce to:

$$d* = (k/c)s* \tag{7.27}$$

and:

$$s^\wedge = s*/2. \tag{7.28}$$

The direct effects to the household located directly beyond where the node is introduced using a gratis pricing scheme will be to increase the budget line so long as $ks* > 0$.

This last case of the zero fee for using the network is analogous to introducing a multinucleated landscape into the CTLR model. The definition of the CBD and node become equivalent. The household will travel to either the CBD or node whichever is nearer (equation (7.28)) or the node whose cost of access is least (equation (7.27)). This result can be stated in the following principle:

> *Principle 7.6*   On the direct effect of introducing gratis fee transportation nodes: the CBD and the nodes become equivalent destination points with the household choosing to commute to either the nearest node or the node whose cost of access is least.

7.2.3   Summary of direct effects of introducing a node

Annuli $s_1 < s^\wedge < s_x < s^* < s_2$, are represented in Figure 7.1(b), with budget lines for households on these annuli respectively AA, CC, BB, DD, and EE in Figure 7.1(a). These annuli can be transected by a ray extending from the CBD through a node located on annulus s^* (Figure 7.1(b)). A user fee for accessing the CBD by way of the node is equal to $k's^*$.

Households closer to the CBD than $s^\wedge$ would pay greater transportation costs by travelling by way of the node to the CBD. At the intersection of the ray and annulus s_1, the direct effect of the introduction of the node has no effect upon households' budget line AA since they will choose to travel directly to the CBD.

Households located at the intersection of the ray and annulus $s^\wedge$ will find transportation cost the same for traveling directly to the CBD or by way of the node to the CBD. The introduction of the node will, then, also have no direct effect upon budget line CC.

Households located along the ray between the breaking-point $s^\wedge$ and the node s^* will, by principles 7.3 and 7.5, have budget lines increase in direct proportion to proximity to the node. Following the introduction of the node, let the direct effect for households at the intersection of annulus s_x and the ray shift the budget line from BB to $B'B'$. Budget lines for households located along the ray and between s_x and the node will shift greater than $B' - B$ on the ordinate. Budget lines for households located between s_x and $s^\wedge$ will shift less than $B' - B$.

The direct effect for households located at the node will be to shift the budget lines from DD to $D'D'$, where by principle 7.5, $D' - D > B' - B$. For households within distance $d*$ from the node, and on the same annulus as the node, budget lines equivalent to DD will increase in direct proportion to proximity to the node, with the maximum shift being $D'D'$ occurring at the node, and the magnitude of the shift declining in direct proportion to distance along the annulus s^* until at distance $d*$ from the node there is no direct effect from the node.

The direct effect for households located beyond the node, say, at s_2, will be to shift the budget lines from EE to $E'E'$, where by principle 7.5, $E' - E = D' - D$.

By inspection of Figure 7.1(a), households at the CBD, s_1 and $s^\wedge$, remain on the spatial equilibrium level of welfare U, as do households distance d^* from the node. Welfare has increased for households at the intersection of the ray and annuli s_2, s^*, s_x and for households located on the same annulus as the node but within distance d^* from the node.

To derive the subsequent indirect effects, the analysis turns to the definitions of open-interactive and closed-interactive cities.

7.3 Indirect effects of introducing nodes of low transportation cost into an open-interactive city

The budget lines after the direct effects are accounted for have been carried over into Figure 7.2, as well as the initial spatial equilibrium quantity of land $Q[s]$. The system is defined to be within spatial equilibrium when welfare remains at U; hence, locations closer to the CBD than $s^\wedge$ have no indirect effects because budget lines for households there are still tangent to U.

The budget lines for locations where annuli s_x, s^*, s_2 intersect the ray (Figure 7.1(b)), as well as for locations within distance d^* on the same annulus as the node, all shift obliquely to the left to become tangent again to U; to accomplish this, land rents increase from $R[s]$ to $R'[s]$. The changes in spatial equilibrium land rents are represented in Figure 7.2(b) for locations along the ray, and in Figure 7.2(d) for locations along annulus s^*.

By inspection of the bottom axis in Figure 7.2(a), consumption of land can be seen to decline for those locations that have also had an increase in land rents. This translates into an increase in population density, and is represented in Figure 7.2(c) for locations on the ray and in Figure 7.2(e) for locations on annulus s^*. Spatial equilibrium population increases because of both radius and density effects.

The above results describing the ideal city and the effect upon it by introducing a low transportation cost node can now succinctly be summarized in the following principle:

Principle 7.7 On the indirect effect of introducing low-cost transportation nodes in an open city:
  (i) The inner core of the city remains unaffected by the node.
  (ii) Along a ray extending from the CBD through the node, beginning at a breaking-point between the node and CBD, land rents and population density increase.
  (iii) The city has an extension of urban radius directly beyond the node.
  (iv) Because of radius and density effects, population increases.

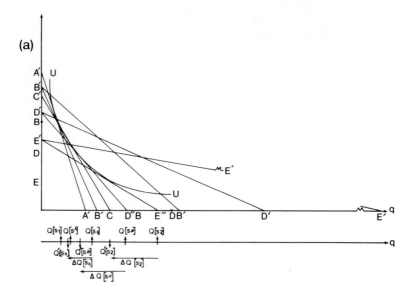

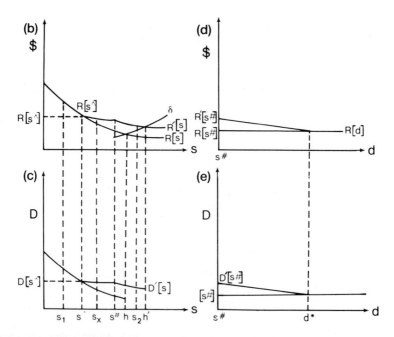

Figure 7.2 The indirect effect in an open-interactive city from introducing a low-cost transportation network accessible by a single node

7.4 Indirect effects of introducing nodes of low transportation cost into a closed-interactive city

Following the introduction of the node on annulus s^*, budget lines increase for locations beyond $s^\wedge$ along a ray through the CBD and the node. By principle 4.9, somewhere the direct effects will be sufficient to satisfy conditions of spatial equilibrium. Let budget line BB shift to $B'B'$ as a result of direct effects of introducing the node to the landscape. $B'B'$ is tangent to $u[s_x] = U'$ (Figure 7.3(a)). Because of the higher welfare, no change in land rents, and greater disposable income, households at s_x allocate some of the increase in disposable income to purchase land. Hence, population density at s_x will decline.

In Figure 7.3, the arrows beneath the abscissa indicate the direction and extent of shift of the intercepts of the budget lines along the abscissa starting from the resting point resulting from the direct effects and ending at the final point necessary to accommodate indirect requirements. A rightward shift indicates a reduction in rent, and a leftward shift indicates an increase in rent. The lower axis is a duplicate of the abscissa drawn to differentiate clearly the initial (from Figure 7.1(a)) and final spatial equilibrium quantity of land consumed; arrows indicate the direction of change in land consumption.

Along the ray transecting the CBD and the node households within distance $s^\wedge$ were not directly affected by the introduction of the low transportation cost node at s^*. After the introduction of the node, it is not necessary for households between the CBD and $s^\wedge$ to pay as great a premium for proximity to the CBD; by outmigrating along the ray beyond $s^\wedge$, access to the CBD because of the node may not diminish. Land rents (Figure 7.3(b)) and population density (Figure 7.3(c)), therefore, decline between the CBD and $s^\wedge$, namely budget lines $A'A'$ and $C'C'$ for locations s_1 and $s^\wedge$ shift obliquely to $A'A''$ and $C'C''$ (Figure 7.3(a)).

At the node on annulus s^*, the direct effects leave households with a greater increase in welfare than locations along the ray closer to the CBD. This leads to an increase in land rent because of the otherwise greater desirability of locating at the node. Budget lines for households at the node shift obliquely from $D'D'$ to $D'D''$. All of the households' increase in disposable income, however, does not go into increased land rents because if this were the case welfare could not increase at s^* to the new higher spatial equilibrium level of $U' = u[s_x]$. Rather the household will allocate the remaining additional disposable income between purchases of land and composite good. Since land consumption increases, then population density at the node decreases. This is indeed a remarkable result and not at all intuitive or easily reached without the CTLR reasoning.

For locations beyond the node but along the ray, such as s_2, the node leaves households with greater disposable income and a level of welfare higher than that attainable at s_x. The desirability of these locations necessitates an

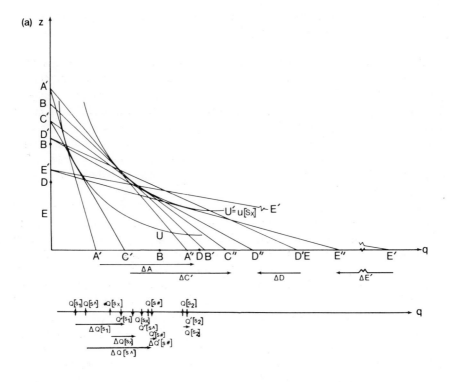

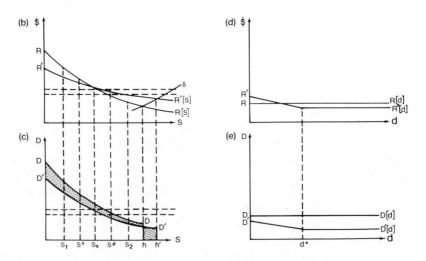

Figure 7.3 The indirect effect in a closed-interactive city from introducing a low-cost transportation network accessible by a single node

increase in urban radius, thereby shifting the budget line from $E'E'$ to $E'E''$; the increase in land rents is commensurate with the necessary urban radius expansion from h to h' to accommodate the outmigration of households occurring along the ray between the CBD and h.

Land rent at the node increases and declines with increasing distance along the annulus of the node (Figure 7.3(d)). Population density everywhere declines, even at the node. The greater the distance from the node, along the annulus of the node, the greater the decrease in population density to compensate households there for not being able to receive an increase in welfare directly because of the introduction of the reduced-rate transportation network. The following principle can be used to summarize the effect of introducing a low-cost transportation node into the landscape of the ideal closed city:

Principle 7.8 On the indirect effect of introducing low-cost transportation nodes in a closed city:

(i) Population density everywhere in the city declines.

(ii) Along a ray from the CBD through the node the land rents increase near to and everywhere beyond the node. Somewhere between the node and the CBD land rents do not change, and closer to the CBD land rents decline.

(iii) The urban radius near to the ray sufficiently expands to accommodate the decrease in population elsewhere in the city.

(iv) Rent and population density both decline at the city center.

7.5   Conclusion

Following the introduction of the node, disposable income increases by the savings in the cost of transportation attributable to the new node. Some households relatively remote from the new node will still find it less expensive to travel directly onto the CBD.

In the open city, the resulting higher disposable income at some locations translates into households moving to those locations. The collective result of the migration is to drive up land rent and population density in direct proportion to the savings in transportation costs, thereby re-establishing the initial level of welfare. By definition, households will be no better off following the introduction of the low-cost transportation node. Nevertheless, the node will have changed the geography of the city.

Actual cities whose periods of rapid growth have been commensurate with investments in low-charge public transportation systems, such as Toronto, London, Paris, and so on, have had their urban spatial structures strongly influenced by the presence of a transit system. These cities have high population densities and land rents clustered about the nodal subway sites.

The clustering is in part a result of persons not willing or able to walk more than several blocks to the rail station. One might then expect that the most extensive geographic impact has been in those cities such as London whose low-charge transit bus and subway systems are within easy walking distance of most households. Limited-access highways, such as in post-1950 Los Angeles, have had much the same effect except that the friction of distance about the freeway on- and off-ramps is much less than about a railway station: the friction of distance from walking is much greater than when driving.

In the closed city, the low-cost transportation node translates into an increase in welfare for all households. Those households at the nodal site will be left with greater disposable incomes; this residual income will be allocated to both higher consumption of land and of composite good. Somewhat counterintuitively, population density will then decline about the node. The lower population density leads everywhere to lower land rents. Nevertheless, the nodal site will be established as a local peak in the reduced land rents. This is because with access costs diminished, households need not pay as great a premium to locate near the CBD. The lower cost of access will lead to suburbanization commensurate with the lower population density function. Yet in many economically depressed cities of the United States with constant or declining population bases, such as Buffalo, light rail rapid transit systems have been installed precisely as an investment to revitalize the city with the hope of reducing outmigration to the suburbs. In such cities, the CTLR would imply that the transportation system would merely hasten the outmigration of persons from the city. If further government policies encouraged new housing development at the nodal sites, it would merely be at the expense of already developed areas of the city. It should be noted, however, that though the node leads to a decline in the premium households are willing to pay to reside in the surrounding area, at the same time it may become an attractive retail location because of the ease of access to the node and the supposedly larger number of households passing through the node; that the node becomes a force for redevelopment of cities with constant population bases, then, depends upon investment by the commercial (PTLR) sector at the nodes, and not by housing in the consumption sector.

References

Fischler (1976)
Gordon, Richardson and Wang (1986)
King (1984)
Werner (1985)

PART III

Government Revenue

Tax expenditure overview

8.1 Introduction

Taxation is introduced into the household's budget constraint in this chapter.
The three principal forms of taxation will be examined: property taxes, sales
taxes, and income taxes. In the Common Market, the value added tax is to the
consumer quite indistinguishable from the sales tax discussed here. Because
deductions of mortgage interest payments from declared income can be an
important aspect of income taxes in some countries, it too will be examined
along with the effect of changing mortgage interest rates.

The Consumption Theory of Land Rent (CTLR) analysis is limited in this
chapter to one of how the various types of taxes are to be included within the
household's budget constraint. In Chapters 9–11 the three taxes will be
examined, in turn, using the CTLR methodology. Each of the different kinds
of tax may affect the geography of the city in a different manner: the property
tax is a tax on land; the sales tax is a tax upon composite good. For purposes
of income tax, in the United States, households can subtract mortgage
interest payments from gross income and thereby arrive at a lower taxable
income; in other countries, such as Canada, deductions of this kind are not
allowed. If the taxes can be shown to have an effect upon the geography of
the city, the tax is not spatially neutral. One of the key insights gained from
the CTLR analysis is whether the tax is spatially neutral, or whether the direct
incidence of the tax is greater at some locations than at other locations:

Definition 8.1 The direct effect (incidence) of a *spatially neutral tax*
upon the welfare of households will be the same for all households that
have the same income and taste preferences. The incidence of a *spatially
biased tax* is conditional upon the relative spatial location of the
household.

In previous chapters a brief empirical illustration has sometimes served to
place into a real-world context the exogenous parameter being analyzed. The
empirical overviews for each of the forms of tax to be analyzed in Chapters
9–11 are agglomerated in the latter part of this chapter.

8.2   Taxation and the households' budget constraint

Let household income be partitioned into expenditures on a sales tax, a property tax, and an income tax. The sales tax is a percentage of composite good expenditures that must be paid to the government; the tax levy can be made either at the cash register, in which case it is visible to the consumer, or added to the price of the good before the cash register, in which case it may be invisible to the consumer. Whether the sales tax is visible or invisible, it can be stated as a percentage t_1 of total expenditures on composite good, namely $t_1 pz$.

Ad valorem property taxes are a percentage of total market value of housing. Housing in the CTLR has been partitioned into the separate components of land and capital that rests upon the land (Chapter 14). Since housing capital is assumed for now to be part of composite good, the tax on housing capital can be viewed as analogous to a sales tax. We will focus upon property tax t_2 as a percentage of land value, namely $t_2 rq$.

Income tax is the percentage t_3 of household income that must be paid to the government, namely $t_3 y$. Income taxes can become more complex than a levy on the mere percentage of income. A government through deductions may allow households to reduce the amount of income that the taxes are based upon; the mortgage interest deduction is interesting in the context of the CTLR.

To accommodate mortgage interest deductions, the budget constraint in equation (2.2) (p. 14) is modified, so that expenditure on transportation, quantity of land, composite good plus the cost of a discounted mortgage irq with interest rate i is equal to household *net income M*:

$$M = pz + rq + irq + ks. \qquad (8.1)$$

The income tax when mortgage interest deductions are allowed is the product of the tax rate t_3 and taxable income I. Net income is the difference between gross income y and income taxes $t_3 I$:

$$M = y - t_3 I. \qquad (8.2)$$

The income tax rate t_3 is used here as a constant proportion of taxable income; in some tax systems t_3 can, in turn, be a function of I and thereby create tax brackets. To minimize the complexity of this CTLR analysis, it will be assumed that unlike the mortgage interest deduction, property taxes and sales taxes are not allowed as deductions from income.

Taxable income is the difference between gross income and proportion m of the mortgage interest payment that the household is allowed to deduct, thus:

$$I = y - mirq. \qquad (8.3)$$

In general, m will range from 0, as is the present case in Canada, to 1, as is the case in the United States for the household's primary residence.

Substitute equation (8.3) into equation (8.2) and rearrange the resulting relationship:

$$M = yw + mirqt_3 \qquad (8.4)$$

where:

$$w = 1 - t_3. \qquad (8.5)$$

The household's budget constraint can now be expressed in terms of income tax and mortgage interest deductions. Substitute equation (8.4) into equation (8.1) and rearrange:

$$yw = pz + rq(1 + i - mit_3) + ks. \qquad (8.6)$$

In addition to income taxes, the household must also pay to the government sales taxes equal to t_1pz and property taxes equal to t_2rq. The added complexity of including property and sales taxes as deductions for the purposes of calculating income taxes will not be considered here.

The budget constraint in equation (8.6) can now be rewritten to accommodate these expenditures as:

$$yw = pz + t_1pz + rq(1 + i - mit_3) + t_2rq + ks. \qquad (8.7)$$

Gathering the terms in equation (8.7), it can be rewritten as:

$$yw = pz(1 + t_1) + rq(\{1 + i - mit_3\} + t_2) + ks. \qquad (8.8)$$

Rearranging equation (8.8) in the form of the budget line yields:

$$z = (yw - ks)/\{p(1 + t_1)\} - (1 + iv + t_2)(r/\{p(1 + t_1)\})q \qquad (8.9)$$

where v is the term used to collect variables with the objective of reducing the apparent complexity of the equation:

$$v = 1 - mt_3. \qquad (8.10)$$

The intercept on the ordinate can be derived from equation (8.9) as:

$$z = (yw - ks)/(p\{1 + t_1\}) \qquad (8.11)$$

and on the abscissa as:

$$q = (yw - ks)/(\{1 + iv + t_2\}r). \qquad (8.12)$$

In Chapters 9–11, each tax is evaluated in isolation from the others. All taxes are initially set to zero, and then individually reset to a nontrivial value greater than zero. Throughout the analysis it will be assumed that changes in the level of taxation do not change the distribution of goods provided by the public sector; the issue of the geographic effects of public expenditures will be evaluated later in Part IV.

The remainder of this chapter is devoted to an empirical examination of the importance to government and to households of income, sales, and property taxes, and spatial inequities in the determination of property taxes.

8.3   The magnitude of taxes

For the United States federal government, individual income and employment taxes represent the major source of revenue; the second largest source is corporation income taxes, followed by total excise taxes. Excise taxes include taxes on alcohol, tobacco, gasoline, automobiles, and parts; they are generally levied as a lump-sum tax per item purchased such as $2.50 per automobile tire. Households by paying income and excise taxes are responsible for about 80 percent of the total federal government revenues.

For state governments in the United States, income taxes and sales taxes are the principal sources of revenue. Total state tax collection and the percentage of those tax collections attributable to individual sales taxes are presented in Table 8.1. At the local government level, most own-source revenue comes from property taxes, sales taxes, and income taxes. Table 8.2 provides a list of effective residential property tax rates, the sales tax rates, and the income tax rates in selected cities of the United States.

One state or city may use income taxes as a revenue source. In another state, there may be no income taxes other than those imposed by the federal government; cities in those states may compensate for this by levying comparatively higher sales taxes or property taxes. There may then be substantial spatial variation in the manner in which revenues are raised; however, because a lower tax may be compensated for by a higher tax, the total amount of tax debt by households with the same income may be the same or may be

Table 8.1   Percentage of total state revenue collections attributable to sales taxes, 1983

State	Total state tax collections ($ million)	Sales taxes % revenue from tax	tax rate
Alabama	2,341	59.2	4
Alaska	2,046	3.7	*
Arizona	2,061	55.6	5
Arkansas	1,338	52.8	4
California	22,260	44.7	4.75
Colorado	1,743	50.8	3
Connecticut	2,538	70.9	7.5

State	Total state tax collections ($ million)	Sales taxes % revenue from tax	tax rate
D.C.	639	14.1	*
Delaware	1,317	32.2	6
Florida	6,225	77.0	5
Georgia	3,504	50.9	3
Hawaii	1,151	65.7	4
Idaho	620	46.6	4
Illinois	7,420	52.1	5
Indiana	3,195	62.9	5
Iowa	2,014	44.1	4
Kansas	1,566	46.5	3
Kentucky	2,602	45.6	5
Louisiana	3,011	45.0	4
Maine	780	54.1	5
Maryland	3,468	44.6	5
Massachusetts	5,156	33.7	5
Michigan	7,023	39.5	4
Minnesota	4,319	39.3	6
Mississippi	1,538	66.5	6
Missouri	2,640	52.6	4.125
Montana	514	20.8	*
Nebraska	987	56.8	3.5
Nevada	779	85.9	5.75
New Hampshire	329	48.3	*
New Jersey	6,128	54.0	6
New Mexico	1,163	56.5	3.75
New York	16,208	35.3	4
North Carolina	4,028	43.8	3
North Dakota	526	41.6	4
Ohio	6,734	54.7	5
Oklahoma	2,627	30.5	3
Oregon	1,784	11.9	*
Pennsylvania	8,430	44.3	6
Rhode Island	726	51.5	6
South Carolina	2,113	54.0	5
South Dakota	325	85.8	4
Tennessee	2,246	75.9	5.5
Texas	9,019	62.9	4
Utah	974	54.1	4.625
Vermont	358	48.9	4
Virginia	3,478	41.4	3
Washington, D.C.	4,191	74.3	6.5
West Virginia	1,470	68.4	5
Wisconsin	4,297	42.5	5
Wyoming	736	32.9	3

* Not applicable.
Source: US Bureau of the Census, State Tax Collections and Statistical Abstract of the USA, p. 274; IPA p. 624.

Table 8.2 Effective tax rates for selected cities in the United States, 1982

City	Effective property tax rate per $100	Assessment level (%)	Sales tax rates (%)	Income tax rate (%)
Birmingham, Ala.	0.69	10.0	1.0	1.0
New York, N.Y.	1.66	18.5	4.25	0.9–4.3
St. Louis, Mo	1.56	24.9	1.0	1.0

Source: US Bureau of the Census, *State Tax Collections and Statistical Abstract of the USA*, p. 283; IPA, p. 625.

Table 8.3 Estimated taxes paid by a family of four, by income level for selected cities in the United States, 1982

City	$17,000 Income total tax paid	(percentage of income)	$50,000 Income total tax paid	(percentage of income)
Albuquerque, N.M.	1231	7.2	4003	8.0
Atlanta, Ga.	1510	8.9	4883	9.8
Baltimore, Md.	1788	10.5	5291	10.6
Boise City, Ida.	1103	6.5	4446	8.9
New York City	1984	11.7	7424	14.9

Source: US Bureau of the Census, *State Tax Collections and Statistical Abstract of the USA*, p. 283; IPA, p. 625.

different between places. Since a large amount of revenues is generated by the three forms of taxes, what then is the expected tax debt for the household? Total estimated taxes paid by individual households in selected cities of the United States are presented in Table 8.3.

8.4 Structural form of local taxes

8.4.1 Sales and income taxes

The determination of household debt attributable to income and sales taxes can be a relatively straightforward accounting problem. If the sales tax is $t_1 = 5\%$, and the household expenditure is $pz = \$10,000$ per year on taxable goods, then the household has paid $t_1 pz = \$500.00$ in sales taxes.

Determination of the income tax for some households can, analogous to the sales tax, be a straightforward product of tax rate and income. However, for other households the calculation is not so straightforward because of legal deductions. Deductions serve to create a differential tax between persons with identical gross incomes. This is done to encourage the allocation

Table 8.4   Home mortgage interest rates in the United States, 1965–84

Year	Interest rate on conventional loan[1]	Year	Interest rate on conventional loan[1]
1965	5.83	1978	9.68
1970	8.52	1979	11.15
1971	7.75	1980	13.95
1972	7.64	1981	16.52
1973	8.30	1982	15.79
1974	9.22	1983	13.43
1975	9.10	1984	
1976	8.99	1985	
1977	8.95		

Source: US Bureau of the Census, *Statistical Abstract of the United States*, table 799, "Conventional existing home loans."

of households' resources in particular directions such as investment; or to differentiate households because of need; or to recognize that many households' income has been arrived at by first having necessary up-front business expenditures.

The following formula can be used to approximate the yearly mortgage payment (Thrall, 1983a, 1985):

$$\text{Yearly mortgage} = \frac{(\text{interest rate})(\$ \text{ amount of loan})}{1 - (1/(1 + \text{interest rate}))^{(\text{years to mature})}}$$

(8.13)

A household that assumes an $85,000.00 loan for 30 years to purchase a dwelling at an interest rate of 9.5 percent will pay to the loan agent each year $8642.85. At the end of 30 years the household would have paid $259,285. As a rough estimate, this works out to be about ($259,285–$85,000)/30 = $174,285/30 = $5809.50 per year in interest payments. Say that the household has an earned income of $25,000; and also say that this places the household in a 15 percent tax bracket. Hence, this household would owe to the government (0.15)($25,000) = $3750. However, the household paid about $5809.50 in interest payments for that year. Therefore, the household would declare as taxable income only $19,190.50 = ($25,000 – $5809.50). In many instances, the lower income would also be taxed at a lower percentage. Say that, however, the income was still taxed at 15 percent; the income tax payment to the government would then be $2878.58, a saving of $871.42. Without the mortgage interest deduction, the household's effective income tax rate was 15 percent; with the deduction, the effective income tax rate reduces to about 11.5 percent, and even lower still if the income with the deduction places the household in the lower bracket. Moreover, the effective yearly owner's mortgage payment is ($8642.85 – $871.42) = $7771.43.

8.4.2   Property taxes

Determination of property taxes is not, in practice, a straightforward product of tax rate and true land or housing value. It is worthwhile to consider several problems associated with how property taxes are determined in practice. The remainder of this chapter concerns issues related to determining households' property taxes.

In practice, unless property has recently sold, the value of land or housing must be guessed at, which is known as the assessed value. Generally the assessed value is defined as the amount that the property is expected to realize if sold in the open market by a willing seller to a willing buyer. The assessed value is often calculated as in the United States and Canada by an accounting procedure: the characteristics of housing (wall-to-wall carpet, brick façade, patio, and so on) whose prices are known in some base year are added up yielding a total value. The total value becomes the assessed value.

There are many problems in practice with guessing market value in this manner. The price of new housing capital p may be the same everywhere in the city; however, once that capital is in place, its value to a consumer depends upon where it is, thereby conforming to the problem of spatial variation in land value. Furthermore, what accounting value is to be used for the value of land?

Assessed value, AV, is generally required to be a constant proportion χ of market value, MV; χ is known as the assessment level and is presented in Table 8.2 for a selection of cities in the United States. A distinction is made between MV and $R[s]Q[s]$ because MV may also contain the estimate of house capital as well as land value. However, if it is only land that is being assessed, then we can set $MV = R[s]Q[s]$; local governments in practice may or may not distinguish between house capital assessment and land value assessment. Assessed value may then be stated as:

$$AV = \chi(MV). \tag{8.14}$$

The property tax, Ω, that a household must pay to the local government is the product of the millage rate, ζ, and the assessed value:

$$\Omega = \zeta(AV). \tag{8.15}$$

By substituting equation (8.14) into equation (8.15), the property tax that the household must pay can be expressed in terms of the market value of the dwelling:

$$\Omega = \zeta\chi(MV). \tag{8.16}$$

The millage rate generally is the ratio of the total cost of the local public sector, $C[G]$, and the total assessed land value, $ATLV$, of a city, namely:

$$\zeta = C[G]/(ATLV) \tag{8.17}$$

where:

$$ATLV = \sum_{j=1}^{N} x(MV_j). \tag{8.18}$$

Equation (8.18) states that $ATLV$ is the summation of the product of market values for all N households' properties and the assessment rate. The lower is $ATLV$ in equation (8.17), the greater must be the millage rate to generate the same amount of revenues.

Substitute equations (8.17) and (8.18) into (8.16):

$$\Omega = C[G](MV)\chi \left/ \sum_{j=1}^{N} \chi(MV_j). \right. \tag{8.19}$$

For χ not to be a component of taxes, it must be the same for all households. If χ is the same constant for all households, it can be pulled out of the summation in the denominator in equation (8.19) and then divided out. Household property taxes should then be a constant proportion of the market value of one's property and not dependent upon the assessment rate. In other words:

$$\Omega = C[G](MV) \left/ \sum_{j=1}^{N} (MV_j). \right. \tag{8.20}$$

Ω in equation (8.20) is independent of the assessment rate χ; the effective tax rate as a percentage of MV is then F/MV. See Table 8.2 for a sample of effective property tax rates.

If χ is a constant, then the ratio of assessed value to market value will be the same for all households. Solve equation (8.14) for χ:

$$\chi = (AV/MV). \tag{8.21}$$

Otherwise, if χ varies between properties, then some households will be charged a greater (smaller) proportion of market value than other households; such households will be paying more (less) than what is equitable between households. The effective tax rate would then vary between households.

In practice, no method of assessment is perfect in "guessing" what the true market value is. Some variation in χ between households is likely to exist. However, a goal should be to minimize the variation in χ as much as technology and administrative budgets will allow.

I presented this geographic criteria for assessments to be equitable between households in Thrall (1979d). A contour map of χ, the assessed value to market value ratio, should reveal a flat surface. If the surface is not flat, then those locations will be revealed where households are either overassessed or underassessed. By comparing a map of χ that contains significant contours

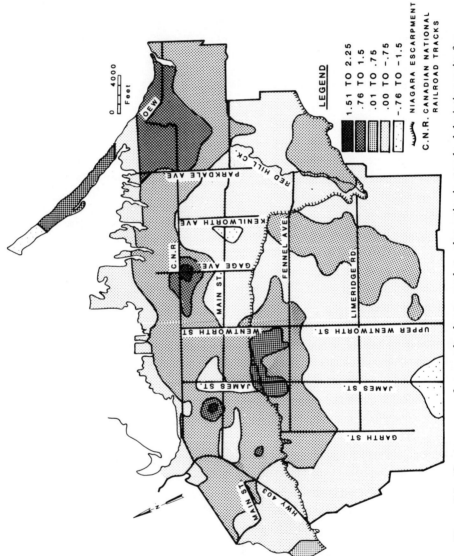

Figure 8.1 Contour map of assessed value to market value ratios in standard deviation units for Hamilton, Ontario, Canada (after Thrall, 1980a)

with maps of housing quality, land values, construction, social indices, income and so on, it may be revealed why the method of assessment is inequitable between households.

Figure 8.1 presents an example of a contour map of assessed value to market value ratios in standardized units. The example is for Hamilton, Ontario. The Hamilton example is based upon a sample of 572 single-family dwellings that sold at about the same time in 1976. The majority of χ for Hamilton falls within 0.75 standard deviation units from the mean; these neighborhoods correspond in large part to middle-income housing, in good maintenance condition, and ranging in vintage from 1850 to 1950.

Several areas are identified as being overassessed at 0.76 and 1.5 standard deviation units above the mean. Several areas are even more overassessed at greater than 1.5 standard deviation units above the mean (Figure 8.1).

The overassessed areas contain residents of low-income and high population density; many of the residents were recent immigrants to Canada. The majority of the dwellings are greater than seventy-five years old and were constructed as row houses. Several of the neighborhoods have intense industrial pollution, being in the smoke plumes from the Hamilton harborfront steel mills. Dwellings here are characteristically going through disinvestment through low maintenance. The other zone of significant high assessment lies along Fennel Avenue and the Niagara Escarpment. This neighborhood, too, contains lower-income residents and high population density. Dwellings there are small but reasonably well maintained; they are tangential to expensive housing, and assessors may be valuing these houses more like their higher-quality neighbors than low-income housing. All neighborhoods with greater than 0.75 standard deviation units above the mean for the city then correspond to (i) high population density, (ii) relatively small dwelling size, and (iii) lower-income population.

Two neighborhoods are underassessed, lying between −0.76 and −1.5 standard deviation units below the mean. Both underassessed neighborhoods occur in transitional areas, one at the fringe of the central business district (CBD) and the other at the urban fringe. Residents at the urban margins have relatively high incomes and own several acres of land. Sales reflect prices of land entering more intensive use, including townhouse developments. The other underassessed neighborhood, near the CBD, has middle-income residents and is going through land use transition from single-family dwellings to high-rise apartments. In both underassessed neighbourhoods, the expected shift to more intensive land use is reflected in higher selling prices of single-family dwellings. Figure 8.1 demonstrates that the actual tax rate paid by the individual household in practice may be significantly greater or significantly less than the supposedly uniform effective tax rate.

Many parameter changes as demonstrated by the CTLR are not spatially neutral resulting in market values changing at differential rates across space.

If the assessed value does not mirror these changes, spatial inequities in property taxation will be created. However, if in practice assessments were to change accurately with market value trends for all locations, then property taxes paid by households would also mirror the trend in market values.

There is evidence that some local governments have used increasing market values to increase their revenues above those which households would otherwise have preferred. Stress between household preferences and government action is created when there is a differential between public revenues actually collected and those that would have existed if market values had not changed. This stress has been shown (Thrall, 1981b) to have been instrumental in causing Californians on June 6, 1978 to vote 65 percent in favor of the Jarvis–Gann Amendment, the so-called Proposition 13.

The Jarvis–Gann Amendment restricted property taxes to 1 percent of assessed value. In turn, with the exception of resales, new construction, and a 2 percent per year maximum increase in assessments, property assessments were returned to values as they were in fiscal year 1975. The Jarvis–Gann Amendment set off a diffusion of similar property tax "rebellions" across North America. From arguments based upon the CTLR, it would be unusual for market values to change in a spatially uniform manner; also because the year upon which the market value is determined for assessment purposes in practice will be different between dwellings, then it is expected that the Jarvis–Gann Amendment will create spatial inequities similar to those in Figure 8.1. Such a tax policy is not spatially neutral.

A less spatially biased tax policy would have been to have assessed values as accurately as possible to represent true market values. Millage rates could then be indexed, so that aggregate public revenue changes only at the rate at which local residents prefer.

8.5   Conclusion

Taxes enter into the household's budget constraint and thereby affect the choice of what to consume. The major forms of property taxation are sales, property, and income taxes. Income taxes are made more complex by the mortgage interest deduction. Taxes can be considered as being spatially neutral if they everywhere have the same effect; or are spatially biased if their direct (or indirect) effects differ between locations. In Chapters 9–11, the CTLR methodology will be used to derive the effect that taxation, mortgage interest payments, and mortgage interest deductions have upon the geography of the city. The existence of spatial bias in the various types of taxes will be revealed.

References

Black (1972)
Netzer (1966)
Oldman and Aaron (1965)
Paglin and Fogarty (1972)
Peterson (1973)
Puryear *et al.* (1979)
Smith (1972)
Thrall (1979b, 1979c, 1979d, 1980a, 1980b, 1981a, 1981b, 1982b, 1983a, 1985)

Income tax, interest rates, and mortgage interest deductions

9.1 Introduction

In this chapter, the Consumption Theory of Land Rent (CTLR) methodology is used to evaluate the effects that income taxes, interest rates, and mortgage interest deductions have upon the geography of the city.

Real estate interests periodically have campaigned the Canadian Parliament to adopt the practice in the United States of mortgage interest deductions. Paradoxically, economists regularly testify to the American Congress that the mortgage interest deduction should be abolished.

The argument in Canada is that high interest rates and high housing prices make housing too expensive to purchase. Mortgage interest deductions, by reducing taxes, can free up income that, in turn, could be allocated to housing. However, if total government revenues are to remain constant, receipts (taxes) from other sectors of the economy would likely have to increase.

In the United States, opponents to the mortgage interest deduction in contrast argue that the income freed by the mortgage interest deduction merely translates into an increase in the price of housing; future purchasers of housing are then likely to be no better off with the deduction than without the deduction. Moreover, the mortgage interest deduction provides a disincentive (perhaps psychological, hence affecting taste preferences) to rent housing. The following CTLR analysis will demonstrate what the long-term implications will be upon the geography of the city if one such tax system is replaced with the other.

The mortgage interest deduction allows households to deduct from their gross income interest accruing from their home mortgages (see Chapter 8). The income remaining after all deductions have been subtracted is the income that is taxable by the federal government. To calculate income taxes, most provincial and state governments piggyback onto taxable income derived using the deductions allowed by the federal governments. The more deductions, the lower will be the taxable income, marginal rate of taxation, and income taxes. If the rate of taxation is not increased to make up the potentially smaller revenue, the household will be left with a larger disposable income.

A tax system that allows mortgage interest payments to be deducted from gross income in order to determine taxable income will be contrasted with a tax system that does not allow such deductions. The analysis can then be extended to determine what the likely effect would be when market interest rates change within both systems, and when there is conversion from one system to the other.

Let household income be partitioned into expenditures on income tax t_3y as well as on composite good, land, and transportation; in other words:

$$y = pz + rq + t_3y + ks. \tag{9.1}$$

Let disposable income $y*$ be income less transportation expenses as well as income taxes:

$$y* = y - t_3y - ks = y(1 - t_3) - ks. \tag{9.2}$$

Using equation (9.2) in equation (9.1) and rearranging:

$$y* = pz + rq. \tag{9.3}$$

The budget line now becomes:

$$z = (y' - ks)/p - (r/p)q \tag{9.4}$$

where:

$$y' = y(1 - t_3). \tag{9.5}$$

The income tax reduces income. The proportion of income remaining after the income tax is $(1 - t_3)$. The income tax changes the intercept of equation (9.4), but not the slope. A reduction in income tax is equivalent to an increase in income. Because of this, the remaining indirect and direct effects of an income tax can be read from Chapter 4. Of particular interest are principles 4.1–4.3, restated in terms of income taxes:

Principle 9.1 On the direct effect of a spatially uniform increase in income tax: regardless of the household's location, each budget line will move parallel by the same amount, and move in the opposite direction as the change in income tax.

Principle 9.2 On the direct effect of a spatially uniform change in income tax: the change in household welfare is inversely proportional to the change in the income tax and the magnitude of this change is directly proportional to the distance the household is located from the central business district (CBD).

Principle 9.3 On the direct effect of a spatially uniform change in income tax: the change in household consumption of land is inversely proportional to the change in income tax and the magnitude of this change is directly proportional to the distance the household is located from the CBD.

For the indirect effects of the income tax in the open city, principle 4.4 can be modified:

Principle 9.4 Between two open cities whose households obtain identical welfare, the city whose inhabitants have the smaller income tax will have greater population density, land rent, urban radius, and total population than the city with the higher income tax.

For the closed city, indirect effects of the income tax can be written with minor modifications of principles 4.11–4.13:

Principle 9.5 Land rent in the closed city is inversely proportional to the income tax at the urban margins and directly proportional to the income tax at the urban core.

Principle 9.6 The greater the income tax for households in the closed city, the more steep will be the rent gradient.

Principle 9.7 The greater the income tax for households in a closed city, the more steep will be the population density gradient.

It is evident from principles 9.1–9.7 that the income tax is not spatially neutral. An increase in income tax reduces household welfare more at the urban margins than at the urban center. For the direct effects of the income tax to be spatially neutral, that is if households at the urban core are to have the same reduction in welfare as households at the urban margins, then the income tax must be higher in the urban core and less at the urban margins; in the United States such a tax would be unconstitutional. All other things being equal, the analysis would imply that the higher the income tax, the greater will be the bias toward living in small cities and the greater the bias against living at the urban margins.

9.2 Interest and interest deductions

9.2.1 The setting

The budget constraint in equation (9.1) must be modified to accommodate mortgage interest deductions. This was done in equation (8.9) (see p. 105). Set all taxes except income tax to zero; the mortgage interest deduction is not here equal to zero. Interest rates are set to be greater than zero. The conditions result in:

$$z = (yw - ks)/p - (1 + iv)(r/p)q. \qquad (9.6)$$

The intercept on the ordinate derived from equation (9.6) is:

$$z = (yw - ks)/p \tag{9.7}$$

and on the abscissa is:

$$q = (yw - ks)/(\{1 + iv\}r). \tag{9.8}$$

First, the direct and then indirect effects of interest rates are determined.

9.2.2 Direct effect of interest rates

Hold constant both the income tax rate and the rate at which the interest on rq can be deducted from gross income. Let the interest rate increase, thus:

$$t_3, m = \text{constant} \tag{9.9}$$

and:

$$i' > i. \tag{9.10}$$

The intercept on the ordinate in equation (9.7) is not affected by an increase in i. The denominator of the abscissa, equation (9.8), will increase causing an oblique shift to the left in the budget line. This direct effect of an increase in i can be verified by contrasting intercepts on the abscissa before and after, A–A', the increase in interest rates:

$$(yw - ks)/(R[s]\{1 + iv\}) -$$
$$(yw - ks)/(R[s]\{1 + i'v\}) <?> 0 \tag{9.11}$$

which reduces to $i' <?> i$; by the definition in inequality (9.10), the direction of the sign of inequality (9.11) is then $>$; hence, $A > A'$.

Next determine between annuli the relative magnitude of the change of budget lines attributable to an increase in interest rate:

$$(yw - ks_1)/(R[s_1]\{1 + iv\}) - (yw - ks_1)/(R[s_1]\{1 + i'v\}) <?>$$
$$(yw - ks_2)/(R[s_2]\{1 + iv\}) - (yw - ks_2)/(R[s_2]\{1 + i'v\}) \tag{9.12}$$

which simplified is:

$$(yw - ks_1)/R[s_1] <?> (yw - ks_2)/R[s_2]. \tag{9.13}$$

The left-hand side of inequality (9.13) is the intercept on the abscissa of the budget line for location s_1; the right-hand side is the intercept on the abscissa of the budget line for location s_2. By principle 2.6 (p. 24), it is known that the abscissa intercept for s_1 is less than that for s_2. Hence, the direction of the sign of inequality (9.13) is $<$. The effect of an increase in i is illustrated in Figure 9.1 where C–$C' > B$–$B' > A$–A', which represents the change in intercepts respectively for annuli $s_2 > s_x > s_1$.

Furthermore, the slope of the budget line $(1 + iv)(r/p)$ in equation (9.6) is related to interest rate i. The greater the change in interest rate, the greater will be the oblique shift in the budget line.

The direct effects of a change in interest rate may be summarized in the following principle:

Principle 9.8   On the direct effect of a change in interest rates:
  (i) The budget line will shift in an oblique and opposite direction as the change in interest rate.
  (ii) The further the household is located from the CBD, and the greater the increase in interest rate, the greater will be the decrease in intercept on the abscissa of the budget line.

9.2.3   *Indirect effects in an open city of a change in interest rates*

Refer to Figure 9.1(a) for an analysis of the necessary indirect effects of a change in interest rate in an open city. Let U be the spatial equilibrium welfare level before and after the change in i. Because of an increase in i, by principle 9.8, intercepts of the budget lines on the abscissa shift from AA, BB, and CC for households located on annuli $s_1 < s_x < s_2$ to budget lines AA', BB', and CC'. In the open city to restore spatial equilibrium, budget

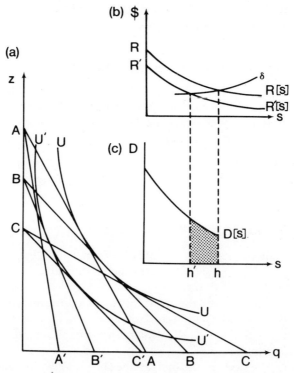

Figure 9.1   Direct effects of an increase in mortgage interest rates (after Thrall, 1982b)

lines will shift back to their initial positions. This is accomplished by house-holds outmigrating, thereby decreasing land rents from $R[s]$ to $R'[s]$. The magnitude of the necessary shift in the budget line increases with increasing distance from the CBD; the proportional change in land rents is then smaller in the inner core than the urban margins. This is illustrated in Figure 9.1(b).

The increase in interest rates leaves land rents insufficient to cover the cost of conversion of nonurban land to urban land utilization between annuli h and h' (Figure 9.1(b)); the urban radius is then smaller the greater the interest rates. The points of tangency between utility function (Figure 9.1(a)) and budget line remain the same before and after the increase in i; spatial equili-brium consumption of composite good and land within the open city are, therefore, unaffected by an increase in i.

When the higher interest rate prevails, population density is zero for distances greater than h' from the CBD. Thus, total urban population is smaller only by the radius effect; there is no density effect. The shaded area in Figure 9.1(c) depicts the difference in total urban population between cases where interest rates i and i' prevail. The indirect effects of an increase in interest rates in an open city can be stated in the following principle:

Principle 9.9 On the indirect effect in an open city of a change in mortgage interest rate:
(i) Land rents and radial extent of the city are inversely proportional to changes in interest rates. The proportional change in land rents will vary inversely with proximity to the CBD.
(ii) Within the city, land consumption is independent of the interest rate because the entire burden of interest rates is transferred into land values.

9.2.4 Indirect effects in a closed city of a change in interest rates

Refer to Figure 9.2(a) for the indirect effects of a change in interest rate in a closed city. Let U be the spatial equilibrium welfare level before the change in i. By principle 9.1, an increase in i results in intercepts of the budget lines on the abscissa shifting for households located on annuli $s_1 < s_x < s_2$ respectively by the amounts $A–A' < B–B' < C–C'$.

Using principle 4.9, say that BB' is tangent to the new level of welfare $u[s_x] = U'$. No indirect adjustment in land rent is required to satisfy spatial equilibrium conditions at s_x.

For the purposes of the geometric solution, define $A–A' = C–C' = B–B'$ on the abscissa (Figure 9.2(a)). The change in intercept on the abscissa as a result of an increase in i at s_1 (s_2) by principle 9.1 must be less than (greater than) that at an intermediate distance, say, s_x. The true intercept must then lie between A' and A for households at s_1 and to the left of C' for households at s_2. If direct effects were to lead to the intersection of the budget constraint on the abscissa for households at s_1 to fall slightly to the left of A, then land rents

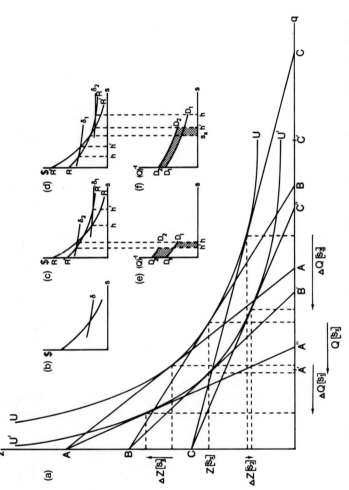

Figure 9.2 Indirect effects in a closed-interactive city from an increase in mortgage interest rates (after Thrall, 1982b)

must subsequently increase to create AA''. However, if A'' were the intercept after the increase in i, then – as was the case at s_x – land rents need no adjustment at s_1 to satisfy spatial equilibrium conditions. If the intercept of the budget line were to fall slightly to the right of A', then indirect effects would require land rents to decrease. By the same reasoning, an increase in interest rates can result in land rents either increasing, remaining the same, or decreasing at s_2.

Therefore, the behavior of land rent following a change in interest rate in the closed city is thus far indeterminate. If the utility curve is very steep for quantities of $z > Z[s_x]$, then it is likely that land rents must increase at s_1. If the utility curve is very flat for quantities of $z < Z[s_x]$, then it is likely that land rents would decrease at s_1.

There is no indeterminacy, however, in the behavior of land consumption following an increase in i. By inspection of Figure 9.2(a), it can be seen that regardless of whether the budget line intersects U', or lies to the left or right of it, land consumption everywhere declines. Hence, population density for all locations within the city also increases. Since density increases and total urban population is constant in the closed city, the radius must decrease. This result is stated in the following principle because it will be used to assist in placing bounds upon what land rent can behave like:

Principle 9.10 In a closed city, population density and the radial extent of the city are inversely proportional to changes in interest rates.

The case of land rent being independent of mortgage interest rates is illustrated in Figure 9.2(b). The radial extent of the city is, therefore, unchanging in Figure 9.2(b). This is inconsistent with principle 9.10 and is, therefore, not a possible solution. Land rents at some locations must, then, change in response to mortgage interest rates.

By similar reasoning, the cases illustrated in Figure 9.2(c) and (d), with cost of conversion δ_1, are not logically possible because a cost of conversion like δ_1 would result in an increase in urban radius in contradiction of principle 9.10.

Two cases that are consistent with the implications of principle 9.10 can be constructed using cost of conversion δ_2. By inspecting Figure 9.2(c) and (d), it is demonstrated that land rents can either decrease at all locations or increase at the CBD and decrease toward the urban margins.

If land rents decrease at all locations (Figure 9.2(c)), then taste preferences of households are such that they are reallocating a large portion of their income to the consumption of composite good which in this analysis is not affected by the interest rate (no nonland consumer loans) and, at the same time, allocating moneys that could be spent on transportation also into composite good consumption.

Alternatively, land rents can increase at the CBD and decrease at the urban margins (Figure 9.2(d)), similar but not identical to the behavior of land rent in Chapter 4 when income declined. The results can be summed up in the following principle:

Principle 9.11 In a closed city, land rents are everywhere inversely proportional to changes in mortgage interest rates with the exception of the inner core of the city where it is possible that they will be directly proportional to changes in the mortgage interest rate.

9.2.5 Effects of mortgage interest deductions

Let:

$$t_3, i = \text{constant} \tag{9.14}$$

and:

$$m' > m. \tag{9.15}$$

Like a change in i, an increase in m does not affect the intercept of the budget line on the ordinate. A change in m does affect the slope of the budget line and also the intercept of the budget line on the abscissa. By the same reasoning as that regarding mortgage interest rates, it can be shown that a decrease in m will shift the budget line to the left, with the change in intercept on the abscissa increasing with increasing distance from the CBD. Direct and indirect effects of an increase in m are then the opposite of an increase in i. Nevertheless, the principles will be summarized for open and closed cities. The results summarized in the following principles for the open city are:

Principle 9.12 The indirect effect of the mortgage interest deduction is the opposite of the mortgage interest rate.

Principle 9.13 On the indirect effect in an open city of a change in mortgage interest deduction:
    (i) Land rents and radial extent of the city are positively related to the mortgage interest deduction. The proportional change in land rents will vary inversely with proximity to the CBD.
    (ii) Land consumption in the interior of the open city is independent of the mortgage interest deduction.

In the open city, what is the change in land rent necessary for the system to regain spatial equilibrium? Since in the open setting the intercept of the budget constraint on the abscissa remains the same after the change in parameter m, the land rent following a change in m, or i, can be derived in terms of the initial land rent:

$$(yw - ks)/(R[s](1 + iv)) = (yw - ks)/(R'[s](1 + i'v'))$$

or:

$$R'[s] = R[s](1 + i\{1 - mt_3\})/(1 + i\{1 - m't_3\}) \qquad (9.16)$$

The results stated in the following principles for the closed city are:

Principle 9.14 In a closed city, population density and the radial extent of the city are directly related to changes in the mortgage interest deduction.

Principle 9.15 In a closed city, land rents are everywhere directly proportional to the level of mortgage interest deduction with the exception of the inner core of the city where it is possible that they will be inversely proportional to changes in the mortgage interest deduction.

9.3 Increasing interest rates with and without mortgage interest deductions

Compare now the impact of increasing interest rates between two cities, one where households may deduct mortgage interest payments and a second where households may not. Therefore:

$$i' > i \qquad\qquad\qquad (9.17)$$
$$\left.\right\} \text{ case 1}$$
and: $\qquad m \geqslant 0. \qquad\qquad (9.18)$

As in the discussion related to Figure 9.2(a), the condition in equation (9.17) brings about the budget constraint at s_x shifting from *BB* to *BB'*, when $m = 0$; the direct effect is for the household to have welfare drop to welfare U_3 (Figure 9.3(a)). When $m > 0$, the change in the intercept on the abscissa of the budget constraint for the same increase in i will be smaller ($<$) as demonstrated by

$$(yw - ks)/R[s] - (yw - ks)/(R[s](1 + iv))$$
$$<?> (yw - ks)/R[s] - (yw - ks)/(R[s](1 + i)) \quad (9.19)$$

which reduces to:

$$1 + i <?> 1 + i(1 - mt_3), \text{ or } 0 < mt_3. \qquad (9.20)$$

Thus, when $t_3 > 0_1$, $i' > i$, and $m = 0$, the direct effects are to shift budget line *BB* to *BB'* (Figure 9.3).

For $m > 0$, $t_3 > 0$, and $i > 0$, budget line *BB* is drawn to change only to *BB''*; the resulting level of welfare is U_2, where by inspection, $U_1 > U_2 > U_3$.

The incidence of the direct effects from an increase in interest rate is greater in a city without mortgage deductions than with mortgage deductions. The obtainable level of welfare for a closed city will therefore be greater when households are able to deduct mortgage interest rates from gross income to

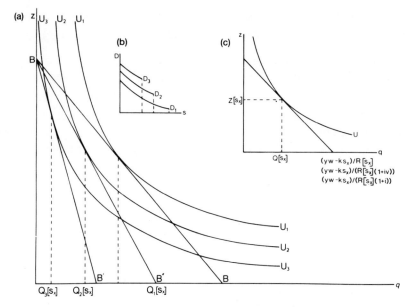

Figure 9.3   Comparison of an increase in mortgage interest rates between settings with and without the mortgage interest deduction (after Thrall, 1982b)

derive taxable income (Figure 9.3(a)). In the closed city, since $Q_3[s_x] < Q_2[s_x] < Q_1[s_x]$, then an urban place will be more dense if households cannot write off mortgage interest rates. This may be a contributing factor in explaining why population densities in the United States where mortgage interest deductions are allowed are generally less than cities in other countries, such as Canada, with similar demographic and economic bases but where mortgage interest deductions are not allowed.

In an open city, a consequence of the definition that indirect effects restore welfare back to the initial level is that land consumption and hence population density are not affected by either i or m.

9.4   Malleability

Generally in this book, it is assumed that housing is composed only of land; in Chapter 14 it will be demonstrated how the CTLR can more realistically and easily define housing as the decomposition of land and capital. Capital has vintage and is not easily replaced in the short run. Furthermore, once lots of a particular size have been purchased, the lot size cannot subsequently be easily changed. Capital allows households to live in higher density than would otherwise be possible, such as a high-rise building. Because population density then depends upon both the consumption of capital and land, once population density has been established it cannot change in the short run. Once population density has been set, the remaining choice to households reduces to whether the region should be inhabited at the prevailing density, or not inhabited. Such a city would be referred to as *nonmalleable*. In the long run, the capital can be maintained, allowed to deteriorate, changed into housing units of different sizes, or replaced.

Forces that contribute to development of the urban margins, such as declining *i* or increasing *m*, can lead to abandonment in the previously

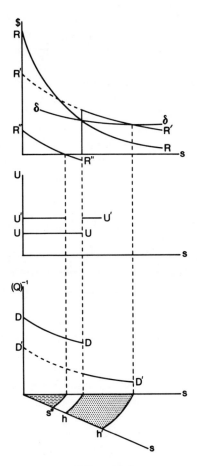

Figure 9.4   Effect of the mortgage interest deduction in a nonmalleable closed–interactive city (after Thrall, 1982b)

developed part of the city. For illustration, prior to an increase in m, let the land rent schedule be $R[s]$ and population density $D[s]$ and welfare U. In a closed-interactive, perfectly malleable city, following an increase in m, let the new land rent be $R'[s]$ and population density $D'[s]$ (Figure 9.4). Say the increase in m leads to an increase in welfare to U'.

But consider the difficulties of this transformation in a closed-interactive, nonmalleable city. Lot size and, therefore, population density between the CBD and h cannot change; households over this range, then, must be compensated if they are voluntarily going to reside in a population density greater than they otherwise would have chosen (see Chapter 12 on involuntary situations, and Chapter 13 on a more formal presentation of compensation). The compensation is for land rent to fall, say, to $R''[s]$ between the CBD and h. The compensated land rent allows two things: first, welfare within radius h to increase to U'; and second, population to outmigrate from within h to the new developments in the old transition zone.

Land rents will adjust, following population movement and the change in demand, until spatial equilibrium conditions are satisfied. A decrease in land rents to $R''[0 < = s < = h]$ is necessary compensation for households not to continue to relocate to the new lower population density environment. A zone of abandonment $s^* \leqslant s \leqslant h$ will be created; the zone exists over that region where land rents could not decline in compensation and still be positive. Rents beyond h become equal to $R'[h < s < = h']$ and population density equal to $D'[s > h]$.

The cost to society as a result of the government policy to increase m may be substantial. Land that otherwise would have value may be abandoned between s^* and h. The zone of abandonment may create problems (negative externalities, see Chapter 13) for areas tangential to the abandoned zone. Property tax revenues will decline for the region interior to s^*, and be totally lost for the region between s^* and h. The cost of distributing public goods may increase due to the discontinuity in the settled area. Once these and other costs are included in the model, there may be a net decrease in welfare. These negative effects may be minimized by limiting the expansion of the urban fringe, as will be discussed in Chapter 12 on planning. It may be sufficient to impose a radial constraint on the urban area using the criterion that if the vacancy rate exceeds, say, 3 percent for a particular land use category, then similar development at the periphery of the urban area will not be allowed until the vacancy rate falls below that level.

If an increase in m occurs within a nonmalleable, open-interactive city, then welfare remains at U and the analysis is the same as the malleable case. This is because density in the open city is independent of m. It is easy to extend all the perfectly malleable analyses to the nonmalleable setting, as above.

9.5   Conclusion

This chapter has investigated the change in the geography of the city as a result of a change in two factors within the household budget constraint. Changes in market interest rates were contrasted with a public policy of deducting interest payments from gross income in order to derive a reduced taxable income.

In the open city, increasing interest rates have the same effect as reducing the ability of households to use mortgage interest rates to reduce income taxes; both factors decrease land rent, decrease the radius of the city, and decrease equilibrium total population. Those who claim that the mortgage interest deduction only increases land rent in direct proportion to the deduction are implicitly referring only to the extreme polar case of the perfectly open city.

In the closed city, a decrease in the interest rate and an increase in the mortgage interest rate deduction have the same impact upon urban form and land rent. Land rent may either increase or decrease in the central part of the city, while land rent will increase at the urban margins. The radius of the city increases. Population density everywhere decreases.

Mortgage interest deductions can offset the incidence of a decline in welfare attributable to an increase in mortgage interest rates. In the closed-interactive nonmalleable city, zones of abandonment may be created when either interest rates decrease or mortgage interest rate deductions increase unless planners take the initiative to limit suburban expansion.

References

Thrall (1980b, 1981a, 1982b)

10

Sales tax

10.1 Direct effects of the sales tax

This chapter continues the analysis from Chapter 8 on the effect of the sales tax upon the geography of the city.

Let household income be partitioned into expenditures on sales tax $t_1 pz$ as well as on composite good, land, and transportation; all other taxes as discussed in Chapter 8 are set to zero. The budget line with positive sales tax becomes:

$$z = (y - ks)/(p\{1 + t_1\}) - (r/(p\{1 + t_1\}))q \qquad (10.1)$$

with intercepts:

$$z = (y - ks)/(p\{1 + t_1\}) \qquad (10.2)$$

and:

$$q = (y - ks)/r[s]. \qquad (10.3)$$

When there is an increase in the sales tax, intuitively the budget line would be expected to decrease. This intuition can be verified by considering the slope of the budget line and the intercepts in equations (10.1)–(10.3). An increase in t_1 increases the denominator of the slope; the budget line becomes more flat. Also the denominator of the ordinate intercept increases, thereby decreasing the point of intersection of budget line and composite good axis. There is no direct effect upon the intercept of the budget line on the abscissa. This is illustrated in Figure 10.1 for annulus s_x. The budget line for households on annulus s_x shifts obliquely from BB to $B'B$. The new budget line allows households' only level of welfare $u[s_x] < U$. These results on the direct effect of a change in a sales tax can be summarized by the following principle:

Principle 10.1   On the direct effect of a change in sales tax: the maximum possible consumption of composite good is inversely related to the level of sales tax, while the maximum possible consumption of land is independent

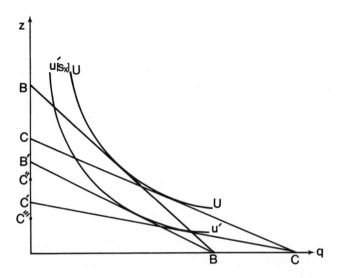

Figure 10.1 Direct effects of an increase in the sales tax (after Thrall, 1981a)

of the sales tax. The households' budget line then changes obliquely in the opposite direction as the change in sales tax.

The change in intercepts on the ordinate can be demonstrated to be greater for annuli closer to the city center than for annuli relatively more distant from the city center. Between two locations, $s_1 < s_x$, determine:

$$(y - ks_1)/p - (y - ks_1)/(p\{1 + t_1\}) <?>$$
$$(y - ks_x)/p - (y - ks_x)/(p\{1 + t_1\}). \qquad (10.4)$$

Multiplying inequality (10.4) through by $(1 + t_1)p/t_1$ and rearranging the result leaves:

$$y - ks_1 > y - ks_2. \qquad (10.5)$$

When disposable income increases with proximity to the central business district the direction of the sign of inequality (10.5) will be $>$.

Figure 10.1 has been drawn with budget lines CC and BB respectively for annulus $s_2 > s_x$. Because of the discussion concerning inequalities (10.4) and (10.5), the figure has been drawn with $B\text{-}B' > C\text{-}C'$ on the ordinate. Figure 10.1 demonstrates that following the introduction of the sales tax, households at s_1 and s_x can be reduced to the same lower level of welfare, namely $u[s_2] = u[s_x]$. Hence, it is possible that the incidence of the effect of the sales tax upon household welfare is spatially neutral. It would also have been consistent with inequality (10.4) that the budget line for households at s_2 had diminished only to $C\text{-}C'' < B\text{-}B'$, thereby creating a state of inequity where $u[s_2] > u[s_x]$. A third case is also possible of $C\text{-}C''' < B\text{-}B'$ leaving $u[s_2] < u[s_x]$. The direct effect of the sales tax upon household welfare is not necessarily spatially neutral.

The actual incidence depends upon household taste preferences which are reflected in the shape of the utility curve. While throughout this book households are assumed to have constant taste preferences, one can speculate that a spatially biased incidence can contribute to households changing their taste preferences.

10.2   Indirect effects of the sales tax in an open city

The direct effect of introducing a sales tax has been to reduce budget line BB to $B'B$ (Figure 10.2(a)). The resulting lower level of obtainable welfare provides a disincentive for households to remain at s_x. Household relocation leads to a decrease in land rents from $R[s_x]$ to $R'[s_x]$. Land consumption increases from $Q[s_x]$ to $Q'[s_x]$. Population density, therefore, decreases at s_x. The revealed effect is to shift density from $(Q[s_x])^{-1}$ to $(Q'[s_x])^{-1}$.

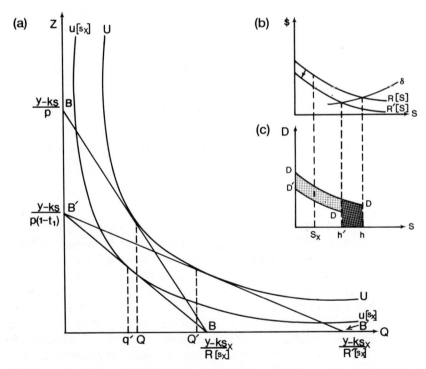

Figure 10.2 Indirect effects in an open-interactive city from an increase in the sales tax (after Thrall, 1981a)

The same process can be demonstrated for all locations within the city. Because the direct incidence upon household welfare is indeterminate, without empirical information concerning household taste preferences, the relative magnitude of the change in population density and land rent between locations is also indeterminate.

The resulting indirect effect upon land consumption and rent from an increase in sales tax in an open city is the same as the introduction of an income tax (Figure 10.2(b)). Land rents are everywhere smaller. The urban radius is smaller by the amount $h - h'$. Population density is everywhere less. Hence, total population is smaller by both radius and density effects with increases in the sales tax. The results can be stated in the following principle:

Principle 10.2 Between two open cities with identical characteristics except for sales taxes, the city with the higher sales tax will have lower land rents, smaller radial extent, lower population density, and also smaller total population.

10.3 Indirect effects of the sales tax in a closed city

Budget constraints for households on annuli $s_1 < s_x < s_2$ are initially respectively A_1A, B_1B, and C_1C (Figure 10.3). Using principle 4.9 (p. 48), let budget constraint B_1B shift to B_2B, tangent to the new spatial equilibrium welfare U'. The intercepts on the ordinate for location s_x have shifted from B_1 to B_2. By principle 10.2, the decrease must be greater for locations closer to the CBD than s_x, and smaller for locations further from the CBD than s_x.

Draw $A_1-A_2 = B_1-B_2$ (Figure 10.3). The direct effect of the downward shift in the intercept on the ordinate of the budget constraint for s_1 must be greater than that indicated by A_1-A_2. If drawn, the line A_2A would twice cross U'; hence, the direct effect at s_1 may result in welfare $u[s_1] < = > U'$. The effect upon land rents from an increase in sales tax in the closed city is then indeterminate; land rents can increase, remain the same, or decrease at s_1.

Similarly, draw $C_1-C_2 = B_1-B_2$. The downward shift in C on the ordinate for households at s_2 must actually be less than $C_1 - C_2$. Since line C_2C lies below U', then land rents in the closed city can either increase, remain the same, or decrease.

From inspection of Figure 10.3, the following principle about the behavior of population density with respect to changes in sales taxes in a closed city can be stated:

Principle 10.3 Following an increase in a sales tax in a closed city, population density increases in the inner core of the city and decreases at the urban margins.

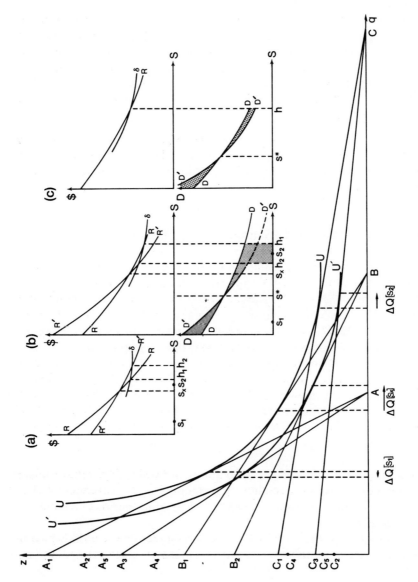

Figure 10.3 Indirect effects in a closed-interactive city from an increase in the sales tax (after Thrall, 181a)

Refer to that location as s^* where in spatial equilibrium no changes are observed in land consumption following the introduction of a sales tax. The following principle summarizes the possible behavior of land rent:

> *Principle 10.4*   Following an increase in a sales tax in a closed city: land rents and the radial extent of the city can increase, remain constant, or decrease, so long as the constant population requirement is maintained that the increase in population attributable to an increase in population density interior to location s^* is exactly balanced by a decrease in population beyond s^*.

10.4   Conclusion

This chapter has continued the discussion of the effect upon the geography of the city attributable to the public sector's policy of revenue collection with an examination of the sales tax.

The direct effect of an increase in sales tax was an oblique and downward shift in the households' budget line. The maximum possible consumption of composite good was reduced, while the maximum possible consumption of land in this setting is independent of the sales tax.

In the open city, higher sales taxes decrease land rents and urban radius leading to a smaller spatial equilibrium population. For the closed city, population density increases in the inner core of the city and decreases at the urban margins. The behavior of land rent, however, is indeterminate. Household taste preferences are likely a major determinant in whether land rents increase, remain constant or decrease because of an increase in sales tax.

References

Thrall (1980b, 1981a)

11

Property tax

11.1 Introduction

This chapter completes the analysis begun in Chapter 8 on the effect upon the geography of the city attributable to government revenue collection; analyzed here is the property tax.

Before developing the Consumption Theory of Land Rent analysis, reflect first on the aspatial view of the property tax; the analysis is generally attributed to the great nineteenth-century economic geographer and newspaper journalist Henry George and is still an integral part of the belief system of many contemporary economists. The supply of land is considered to be perfectly inelastic as nature has been fit to provide only so much land, and that is all there is. The demand of land is a function of the productivity or returns to the land. A property tax on the land will decrease the return to the land by the dollar amount of property tax (Figure 11.1).

In Figure 11.1, R is the land value before the tax, and R' is the land value after the tax. The difference between new and old taxes is equal to the difference in the dollar amount of the tax. If the dollar amount of the tax is changed from t to t', then the change in land rent can be expressed as:

$$R - R' = t - t'. \tag{11.1}$$

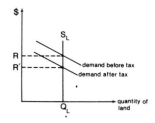

Figure 11.1 Classical aspatial economists' derivation of the burden of an increase in the property tax (after Thrall, 1981a)

Divide both sides of equation (11.1) by the difference in the tax:

$$B = (R - R')/(t - t').$$ (11.2)

If the change in taxes are 100 percent translated as implied by Figure 11.1 into the change in rents, then the ratio in equation (11.2) must be:

$$B = -1.$$ (11.3)

Equation (11.2) is referred to as the *index of burden*. Confirmation by empirical analysis that $B = -1$ would indicate that the burden of an increase in tax is *passed backward* onto present landowners. Future landowners in this scenario would find that they need not be concerned about the tax because the land rent will be reduced by the amount of the tax; this is often known as the Henry George theorem. If $B \neq -1$, then the argument concerning Figure 11.1 is somehow in error. For example, if instead the empirical results were to show that $B = +1$, then the tax would be shifted forward onto future owners of the land. There are two reasons why within the context of the CTLR the theory underlying the index of burden is unsatisfactory.

First, and most important, once space is introduced into the argument, the supply of land is not perfectly inelastic as portrayed in Figure 11.1. The implicit underlying assumption of the paradigm of economics that all economic activity occurs at a singular point in space is a great falsehood: *the geographic argument of this book is that relative spatial location is a primary characteristic in determining how land and land rent will be affected by changes in the parameters of the system*. Less abstract than relative spatial location is that the urban fringe can expand and contract in response to changing conditions and thereby increase or decrease the supply of urban land.

Second, arguing in terms of the productivity of land does not directly translate to the consumption sector. As was pointed out in sections 1.2.1 and 4.5, the underlying motivation and structure of the production sector is not the same as the consumption sector. The belief that the returns to land decrease because of a tax does not provide sufficient information as to what the reaction will be from the consuming household.

11.2   Direct effects of the property tax

Let the property tax be set equal to a percentage of the market price of land. Household income is then partitioned into expenditures on property tax t_2rq, composite good, land, and transportation; all other taxes, as discussed in Chapter 8, are set to zero. The budget line becomes:

$$z = (y - ks)/p - (r/p)(1 + t_2)q$$ (11.4)

with intercepts:

$$z = (y - ks)/p \qquad (11.5)$$

and:

$$q = (y - ks)/(r[s]\{1 + t_2\}). \qquad (11.6)$$

An increase in the property tax increases the numerator of the slope; the budget line becomes more steep. The denominator of the intercept on the abscissa increases, thereby decreasing the point of intersection of budget line and land axis. There is no direct effect upon the intercept of the budget line on the ordinate. This is demonstrated in Figure 11.2 for annulus s_x. The budget line for households on annulus s_x shifts obliquely from BB to BB'. The new budget line allows households only level of welfare $u[s_x] < U$.

The relative magnitude of the change in intercepts on the abscissa can be demonstrated to be inversely proportional to the proximity of the annulus the household is located on and the central business district. Between two locations, $s_1 < s_x$, determine:

$$(y - ks_1)/R[s_1] - (y - ks_1)/(R[s_1]\{1 + t_2\}) <?>$$
$$(y - ks_x)/R[s_x] - (y - ks_x)/(R[s_x]\{1 + t_2\}). \qquad (11.7)$$

Factor out from both sides of inequality (11.7) the ratio of disposable income to land rent. This results in:

$$\{(y - ks_1)/R[s_1]\}\{1 - 1/(1 + t_2)\} <?>$$
$$\{(y - ks_x)/R[s_x]\}\{1 - 1/(1 + t_2)\}. \qquad (11.8)$$

For $t_2 > 0$, dividing both sides of inequality (11.8) by $\{1 - 1/(1 + t_2)\}$ results in:

$$(y - ks_1)/R[s_1] <?> (y - ks_2)/R[s_2]. \qquad (11.9)$$

By inspection of Figure 2.12 and by principle 2.6, the sign of inequalities (11.7)–(11.9) must be $<$. The shift in the budget line is less the closer the household is to the central business district.

The direct effect of a change in property tax can be summarized in the following principle:

Principle 11.1   On the direct effect of a change in property tax:
  (i) The maximum possible consumption of composite good is independent of the property tax; the maximum possible consumption of land is inversely related to the property tax.
  (ii) The household's budget line changes obliquely in the opposite direction as the change in property tax.
  (iii) The magnitude of the oblique shift of the budget line is directly proportional to the distance separating the household from the CBD.

Consider the intuition of principle 11.1.iii. In Chapter 2 it was

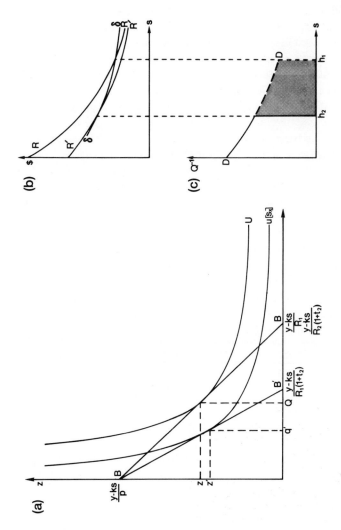

Figure 11.2 Direct effect on annulus s_x of an increase in property tax using the explicitly spatial CTLR methodology, and indirect effects in an open-interactive city (after Thrall, 1981a)

demonstrated that composite good consumption decreases with increasing distance from the CBD; since composite good price has been assumed to be everywhere the same, expenditures on composite good must then also decrease at a decreasing rate. The proportion of income allocated to composite good expenditures then decreases at a decreasing rate with increasing distance from the CBD. Transportation expenditures increase with increasing distance to the CBD and thereby offset, in part, the decreasing composite good expenditures. Because transportation expenditures have been assumed to increase at a constant rate, and composite good expenditures decrease at a decreasing rate, then land plus transportation expenditures must increase but at a decreasing rate with increasing distance to the CBD. This means that the further the households are from the CBD the greater is the total proportion of welfare attributable to land, the taxed good (see Chapter 14).

Figure 11.3(a) has been drawn with budget lines AA, BB, and CC respectively for annulus $s_1 < s_x < s_2$. The figure has been drawn with $A-A' = B-B' = C-C'$ on the abscissa. However, by principle 11.1, it is known that $A-A' < B-B'$, therefore, the resulting intercept for the budget line of households on annulus s_1 must lie somewhere between A' and A on the abscissa. This means that the budget line can be tangent to $u[s_x]$, or lie above or below $u[s_x]$. The direct effect at location s_1 upon household welfare from an increase in property tax can be greater than, equal to, or less than the direct effect at location s_x. Also by principle 11.1, $C'-C > B'-B$; hence, the intercept on the abscissa for the budget line of households on annulus s_2 can lie anywhere to the left of C' as drawn (Figure 11.3(a)). Since CC' intersects $u[s_x]$, then the resulting budget line can lie above, be tangent to, or lie below $u[s_x]$. This result can be stated in the following principle:

Principle 11.2   On the direct effect of a change in property tax:
(i) Household welfare is inversely proportional to the change in property tax.
(ii) The relative change in welfare between locations is indeterminate. As proximity to the CBD declines, the household welfare may increase, remain constant, or decrease.

The implications of principle 11.2 are portrayed in Figure 11.3(b). There are three possible cases: case 1, where the direct incidence of the property tax is spatially neutral; case 2, where it is spatially biased against the inner core of the city and spatially biased in favor of the urban margins; and case 3, where the incidence is greater at the urban margins and less at the inner of the city. Further analysis requires consideration as to whether the city is open or closed.

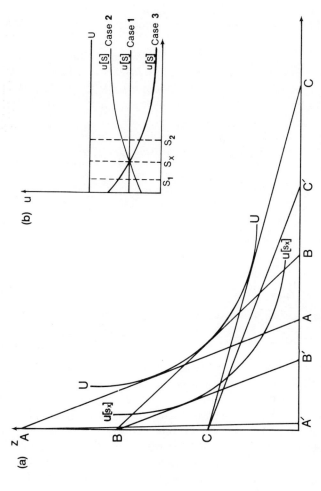

Figure 11.3 Direct effects on annuli $s_1 < s_x < s_2$ from an increase in property tax using the spatial CTLR methodology, and indirect effects in an open-interactive city (after Thrall, 1981a)

11.3   Indirect effects of the property tax in an open city

11.3.1   Ad valorem *property taxes*

Consider again Figure 11.2. The direct effect of an increase in t_2 was to shift the budget line from *BB* to *BB'*. By principle 11.2, the direct effect upon household welfare was indeterminate. Hence, the shift in budget lines at other locations could result in obtainable levels of welfare greater than, equal to, or less than $u[s_x]$. Regardless, all resulting welfare levels were less than *U*; s_x in Figure 11.2 can then be taken as representative of all locations in the ideal city.

Because the level of welfare is fixed at *U* in the open city, and because all terms in the intercepts and slope of budget line *BB'* are constant at location *s* except for $R[s]$, then land rents must decrease to $R'[s]$. This swings the budget constraint back to the right to become coincident with the initial no-tax budget line *BB*.

Because the new and old intercepts on the abscissa are equal, the new land rents $R'[s]$ and the old rents $R[s]$ must be proportional, that is equating new and old intercepts:

$$(y - ks)/R[s] = (y - ks)/(R'[s]\{1 + t_2\}). \qquad (11.10)$$

Solve equation (11.10) for the new land rent:

$$R'[s] = (1/\{1 + t_2\})R[s]. \qquad (11.11)$$

Equation (11.11) may be rewritten as:

$$R'[s] = W R[s] \qquad (11.12)$$

where:

$$W = (1/\{1 + t_2\}). \qquad (11.13)$$

W is an index of proportionality between new land rents and old land rents. If $t_2 = 0$, then old and new land rents are the same. If $t_2 > 0$, then $W < 1.0$. The greater the tax, the smaller is W and the smaller is the new land rent. Note that W decreases at a decreasing rate as the property tax increases.

Land rents will decline by a constant proportion, regardless of location, because by inspection of equation (11.13) W is constant over space for any given t_2; Figure 11.2(b) portrays this change in land rent, from R to R'. Because a constant proportion of relatively small urban fringe land values is less than that of relatively large CBD land values, land rents in absolute terms decline more in the CBD than at the urban fringe. The radius of the open-interactive city will decline from h to h_1 because urban land rents are no longer sufficient to cover the cost of conversion over that range.

The total land expenditure per unit of land by each household remains at $R[s]$, though it is partitioned into taxes to the government and dollars to the landowners; consequently, there will not be any density effect with regard to determining total urban population. Total urban population declines here only as a result of the radius effect (Figure 11.2(c)).

The above results may be placed in context of the index for burden and the Henry George theorem discussed in equations (11.1)–(11.3). Burden is here defined as the ratio of land rents to tax expenditures per unit of land:

$$B = (R[s] - R'[s])/(t_2 R[s] - t_2 R'[s]). \tag{11.14}$$

Substitute equation (11.12) into (11.14):

$$B = (R[s] - W^{\cdot}R[s])/(t_2 R[s] - t_2' W^{\cdot}R[s]). \tag{11.15}$$

Substitute the expression for W from equation (11.13) into equation (11.15), multiply the result by $(1 + t_2')$ and rearrange:

$$B = 1/(t_2 - 1 + t_2/t_2'). \tag{11.16}$$

Say that the tax is initially $t_2 = 0$; equation (11.16) then reduces to equation (11.3). Therefore, the Henry George principle on passing the cost of taxes 100 percent back onto present landowners holds for the open city when taxes are a percentage of present market value and where the initial tax is zero.

However, B in equation (11.16) depends upon both the initial value of t_2 and the subsequent value of t_2'; if t_2 is not restricted to zero, then B can take on values other than -1.

These results for a closed city may be summarized in the following principle:

Principle 11.3 On the indirect effect of a change in property tax in an open city:

(i) The resulting budget line is coincident with the initial budget line. There is no change in intercepts of the budget line or consumption of goods.

(ii) The summation of taxes paid and resulting land rents to owners equals the initial total land expenditure.

(iii) Land rent and urban radius are inversely related to property taxes. Because of the radius effect, population is inversely related to the property tax.

Also related to the index of burden in equations (11.1)–(11.3) is:

Principle 11.4 The Henry George theorem of the incidence of the property tax is a special case of *ad valorem* property taxes in the open city where the initial property tax is zero.

Principle 11.4 implies that the results may be dependent upon whether the initial land rent had itself taken on a value attributable to tax levied against a prior value. This is the subject of the next section of this chapter.

11.3.2   An assessment function

In the foregoing analysis, the value of land that is taxed continually changes as the tax is changed. Consider an alternative taxing scheme where land is taxed continuously at the spatial equilibrium pretax level. This modification to the above analysis can be accomplished in the following manner. As in equation (8.14), let assessed value per unit of land be:

$$AV[s] = \chi^{\cdot} R[s]. \tag{11.17}$$

The budget constraint now becomes:

$$y = pz + rq + t_2(AV[s])q + ks. \tag{11.18}$$

Following the introduction of the property tax, the intercept on the abscissa of the budget line becomes:

$$q = (y - ks)/(R'[s] + t_2 AV[s]). \tag{11.19}$$

Substituting $\chi^{\cdot} R[s]$ in equation (11.17) for $AV[s]$ in equation (11.19) results in:

$$q = (y - ks)/(R'[s] + t_2 \chi^{\cdot} R[s]). \tag{11.20}$$

By principle 11.2, the resulting intercept in equation (11.14) must equal the initial intercept on the abscissa:

$$(y - ks)/(R'[s] + t_2 \chi^{\cdot} R[s]) = (y - ks)/R[s]. \tag{11.21}$$

The resulting land rents can then be expressed as a percentage of initial land rents using equation (11.21):

$$R'[s] = (1 - t_2\chi)R[s]. \tag{11.22}$$

If assessed values are 100 percent of initial land values, namely $\chi = 1$, then an increase in property taxes will reduce land rents by the exact amount of the property tax.

Refer back to Chapter 8 where it was argued that χ must be spatially invariant for property taxes to be equitable between households. In equation (8.21) (p. 111), χ was defined as the assessed value to market value ratio. The assessed value to resulting market value ratio can then be found by dividing equation (11.17) by (11.22):

$$
\begin{aligned}
AV[s]/R'[s] &= \chi^{\cdot} R[s]/(R[s]\{1 - t_2\chi\}) \\
&= 1/(1/\chi - t_2).
\end{aligned}
\tag{11.23}
$$

The assessed value to market value ratio in equation (11.23) conforms to the geographic criteria of equitable assessment so long as χ is everywhere the same.

Compare the equation for burden with that derived in the previous two sections. Substitute equation (11.22) into (11.14):

$$B = \frac{(R[s] - (1 - t_2x)R[s])}{t_2 AV[s] - t'_2 AV[s]}.$$ (11.24)

Equation (11.24) can be rearranged to become:

$$-1/(1 - t_2/t'_2).$$ (11.25)

Say that $t_2 = 0$ and property tax is subsequently raised to $t'_2 > 0$. Equation (11.25) becomes -1.0. The index of burden in equation (11.25) depends upon both the initial value t_2 and the subsequent value t'_2; therefore, empirically B can take on values other than zero, and values other than Henry George's negative one.

11.3.3 Comparison of ad valorem *and assessment function*

In the following analysis, the two methods of determining property taxes will be compared for the open city.

Determine if the land rent that results from the *ad valorem* method is greater than, equal to, or less than the land rent that results from the assessment function, namely:

$$R'[s]_{ad\,valorem} <?> R'[s]_{assessment}.$$ (11.26)

Using the two different calculations for $R'[s]$ from equations (11.12) and (11.22) in equation (11.26) results in:

$$R[s]/(1 + t_2) <?> R[s](1 - t_2).$$ (11.27)

Equation (11.27) can be rearranged to become:

$$1 <?> (1 - t_2)(1 + t_2)$$ (11.28)

and:

$$0 > -(t_2^2).$$ (11.29)

So long as $t_2 > 0$, the resulting sign for inequality (11.26) is $>$: the *ad valorem* approach discussed in section 11.3.1 will return land rent values greater than the assessment approach discussed in section 11.3.2.

11.4 Indirect effects of the property tax in a closed city

Let AA, BB, and CC represent budget lines for households located on annuli respectively $s_1 < s_x < s_2$ in a closed-interactive city (Figure 11.3). Following an increase in the property tax, the budget constraint for s_x shifts to BB'; the direct effect upon budget line for annulus s_x is used to find the new spatial equilibrium level of welfare $u[s_x] = U'$. BB' is tangent to U'.

Because of principles 11.1 and 11.2, it is indeterminate whether land rents must increase, remain the same, or decrease in the inner city in order to re-establish spatial equilibrium and tangency between budget line A and welfare $u[s_x]$. Consider now the three possible cases.

11.4.1   *Case 1:* ad valorem *property tax, closed city, no change in land rent*

Let direct effects shift all budget lines (Figure 11.4(a)) to become tangent to $u[s_x] = U'$ namely by the amount on the abscissa A–A'', B–B', and C–C'', for $s_1 < s_x < s_2$. Land rents will not then change from subsequent indirect effects. That land rents are independent of the tax also requires the urban radius to be independent of the tax.

It is seen by inspection of Figure 11.4(a) that in this case a decrease in land consumption occurs at every location thereby creating an increase in population density. This density effect results in a net increase in population within any annulus about the CBD. Since land rents do not change, the urban radius must remain constant, yet population density everywhere increases, yielding an increase in total population in violation of the definition of a closed city. Case 1 then is inconsistent and, therefore, not possible.

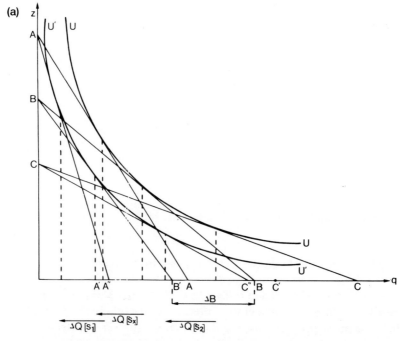

Figure 11.4 Indirect effects from an increase in property tax in a
closed-interactive city: the case where land rent decreases
at the city center (after Thrall, 1981a)

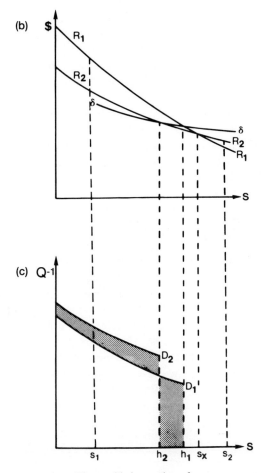

Figure 11.4 *continued*

11.4.2 *Case 2:* ad valorem *property tax, closed city, land rent decreases at the CBD*

In this case, direct effects result in a greater reduction in welfare at the inner core of the city than elsewhere. Budget lines shift as a result of direct effects by $A–A'$, $B–B'$, and $C–C'$ on the abscissa for locations respectively $s_1 < s_x < s_2$ (Figure 11.4(a)). In compensation, land rent decreases at s_1 to $R_2[s_1]$. The budget line stabilizes at AA'' for households at s_1. Households at s_1 consume more land than would be the case from only direct effects, though the overall revealed effect is for land consumption to decrease. Population density increases at the urban core, s_1, as it does at s_x.

The reduction in welfare directly attributable to the tax is less for locations at the urban margins than at the inner core of the city. Land rent then increases for locations beyond s_x, resulting in the budget line for households stabilizing at CC'''.

Population density is revealed to increase everywhere. This information can be used to deduce the possible behavior of land rent relative to the cost of conversion δ.

Land rents relative to cost of conversion δ must lead to a reduction in urban radius to balance the demonstrated increase in population density in this closed city. Land rents must then unfold across space relative to δ, so that $s_x > h$, as in Figure 11.4(b). Land rents everywhere in the city then decrease and the urban radius contracts.

11.4.3   Case 3: ad valorem *property tax, closed city, land rent increases at the CBD*

Consider now the case where direct effects are that household welfare declines less at the CBD than elsewhere. Land rents increase at the CBD (Figure 11.5(a)). Land rents remain the same at s_x. At locations $s > s_x$, land rents decrease. Land rents must unfold across space such that the cost of conversion δ provides for $s_x < h$. There is a reduction in urban radius. Land consumption everywhere decreases, creating greater population density. The increase in population attributable to the increase in density (Figure 11.5(b)) must be exactly balanced by the decrease in population at the urban margins attributable to the decrease in radial extent of the city.

The indirect effects of cases 2 and 3 are summarized in the following principle:

> *Principle 11.5*   On the indirect effect of a change in property tax in a closed city:
> (i)   The incidence of the property tax is not spatially neutral. Land rents are inversely related to the property tax at the urban margins. Land values can be either inversely or directly related to the property tax at the urban core.
> (ii)   The radial extent of the city is inversely related to the property tax.
> (iii)   Population density is directly related to the property tax.
> (iv)   Since land rents can increase, remain the same or decrease because of changes in the property tax, then the index of burden can be positive, negative or zero. The numerical value of the index of burden depends upon relative spatial location of the property.

11.5   Conclusion

The purpose of this and the previous three chapters has been to derive the

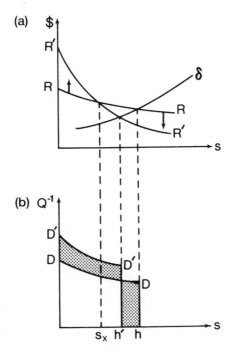

Figure 11.5 Revealed indirect effects from an
increase in property tax in a closed-
interactive city: the case where land
rent increases at the city center (after
Thrall, 1981a)

effects on the geography of the city of property taxes, sales taxes, and income
taxes, as well as mortgage interest deductions and interest rates.

The effect of the property tax upon land values has long been an issue
concerning scholars and practitioners of public finance. Henry George
campaigned quite successfully for the "single tax movement," where the
property tax would return to the community exactly the value that land
received because of the community. This was demonstrated in the above
CTLR analysis to be a special case of the open city. It is not, then, surprising
that empirical evidence has failed to confirm the Henry George theorem;
empiricists should look for support in those cities that conform most closely
to being open. It would then be worthwhile for an empirical study on the
incidence of the property tax to compare two cities that are very similar
except in property taxes: the city with the higher property tax would be
expected to have lower land rents at the urban margins, a greater population
density, while urban core land rents can be either higher or lower relative to
the city with the lower property taxes. An empirical study on the incidence of

the property tax within a single city would require clear spatial delineation of the case study sites.

References

Barr (1972)
Carlton (1981)
Thrall (1979a, 1980b, 1981a)

PART IV

Government Services

12
Planning

12.1 Introduction

City planning generally is associated with being a complex tangle of laws and regulations. In practice, the particular laws in force within a community are the result of decades of tug-o'-war battles and short-term collusion between special interest groups. How the laws originated can best be examined in the context of game theory and history. Regardless as to how the laws came about, the laws affect urban spatial structure and, consequently, the welfare of the household and of the general community.

An objective of the theorist of spatial public policy analysis is to present tools that can change in a predictable manner the spatial structure of cities or systems of cities. A responsibility falls upon the theorist to determine the underlying and not so obvious implications that are likely to result from the implementation of various policies; many of the implications on first evaluation may appear counterintuitive. A responsibility of the theorist is to be one of the guides of society toward establishing social objectives and criteria; goals that include: greater efficiency; the choice of transfer effects; equity; fairness; and, in this process, the maximization of individual welfare and the maximization of the general social welfare, and the trade-off between the two. The tools to accomplish these tasks that are available to the urban theorist fall within three broad categories: design, social, and institutional.

Design includes physically structuring space to achieve some criteria of optimality. One example of design was discussed in Chapter 7, the introduction and placement upon the landscape of low-cost transportation nodes.

Social tools include biasing information process and modifying values. This tool serves to modify household taste preferences thereby altering the curvature of the household utility function. In the context of the Consumption Theory of Land Rent, this includes changing the trade-off between goods such as composite good and land, and the desirability or disutility of certain externalities.

Institutional tools include taxation, income redistribution (Chapter 4), the legal system, and zoning: knowing the spatial bias of a tax and employing this knowledge to obtain or avoid some land use effect (Chapters 8–11) including taxes on private transportation (Chapter 5); knowing the intended and indirect effects of income change (Chapter 4); and controlling or providing externalities through zoning, part of the larger problem of public goods and externalities (Chapter 13).

Three pure institutional tools are analyzed in the context of the CTLR in this chapter:

(1) limiting the areal extent of a city by restricting the diameter of the city to be less than would normally prevail within a freely operating market;

(2) adjusting the cost of conversion of nonurban to urban land utilization;

(3) requiring land rent and/or population density to be other than that which would normally occur in a freely operating market.

The first tool creates a radially constrained city, introduced earlier in Chapter 3. This type of city is analogous to Anglo-Canadian cities and those in the United Kingdom that are circumscribed by green belts. Some cities become naturally radially constrained by boundaries of mountains and sea.

Radially constraining cities in Ontario, Canada, has been since the mid-1950s a formal land policy. Ontario Hydro-Electric, in concert with regional municipalities and the province, effectively restricts development at the urban margins by not extending power lines to those properties. Provincial zoning often constrains radial expansion of cities to protect orchards and vineyards; southern Ontario is one of the few regions where these agricultural products can be grown in Canada. Adding to the pressures to radially constrain the urban margins is the reality that as much as 85 percent of land at the urban margins of most major cities in Canada is owned by only six giant development companies. The profit maximization strategy of these companies may differ radically from their competitive counterparts in the United States. Monopolistic landowners in Canada may withhold their land from the market with the expectation of higher returns; land may be rented instead of sold. The Canadian developer may make a larger return by limiting the availability of housing, constructing apartments, then receiving greater than normal rents. In contrast, developers in the United States may make the larger portion of their profits from the increase in land values that result from the installation of the necessary infrastructure for conversion of nonurban land to urban land. This infrastructure in the United States is most often paid for by the local taxpayer.

The second tool, subsidizing the cost of suburban expansion, is the single most important planning tool used in the United States. In practice, subsidies come from development of extensive highway networks, extending light rail transit lines to the suburbs, governments paying the cost of installing new roadways, utility, sewer and water trunk lines, and so on.

In addition to the cost of converting nonurban land to urban land in the United States being borne by federal, state, or local governments, the federal government has also historically subsidized new housing capital construction in the suburbs thereby generating a bias against housing renovation and redevelopment in the inner core of the city. The single federal policy most responsible for the bias toward the suburbs has been the availability of low-interest loans to discharged military personnel. When applied following World War II, this federal policy had two intended effects: first, to assist military service personnel in the start-up costs of civilian life; and second, to subsidize the labor-intensive housing industry because it employs large numbers of low-skilled blue-collar workers. The indirect effect of this policy has been to change the American city. (See also Chapter 9 for the analysis of mortgage interest rates.)

A dwelling to qualify as security against a low-interest loan had to fall within certain specifications. The two most important specifications were: that fire-impeding blocks had to be placed at prescribed intervals in the walls of the dwelling; and the dwelling had to be a detached unit. To the layman, the specifications appeared as reasonable and fair since the government had to secure its investment. The indirect effect of these two requirements by themselves, however, made a large part of the pre-1945 American city obsolete. Many dwelling units constructed before 1945 did not qualify for the low-interest loans. Much of the housing that did qualify was in the suburbs, and the new interstate highway system provided access to these new suburbs.

The third planning scenario, incidental in capitalist countries, allows a central authority to determine land rent and population density. A few capitalist countries have periodically used rent controls, particularly for the duration of wars and during periods of unusually high inflation.

In theory, zoning laws can restrict population density to be less than the market would otherwise create, or restrict a particular land use from occurring at a certain location and thereby generate negative externalities (see Chapter 13) about the site. Zoning laws more often serve to provide a sign for those who otherwise cannot read the landscape as to what type of land use is presently willing and able to pay the highest for the land; when this changes, so does the zoning.

The third planning scenario is dominant in centrally planned nonmarket economies, often champions of Marxist or socialist values, where the government constructs kilometers of medium-rise and high-rise apartments, creating a population density greater than that which would prevail in a freely operating market. These centrally planned economies also generally set rent to be less than would otherwise prevail in a freely operating market economy.

In this chapter, each of the three pure planning scenarios is contrasted to the pure or freely operating market solution. The pure market city is the basic CTLR open-interactive or closed-interactive city, where the cost of conversion is entirely borne by the individual resident.

The scenario of the radially constrained city is derived first. Next the derivation is presented of the effect of subsidizing thé cost of converting nonurban to urban land. The third scenario is a collage of analyses where either population density and land rent, or both, are restricted by the central authority. Lastly, the welfare effects for closed cities of each of these scenarios will be contrasted.

12.2   Radially constrained city

12.2.1   *Direct effects of a radial constraint*

The "radially constrained" city from definition 3.2 (p. 28) is limited to a smaller radius than that which would otherwise occur in an unbounded market city. In practice, a city can become radially constrained because of zoning regulations, or through conspiratory urban-fringe landowners, or because of natural features of the landscape. Instead of the city extending to the usual h, where the cost of conversion is equal to urban land rents, a radially constrained city may be limited in radius to h', where $h' < h$.

A decrease in radius from h to h' decreases the area of the city by $\pi (h^2 - (h')^2)$. Say that the households initially located between annuli h' and h attempt to relocate to the remaining inner core of the city, between 0 and h'. Intuitively, we would expect population density to increase because of a constant number of people being crowded into a smaller area. Since land rents and population density are directly related, then land rents would be expected to increase; and because the general level of land rents and welfare are inversely related, welfare would be expected to decrease.

To derive the direct effect that a radial constraint has upon household welfare, it is necessary to determine if our intuition about welfare is correct, that is will the direct effect of a radial constraint increase, leave unchanged or decrease household welfare?

Determine whether the direct effect of a radial constraint is to increase household welfare. Let AA, BB, and CC represent the initial budget lines for households located respectively on annuli $s_1 < s_2 < s_3$ (Figure 12.1). Prohibit the urban area from extending beyond h', instead of out to h (figure 12.2). If welfare were to increase, say, from U to U', indirect effects would require budget constraints to shift obliquely to AA', BB', and CC' to become tangent to U' (Figure 12.1). Land consumption thereby increases from $Q[s]$ to $Q'[s]$, decreasing population density from $D[s]$ to $D'[s]$ (Figure 12.2(a)), while land rent would decrease from $R[s]$ to $R'[s]$ (Figure 12.2(b)). The shaded area (Figure 12.2(a)) represents the population that cannot then be accommodated within a radially constrained city whose welfare increases. In the closed city, the number of households must remain constant thereby

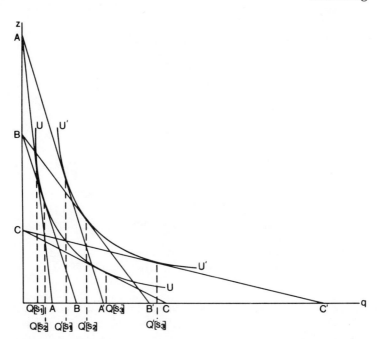

Figure 12.1 Derivation of welfare effects from radially constraining a
closed city (after Thrall, 1983b)

identifying that the direct effect of a radial constraint increasing household welfare is logically inconsistent with the CTLR.

Determine whether household welfare can remain the same as a direct response to the radial constraint. If welfare were to be constant, then for budget constraints to remain tangent to U, they could not shift. Land rent would remain constant at $R[s]$ (Figure 12.2(d)). Land consumption would remain constant at $Q[s]$, thereby keeping population density at $D[s]$ (Figure 12.2(c)). The shaded area (Figure 12.2(c)) represents the population that cannot be accommodated within a radially constrained city whose welfare remains constant. The direct effect of a radial constraint leaving household welfare unchanged is therefore logically inconsistent with the definition of a closed city.

The only remaining possibility is for household welfare to decrease because of the radial constraint. The following analysis assumes that the radial constraint decreases household welfare; if no subsequent logical inconsistencies are discovered, then because there is no other possibility, it can be stated as a principle that the direct effect of a radial constraint is to reduce welfare.

Because the logical inconsistency of the direct effect of household welfare either increasing or remaining the same hinges upon arguments related to the

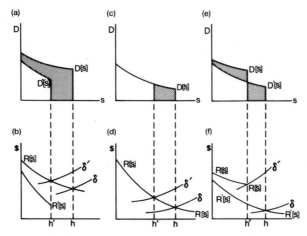

Figure 12.2 Radius and density effects considered from radially
constraining a closed city (after Thrall, 1983b)

closed city, then the indirect effect of introducing a radial constraint into a
closed city will be evaluated first; this analysis will then be followed by an
analysis of an open city.

12.2.2   Closed radially constrained city

The radial constraint requires households to outmigrate from the restricted
area to the unrestricted inner core of the city. The shaded area (Figure
12.2(e)) to the right of h' represents the population that cannot be accommodated there because of the radial constraint. The closed city scenario must
then be associated with an increase in density to the left of h' that can accommodate these displaced persons.

Consider the implications if the direct effect of a radial constraint is that
household welfare is reduced from U' to U (Figure 12.1). The indirect effects
would be to have budget lines for households on annulus $s_1 < s_2 < s_3$ about
the central business district (CBD) obliquely shift downward from AA' to
AA, BB' to BB, and CC' to CC, thereby becoming tangent to U. To accomplish this, land rent must increase from $R'[s]$ to $R[s]$ (Figure 12.2(f)).

Land consumption decreases from $Q'[s]$ to $Q[s]$ (Figure 12.1) thereby
increasing population density from $D[s]$ to $D'[s]$ (Figure 12.2(e)). By
inspection of Figure 12.1, land consumption is revealed to decrease proportionately more at the urban margins than at the inner core of the city, namely:

$$Q'[s_3] - Q[s_3] > Q'[s_2] - Q[s_2] > Q'[s_1] - Q[s_1].   (12.1)$$

Because population density increases proportionately more at the urban
margins than at the city center, the population density gradient becomes

more flat (Figure 12.2(e)). Since the population is constant, the shaded area to the right of h' is equal to the shaded area to the left of h'.

The indirect effects of a radial constraint on a closed city can now be summarized by the following principle:

Principle 12.1 On the indirect effect of a radial constraint in a closed city:

(i) Household welfare decreases.

(ii) Land rents everywhere increase.

(iii) Land consumption decreases proportionately more at the urban margins than at the inner core of the city. The population density gradient becomes more flat.

The direct effect of imposition of a radial constraint upon the city is thus far logically consistent with decreasing household welfare.

12.2.3 Open radially constrained city

The indirect effect upon household welfare in an open city must accommodate a return to the initial level of welfare.

Say that the population beyond radius h attempted to locate within the remainder of the city. This would, as demonstrated in arguments related to the closed city in section 12.2.2, lead to an increase in land rent and a reduction in welfare. There is no opportunity for the intercept of the budget line on the ordinate to change since at any given distance s the disposable income is constant, as is composite good price p. If population were to inmigrate, then the only mechanism to regain welfare level U' (Figure 12.1) is to decrease land rents thereby swinging the budget lines obliquely and regaining tangency to the initial welfare curve. Since the resulting budget line is coincident with the initial budget line, land rents and land consumption return to their initial levels.

The indirect effect of a radial constraint in an open city is therefore to exclude households that would otherwise reside further than h' from the CBD. The open city will then have a smaller population because of the pure radius effect. This is represented in Figure 12.2(c) and (d), where land rents and population density are unchanged because of the radial constraint; the city is less those number of persons indicated by the shaded area between h' and h.

The indirect effect of a radial constraint on an open city can be summarized in the following principle:

Principle 12.2 On the indirect effect of a radial constraint in an open city:

(i) Total population is reduced by restricting the outer margins of the city from development.

(ii) The zone interior to the radial constraint is unaffected by the radial constraint.

12.2.4   Overview of the radially constrained city

Now the following principle can be stated regarding the direct effect of introducing a radial constraint into the ideal city:

Principle 12.3   On the direct effect of introducing a radial constraint into the ideal city: welfare decreases in response to the displaced persons at the urban margins.

The burden falls upon the planner to demonstrate that the benefits attributed to radially constraining a city are not outweighed by the costs. Costs of this policy in a closed city include a lower level of welfare, higher land rents, and a population density gradient that is both higher and flatter than the closed market city. The open radially constrained city results in a smaller population base than would otherwise be the case. Since cities in actuality fall somewhere between these polar cases, a combination of these costs will be borne.

In practice, a desirable application of the radial constraint is to moderate the vacancy rate for housing and office space. Once the vacancy rate exceeds a critical level, say 3 percent, then further development at the urban margins can be prohibited until the vacancy rate of the remainder of the city returns to a more desirable level. In this way, abandonment in nonmalleable cities can be minimized. It is interesting to consider such a policy in the light of Table 12.1 which lists the national average vacancy rates of office buildings in the United States, and Table 12.2 which lists the 1980 rental property vacancy rate in selected metropolitan areas of the United States. Rental vacancy rate is a better index of unused housing than vacant owner property because often an owner who is unsuccessful in selling a dwelling will attempt instead to rent the property.

Table 12.1   Vacancy rate of office buildings in the United States, 1977–84

Year	Office buildings (%)	Year	Office buildings (%)
1977	7.6	1981	5.6
1978	6.4	1982	13.0
1979	4.7	1983	15.2
1980	5.0	1984	16.4

Source: "The Office Network", News America Syndicate, 1985.

Table 12.2 Vacancy rate of rental property by selected standard metropolitan statistical area in the United States, 1980

Metropolitan area	Vacancy rate of rental property (%)
Albany, Schnectady, N.Y.	7.1
Anaheim, Santa Ana, Calif.	4.6
Baltimore, Md.	5.0
Boston, Mass.	4.8
Buffalo, Niagara Falls, NY	6.5
Chicago, Ill.	6.5
Cincinnati, Ohio	7.7
Cleveland, Ohio	7.0
Columbus, Ohio	7.9
Dallas–Fort Worth, Tex.	10.4
Denver, Colo.	7.6
Detroit, Mich.	7.5
Fort Lauderdale, Fla.	7.3
Gainesville, Fla.	6.8
Hartford, Conn.	4.1
Houston, Tex.	14.7
Indianapolis, Ind.	9.8
Jacksonville, Fla.	11.2
Kansas City	9.4
Louisville, Ky.	7.8
Memphis, Tenn.	6.8
Miami, Fla.	5.4
Milwaukee, Wis.	4.2
Minneapolis–St. Paul	4.2
Nashville, Tenn.	6.8
New York City, Long Island, NY	3.2
Ocala, Fla.	10.8
Oklahoma City, Okla.	11.8
Orlando, Fla.	7.6
Philadelphia, Penn.	7.5
Phoenix, Ariz.	11.8
Portland, Ore.	6.1
Providence, R.I.	7.4
Rochester, N.Y.	5.1
Tampa, Clearwater, Fla.	10.5

Note: See also Table 15.1.

Source: United States Department of Commerce, Bureau of the Census, 1980, *Census of Housing, General Housing Characteristics HC80-1-A1*, table 1, Summary of general housing characteristics, 1980; vacancy rate of rental housing, Washington, D.C., USGPO.

12.3   Subsidized cost of conversion

By inspection of Figure 12.2(d) and (f), it can be seen that a radius constrained to h (or h') has the same effect as the cost of conversion being set at δ
(or δ'). If the cost of conversion is initially δ' and is subsidized exogenously to
the level of δ, then the urban radius will increase from h' to h.

The cost of converting nonurban land to urban land includes the cost of
agricultural capital, speculators' wages, improved access, sewers, pipes for
gas and water, and electric lines; a subsidy of any of these items, singly or
collectively, can reduce δ.

Because the effect is the exact opposite as a radial constraint, then the
following corollary to principle 12.3 can be stated to summarize the direct
effect of subsidized cost of conversion:

> *Principle 12.4*   On the direct effect of subsidizing the cost of converting
> nonurban land to urban land: welfare increases in response to the increase
> in developable land at the urban margins attributable to the subsidy.

Further analysis requires the use of open and closed city definitions.

12.3.1   Indirect effects of cost of conversion subsidies in an open city

The open-interactive city with decreasing cost of conversion can easily be
analyzed by referring to Figure 12.2(c) and (d). Let an exogenous subsidy
decrease the cost of conversion from δ' to δ. The land area of the city is
thereby increased. Since the intercept of the budget constraint on the
composite good axis is constant at any given distance s from the CBD, and
since utility is constant, then neither population density nor land rent can
change within the existing regions of the city; otherwise the budget constraint
will become tangent to a level of welfare other than the spatial equilibrium U.
Therefore, the population density and land rent gradients will smoothly
extend beyond h' to h. Population will then increase because of the radius
effect.

As the cost of conversion decreases and approaches the agricultural land
rent gradient, the urban fringe expands to cover that area shown as transition
in Figure 3.1 (p. 28). Because the population density gradient decreases at a
decreasing rate, then as the radius is extended more and more outwards from
the CBD the gradient becomes increasingly flat.

The indirect effect of subsidizing the cost of conversion in an open city is
summarized in the following principle:

> *Principle 12.5*   On the indirect effect of subsidizing the cost of conversion
> in an open city:

(i) Total population is increased by extending the outer margins of the city.

(ii) The greater the subsidy, the flatter becomes the density and rent gradients.

(iii) The remainder of the city is unaffected by the subsidy.

The pattern of urban growth of many cities of the United States since the early 1950s appears to conform to principle 12.5.

12.3.2 Indirect effects of cost of conversion subsidies in a closed city

Subsidizing cost of conversion is the opposite to radially constraining the city. Therefore, a decrease in cost of conversion results in a decline in rent from $R[s]$ to $R'[s]$ (Figure 12.2(f)) and a decline in population density from $D[s]$ to $D'[s]$. The urban radius increases from h' to h (Figure 12.2(e) and (f)). The number of persons in the shaded area to the left of h' is equal to the new suburban residents in the shaded area to the right of h' (Figure 12.2(e)).

As in the open city, with the cost of conversion decreasing to approach the agricultural land rent gradient, the urban area consumes the zone of transition. The population density gradient becomes increasingly flat the further it is extended from the CBD all other things being equal.

The indirect effects of subsidizing the cost of conversion in a closed city are summarized in the following principle:

Principle 12.6 On the indirect effect of subsidizing the cost of converting nonurban land to urban land in an ideal closed city:

(i) Household welfare increases.

(ii) Land rents decrease; the further out the city is subsidized to extend, the flatter becomes the rent gradient.

(iii) The further out the city is subsidized to extend, the flatter becomes the population density gradient.

12.3.3 Commentary on subsidizing the cost of conversion

There are many issues concerning subsidizing the cost of conversion. Some of which include: who is to pay for the subsidy? In the perfectly malleable closed city, all persons benefit from the subsidy regardless of location; should all persons in the city be required to contribute to the subsidy? If so, will the tax nullify any advantages from the subsidy? Is it equitable to expect persons in other regions to subsidize the development of the city?

Is this the best use of transition land? The subsidy biases development that would not have otherwise occurred under normal market processes. Would it be preferred to leave this land undeveloped as though it were in a land bank?

Recall the discussion of Figure 9.4. Subsidizing the cost of conversion of a nonmalleable closed city will result in increased vacancy rates (refer to Tables 12.1 and 12.2) and eventual abandonment.

Even though the fixed cost component of δ may be subsidized, in practice the variable cost component is not. This includes maintenance of the additional kilometers of sewer and water lines, and highway maintenance. Police and fire services have larger areas to patrol likely to lead to higher per capita costs if quality of service is to remain constant.

There is also the opportunity cost that should be considered. Less dense environments generally cannot efficiently support public transportation systems. Subsidizing the cost of conversion also then may lock the city into a single mode of private transportation. There is also the possible loss to merchants from declining consumption of composite goods.

There is also the issue of option demand. Say that once the city is developed it becomes nonmalleable (recall section 9.6 of this book). If the city had been able to develop in the long run under normal market processes, the population density gradient may have been much higher than that resulting from the subsidy. Is the lower population density a misuse of space?

12.4   Constrained density in a planned city

In addition to indirect effects that are particular to the polar cases of open and closed cities, a third type of city can be defined. The *planned city* is now introduced:

> *Definition 12.1*   In a planned city, both population and welfare are endogenous; the particular values they take on are the consequence of decisions made by a central authority concerning population density and the method by which land rent is determined. There is not necessarily a tendency for the planned city to move toward spatial equilibrium. The obtainable welfare surface may differ according to spatial location.

It will be assumed that if the authority can set population density, it can also set migration patterns; this is not a critical assumption. But the assumption does reveal that in the planned city, automatic mechanisms may not exist that guarantee a welfare surface that is spatially invariant. Rather the study of the planned city may take on a geography of disequilibrium.

12.4.1   *Direct effects of constrained density in a planned city*

In this section, the effects of land rent and population density controls are derived. In two examples annuli about the CBD, say, $s_1 < s_x$, determine spatial equilibrium land rent $R[s]$ and quantity of land demanded $Q[s]$ (Figure 12.3). Households on these annuli initially have budget lines respectively AA and BB.

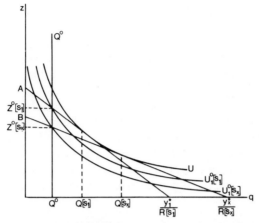

Figure 12.3 Constrained land consumption with market land rents (after Thrall, 1983b)

Constrain the quantity of land consumed to be $Q°$ thereby creating a spatially uniform population density surface $D°$. The analysis of the direct effects for a planned city will proceed by first assuming that land rents are retained at that value which initially prevailed in the pure market city.

Recall from Chapter 2 the argument that indifference curves are everywhere dense, meaning that every combination of goods can be identified as belonging on some utility curve. Since the household at s_1 is required to consume $Q°$ amount of land at price $R[s_1]$, then the remainder of the household's budget will be allocated to the consumption of $Z°[s_1]$ quantity of composite good. Households have a total land expenditure of $R[s]Q°$ and a total composite good expenditure of $pZ°[s_1]$. The budget line then can be written:

$$Z°[s] = y*/p - (R[s]/p)Q° \qquad (12.2)$$

where $y*$ is disposable income from equation (2.1).

The combination of goods $Q°Z°[s_1]$ identified by the intersection of the vertical $Q°$ and the budget line AA restricts the household to be on the indifference curve that also passes through the point $Q°Z°[s_1]$. This identifies for households at s_1 the maximum obtainable level of household welfare $U_1°[s_1]$.

A similar process of determining obtainable welfare is repeated for households located on other annuli about the CBD. For illustration, the household that is located on annulus s_x will have welfare identified by the point at the intersection of $Q°$ and budget line BB. By inspection of Figure 12.3, it is revealed that:

$$U > U_1°[s_1] > U_1°[s_x]. \qquad (12.3)$$

In the planned city, it is not necessarily the case that mechanisms exist or are allowed that ensure an equilibrium location of households comparable to the special case of the automatic spatial equilibrium process in the freely operating market city. Rather, in the planned city, which households locate where may be determined randomly, politically, historically, or through a black market.

In the planned city, and the geography of spatial disequilibrium, the evaluation of the indirect effects of constrained population density requires further specification concerning the alternative possible trajectories of land rent. Land rents can be set by the central planner to increase, decrease, remain at the market levels that prevailed in the direct analysis above, or take on new market values. Each will be evaluated in turn.

12.4.2   Constrained land, market adjustable rents in a planned city

Land rents can be set by a central planner or market, so that all households receive the same level of welfare while, at the same time, land is constrained to be at $Q°$.

Identify locations $s_1 < s_x < s° < s_2 < s_x^* < s_3$, where households are resident with budget lines respectively AA, BB, CC, DD, $B*B*$, and EE (Figure 12.4).

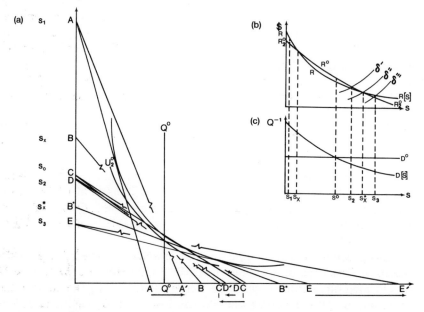

Figure 12.4 Quantity of land is zoned everywhere to be the same in the planned city, while land rents adjust in the market so that all households obtain the same welfare (after Thrall, 1983b)

At s_x, identify the point where budget line BB intersects the new spatial equilibrium welfare and Q°, where $Q^\circ \neq Q[s_x]$. Households at s_x will then be able to obtain welfare:

$$U_2^\circ = u[s_x] < U. \qquad (12.4)$$

Under freely operating market conditions, households at s_1 with budget line AA would have elected to consume $Q[s_1]$ (not drawn), which is less land than the amount Q° allocated by the central authority. Population density decreases at s_1. For the budget line anchored at A on the ordinate to intersect $U_2^\circ Q^\circ$, land rents must decrease from $R[s_1]$ to $R_2^\circ[s_1]$. Regardless of the lower land rents, welfare is driven down to $u[s_x]$ because households are unable to obtain their choice of between Z and Q.

Households at s_2, where $s_2 > s_x$, with budget line DD, under freely operating market conditions would have elected to consume $Q[s_2] > Q^\circ$. Because budget line DD lies above and to the right of point $U_2^\circ Q^\circ$, land rents at s_2 increase from $R[s_2]$ to $R_2^\circ[s_2]$, allowing intersection of budget line DD' with $Q_2^\circ U^\circ$; as elsewhere, households at s_2 then obtain welfare $u[s_2] = U_2^\circ$.

Households at $s_3 > s_x$, with budget line EE, under market conditions would have elected to consume $Q[s_3]$ (not drawn), which is more than the quantity Q° allocated by the central authority. Because budget line EE lies below the point $U_2^\circ Q^\circ$, land rents respond by decreasing from $R[s_3]$ to $R_2^\circ[s_3]$, allowing budget line CC' to cross point $Q^\circ U_2^\circ$. Households at s_3 then obtain welfare $u[s_3] = U_2^\circ$.

Since land rents decrease at s_1 and s_3, and increase in between at s_2, then if space is smooth and continuous there must be two locations, say, s_x and s_x^*, *for* $s_x^* > s_x$, where land rents do not change between alternative states of the freely operating city versus a planned city with these characteristics.

By inspection of Figure 12.4(a), quantity of land consumed at s_1 and s_x increases, and decreases at s_2, then if space is smooth and continuous there is some location s°, $s_1 < s_x < s^\circ < s_2$, where quantity of land consumed and hence population density is unchanged. Draw budget line CC so it is tangent to the point $Q^\circ U$, and CC' tangent to $Q^\circ U_2^\circ$ (Figure 12.4(a)). Since on the abscissa $C' < C$, land rents increase at s°.

Budget line B^*B^* has been drawn for households at location s_x^*, $s_2 < s_x^* < s_3$, where no change in land rent is necessary and population density increases.

Since this is a closed city, the decrease in population to the interior of s° must be exactly balanced by an increase in population beyond s°. This restricts the land rent surface to unfold across space relative to the cost of conversion δ such that the intersection of δ and the urban land rents falls to the right of s°. Costs of conversion δ', δ'', and δ''' are all consistent with this restriction.

To sum up, even though quantity of land has been set to a value by a central authority to be other than that which would otherwise prevail, a spatial equilibrium land rent surface can still be derived. The unfolding across space of land rent and population density surfaces that results from constraining population density to be a constant over space, while at the same time allowing freely floating market land rents, is shown in Figure 12.4(b).

The results can be summarized in the following principle:

Principle 12.7 On the indirect effect of constraining land consumption, but land rents seek a freely floating market level:

(i) The welfare surface will become spatially uniform, but everywhere less than that which would have been the case in a pure market city.

(ii) Land rents can increase (such as at s°), decrease (such as at s_1 and s_3), or remain the same (such as at s_x and s_x^*) depending upon relative spatial location of the household.

12.4.3 Constrained land consumption, land rents set above pure market rents in a planned city

Constrain households to have higher land rents than would otherwise prevail in the market city; thus, $R_3^\circ[s] > R[s]$ for all s. The intercepts of the budget constraints on the abscissa then shift to the left (Figure 12.5). Households are also restricted in population density to $(Q^\circ)^{-1}$.

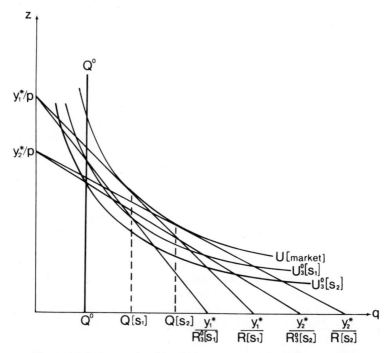

Figure 12.5 Constrained land consumption, land rents set above market rents in the planned city (after Thrall, 1983b)

Household obtainable welfare is identified by the intersection of $Q°$ and the resulting budget constraints; the example welfare surface decreases with increasing distance from the CBD and is everywhere lower than the spatially invariant welfare surface of the freely operating market city, and everywhere less than the welfare surface generated in section 12.4.2, above. Extending equation (12.4), the relationships between different welfare surfaces can be summarized:

$$U > U_2° > U_3°[s] \quad \text{for all } s. \tag{12.5}$$

12.4.4   Constrained land consumption, land rents set below pure market rents in a planned city

In the planned city, often in practice population density is set to be greater than that which would otherwise occur in a pure market city but, at the same time, land rents may be set to be less than pure market levels.

Let the land rent function be $R_4°[s]$ such that $R_4°[s] < R[s]$ (Figure 12.6). "Subsidize" the land rents, so that the resulting budget lines intersect $Q°$ higher than the intersection of $Q°$ and the pure market U. The reduced land rents can create a welfare surface that is greater than that which can be obtained in the pure market city, all other things being equal.

In the limit, as land rent $R_4°[s]$ approaches zero, the budget lines become more flat and asymptotically approach a horizontal line. Draw a horizontal line from the intersection of U and $Q°$. This will be the asymptote that households at s_x approach as land rents approach 0. For $s > s_x$, the intercept of the

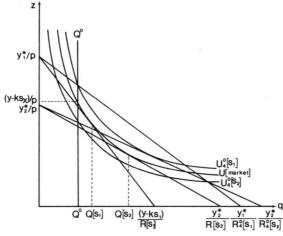

Figure 12.6 Constrained land consumption, land rents set below pure market rents in a planned city (after Thrall, 1983b)

budget line on the ordinate lies below $(y - ks_x)/p$; land rents beyond δ_x would have to be negative thereby generating a positive slope for the budget line in order for a budget line to lie above or on the point $Q°U$. Therefore, so long as land rents are greater than 0, households beyond distance s_x cannot obtain the market welfare level. In this case:

$$U_4^°[s_1] > U = U_4^°[s_x] > U_4^°[s_2]. \tag{12.6}$$

This is an intriguing result and can be stated in the following principle:

Principle 12.8　On the indirect effect of constraining land consumption, but land rents are below pure market levels:
　(i) Welfare can be greater than, equal to, or less than the level of welfare that would occur in a pure market city.
　(ii) Variation in the welfare surface over space depends upon the level of subsidy of land rent.

12.5　Comparison of the pure planning scenarios

The following analysis compares the results of the pure planning scenarios. Several possible welfare solutions and areal dimensions are contrasted in Figure 12.7.
　The city with subsidized cost of conversion will be relatively more dispersed than the market city which, in turn, is more dispersed than the radially constrained city. In the open city, subsidizing the cost of conversion

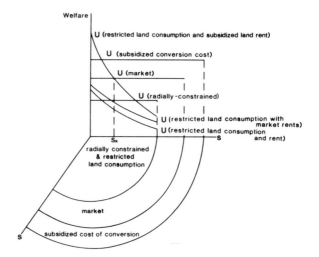

Figure 12.7 Comparison of the pure planning scenarios (after Thrall, 1983b)

will increase total urban population; in the closed city, it may increase household welfare. Radially constrained cities offer the open city a smaller population base, and offer the closed city a reduction in welfare.

If spatial equilibrium were to be obtained in a pure market city, then households would have welfare equal to:

$$U = U_{\text{market}}. \tag{12.7}$$

Those households who reside in a perfectly malleable closed city that received subsidies to convert nonurban land to urban land, and who do not pay for these subsidies through increased taxation, can receive a higher level of welfare than that obtainable in a pure market city, that is:

$$U^* = U[\delta' < \delta_{\text{market}}] > U_{\text{market}}. \tag{12.8}$$

This result holds only if no negative externalities arise and no loss of agglomeration economies occurs as a result of the subsidy policy.

Cities whose planning is limited only to introducing radial constraints allow for welfare:

$$U'[h_{\text{planned}} < h_{\text{market}}] < U_{\text{market}}. \tag{12.9}$$

The process by which households relocate to obtain the highest level of welfare ensures that welfare U' in inequality (12.9) is spatially invariant. The policy of radially constraining a closed city can be used to monitor urban expansion at rates that minimize the deleterious effects of urban decay, including the negative effects that indirectly result from the application of other planning policies, including subsidizing the cost of converting nonurban land to urban land. If the rate of vacancy exceeds a critical level, further development at the urban margins may be curtailed. This policy can be used to "fine-tune" the city analogous to using interest rates in some circumstances to fine-tune an economy. Moreover, this can be used to obtain a solution more equivalent to that which a freely operating market would produce.

The planned city may also not have a spatial equilibrium solution in the sense that obtainable welfare is everywhere the same. A central authority may simultaneously designate land consumption to be less and land rent to be greater than that which would otherwise occur in a pure market city. Such a policy may generate a welfare surface:

$$U[r > R_{\text{market}}, q < Q_{\text{market}}] < U_{\text{market}}. \tag{12.10}$$

In such a planned city, welfare will be everywhere below that which can be obtained in a pure market city.

Instead of the case outlined for equation (12.10), if rents were to prevail that would otherwise occur in a market city, while at the same time planners designate population density to be greater than that which would occur in a pure market city, the welfare surface would be created:

$$U[r = R_{market}, q < Q_{market}] < U_{market} \tag{12.11}$$

that lies below the pure market U. The two welfare surfaces in inequalities (12.10) and (12.11) are not restricted to being uniform over space; therefore, a mechanism other than the market must be introduced to determine which households will reside where. The outcome of the decision as to who will live where also determines which households will receive the relatively higher levels of welfare.

The planning decision to restrict population density to be greater than that which would occur in a pure market city has a negative effect upon household welfare. This negative effect can be counterbalanced at some locations by setting land rents to be less than that which would prevail in the pure market city. This planning policy can create a welfare surface like:

$$U[r < R_{market}, q < Q_{market}] < = > U. \tag{12.12}$$

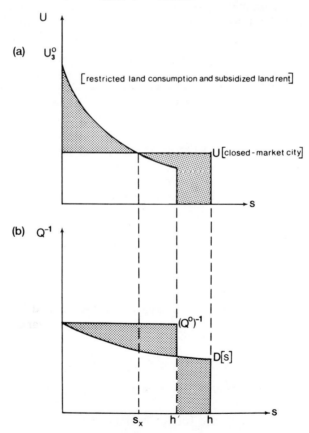

Figure 12.8 Comparison of the spatial welfare surfaces between the pure market solution and the case where land consumption is restricted while land rent is subsidized (after Thrall, 1983b)

Consider in greater detail the implications of equation (12.12). By setting population density to be uniform across space and everywhere greater than that which would occur in a pure market city, while at the same time positioning land rent to be less than the level that would appear in a pure market city, a welfare surface like that presented in Figure 12.8 may be created.

Aggregate social welfare is the area under the welfare function in Figure 12.8. A criterion of the central planner may be to maximize aggregate social welfare. In this analysis, this may be done with land rents set to be near 0. A welfare surface like inequality (12.12) can be created. Yet beyond s_x if the rent is greater than zero, then the welfare in the pure market city remains greater than that in the centrally planned city. If the area to the left of s_x is greater than the shaded area to the right of s_x, then the centrally planned city can be said to have achieved a level of aggregate social welfare that is greater than would occur otherwise in a pure market city. However, this social objective may have been achieved by sacrificing the spatial equilibrium criterion that otherwise identical households will be equally well off.

12.6 Conclusion

This chapter has demonstrated the effect that several pure planning scenarios have upon the internal spatial structure of the city and household welfare. The broad categories of the scenarios are (1) restricting the expansion of the fringe, (2) subsidizing the cost of conversion of nonurban land utilization, and (3) adjusting land consumption or land rent to conform to nonmarket behavior.

The implementation of these planning policies does not necessarily translate into increasing household welfare. Indeed, many reduce individual household welfare to levels lower than those which would have occurred if planning had not occurred. Therefore, the burden falls firmly upon the planner to justify why the particular planning policy is of value.

The planning policy may or may not maximize aggregate social welfare. In the process of maximizing aggregate social welfare, otherwise identical households may result in having different levels of individual welfare depending upon their relative spatial location.

References

Thrall (1983b)

13

Public goods and externalities

13.1   Introduction

The institutional framework within which people live and urban change occurs was demonstrated in Chapter 12 to be a force in the evolving city geography. This chapter continues with the discussion concerning the public sector. Here, in contrast to government institutions, the focus is upon goods and services provided by the government. The same analysis can be used to explain the effect that the general environment has upon the geography of the city. The general environment can include a seascape view; can include a source of noxious emissions such as a chemical dump or waste-disposal site; and can include proximity of households to other households, at least one of which group is prejudiced against the other.

   The geography of the city is determined in part by the mix and scope of such public goods. The densities of environmental attributes or local public goods may be uniformly distributed within the urban area; such local public goods or environmental attributes G are within the tradition of the pure public good. They possess *nonrivalry* and *nonexcludability* in consumption; the densities of environmental attributes or local public goods may at some locations be greater than at other locations, and such local public goods or environmental attributes can be referred to as *externalities*:

> *Definition 13.1*   An externality is a nonpriced good distributed over space. The direct effect of a positive externality can increase household welfare, while a negative externality can decrease household welfare. The density of the externality often conforms to a distance decay function centered on the site of emission or source of the good; the site or source can be fixed as a point or ray in space, or mobile through space.

> *Definition 13.2*   Nonrivalry means that one person's consumption of a good does not compete with (affect the welfare of) another's consumption of the good.

> *Definition 13.3*   Nonexcludable means that one's consumption of a good cannot be restricted or limited.

The externality density function $X[-,s]$ registers the spillin or density of negative externalities at s (Fisch, 1980). The externality density function $X[+,s]$ registers the spillin of positive externalities at s. The benefit or disbenefit that households receive is dependent upon the location of the source of the externality and the unfolding over space of the density function.

In this chapter, the source and characteristics of the externality are assumed to be exogenous and known. The analysis could be extended, however, to investigate the optimal spacing of externality sources, given their known characteristics of distance decay, by combining this analysis with one like the theory of nodes in Chapter 7 along with the criteria of maximizing either individual or social welfare in Chapter 12.

A spatially uniform public good will first be introduced into the Consumption Theory of Land Rent; principles from this analysis will subsequently be used in the analysis of externalities.

13.2   Direct effect of spatially uniform public goods

Consider a spatially uniform local public good G that affects the household welfare. The utility function $u[z,q,G]$ maps the trade-off between private goods z and q and the public good G. The effect that G has upon the household welfare depends upon the interaction between the public good and the combination of private goods. The public good can be either a substitute for or complement to land.

Mosquito abatement and land consumption are examples of complementarity between public and private goods; the eradication of mosquitoes increases the enjoyment one receives from a yard. The larger the yard, the greater will be the private benefit from the public mosquito abatement program. Households with little or no yards, particularly households residing in high-rise buildings, receive little or no benefit from mosquito abatement:

Definition 13.4   A public good is considered a *complement* to land if consumption of the public good increases the utility received from the consumption of land.

A park is an example of substitutability between public and private goods. The greater access a household has to parkland, the less will be the need for a private yard. Households having little or no private yards will benefit significantly from the introduction of neighborhood public parklands:

Definition 13.5   A public good is considered a *substitute* to land if the consumption of land can replaced by an increase in provision of public good with no resulting change in aggregate welfare.

The public good, then, is a component of household utility functions.

Exogenous changes in the provision of public goods translate into changes in the household welfare. The change in utility attributable to the change in provision of public good is known as the marginal utility of public good (MUPG).

> *Definition 13.6*   The marginal utility of public good is the direct change in household welfare attributable to a change in the provision of the public good.

The public good can be a strong or weak substitute for or complement to land consumption. Not all public goods are strong substitutes for or complements to land, as are parks and mosquito abatement. A nuclear aircraft carrier is a weak complement to consumption of land and composite good; by itself the ship is not perceived by the household as a significant component of the utility function. Presumably the aircraft carrier contributes to the safety of the household. Since all households in this analysis have the same income, the MUPG for such a good would increase every household's utility by the same amount, regardless of the particular bundle of private goods consumed.

Recall principle 2.3 (p. 23): Land consumption is inversely related to the proximity of the residence to the city center. If the public good is a complement to land, the utility that the household receives from the consumption of land increases: the more land, the greater the increase in utility. If the public good is a substitute for land, households can obtain a higher level of utility by consuming the public good instead of land, and spend the remainder of income on composite good. This discussion suggests the following principle:

> *Principle 13.1*   On the direct effect of introducing a ubiquitous public good:
> (i) If the public good is a complement to private land consumption, then the MUPG of households who reside at the urban margins will be greater than the MUPG of households who reside at the urban core.
> (ii) If the public good is a substitute for private land consumption, then the MUPG of households who reside at the urban core will be greater than the MUPG of households who reside at the urban margins.
> (iii) If the public good is a weak substitute for or complement to the private good, then the MUPG can be treated as being everywhere the same.

A succinct statement of the above principle is made in the following corollary of principle 13.1:

> *Principle 13.2*   On the direct effect of introducing a ubiquitous public good:
> (i) The MUPG for a public good that is a complement to land is greater the larger the parcel of land consumed.

(ii) The MUPG for a public good that is a substitute for land is greater the smaller the parcel of land consumed.

Let annulus s_x be a base location in the city with which other locations can be contrasted. If the MUPG is an increasing function of distance from the central business district, then households who reside closer to the CBD than s_x will not receive as great an increase in welfare as households who reside beyond s_x. If the MUPG is a decreasing function of distance from the CBD, then households who reside closer to the CBD than s_x will receive a greater increase in welfare than households who reside further than s_x from the CBD. If the MUPG is everywhere the same, then all households have the same direct increase in welfare from the increase in the provision of public goods, regardless of their relative spatial location in the city. These results are summarized in Table 13.1, where the direct effect upon welfare at s attributable to the change in public good provision is to increase welfare to $u'[s]$; the change in welfare is then $u'[s] - U$.

For illustration, assume that the characteristics of the public good follow that of case 1 (Table 13.1): the public good is a complement to land thereby leading the MUPG to increase with increasing distance from the CBD. It is also assumed that the public good is considered as being desirable by the household as opposed to being noxious. If it were noxious, then the direct effect would be to decrease the welfare of households at the urban fringe more than that at the urban core.

Let AA and BB be budget lines for households located respectively on annuli $s_1 < s_x$ (Figure 13.1(a)). Taxation is assumed not to be affected by changes in the provision of the public good. Therefore, the public good does

Table 13.1 Three cases for direct change in welfare as public good provision increases

---

Case 1: Land and public goods are complements, MUPG decreases with proximity to the CBD

$$u'[s] - U \begin{matrix} < \\ = \\ > \end{matrix} u'[s_x] - U \text{ for } \begin{matrix} s < s_x \\ s = s_x \\ s > s_x \end{matrix}$$

Case 2: Land and public goods are substitutes, MUPG increases with increasing proximity to the CBD

$$u'[s] - U \begin{matrix} > \\ = \\ < \end{matrix} u'[s_x] - U \text{ for } \begin{matrix} s < s_x \\ s = s_x \\ s > s_x \end{matrix}$$

Case 3: Land and public goods are neither strong complements nor substitutes, MUPG is independent of household proximity to the CBD

$$u'[s] - U = u'[s_x] - U \text{ for all } s$$

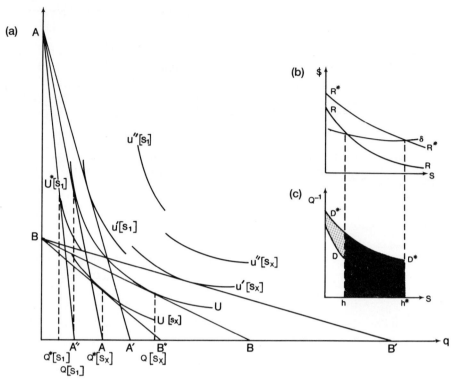

Figure 13.1 Direct effects from the introduction of a public good, and indirect effects in an open city (after Thrall, 1982a)

not have a direct effect upon the household's budget lines. The effect that taxation has upon the geography of the city was evaluated in Chapters 8–11.

The initial level of public good provision is defined to be G^*. Prior to the change in the provision of the local public good G, the initial level of household welfare is assumed to be:

$$U^*[Z[s],Q[s],G^*] = U[Z[s],Q[s]]. \qquad (13.1)$$

An increase in G increases household welfare by the MUPG to $u'[s_1]$ at location s_1 and to $u'[s_x]$ at s_x. Because the MUPG is greater for households located on annulus s_x than s_1, then the increase in household welfare is greater at s_x than it is at s_1; therefore,

$$u'[s_x] - U > u'[s_1] - U. \qquad (13.2)$$

In lieu of household welfare increasing to $u'[s]$ because of an increase in G, the same result could have been obtained by decreasing land rent by the amount $w[s]$. A decrease in land rent of $w[s_1]$ at s_1 would swing the budget line from AA to AA' thereby becoming tangent to $u'[s_1]$. At s_x a decrease in land rents by the amount $w[s_x]$ would be sufficient to swing the budget line from BB to BB' and thereby become tangent to $u'[s_x]$. In other words, on the abscissa in Figure 13.1(a):

$$A' = (y - ks_1)/(R[s_1] - w[s_1]) \qquad (13.3)$$

and:

$$B' = (y - ks_x)/(R[s_x] - w[s_x]). \qquad (13.4)$$

Further analysis of the ubiquitous public good requires the additional definitions of open and closed cities. Following these analyses, the assumption that the public good is ubiquitous will be relaxed in favor of the public good unfolding in some uneven manner over space.

13.3 Indirect effect in an open city of a ubiquitous public good

Indirect effects in the open city must return the household to its initial spatial equilibrium level. It was argued in equations (13.3) and (13.4) that a decrease in land rents by $w[s]$ can increase welfare by the same amount as the increase in the provision of G. Therefore, the addition of $w[s]$ to the initial land rent, simultaneous with the increase in the provision of G, can decrease welfare by an amount necessary to keep it at the initial level U. The term $w[s]$ then represents the capitalization of public good into land rent.

An increase in land rent by $w[s]$ decreases the intercept of the budget constraint on the abscissa for households at s_1 from A to A'', and at s_x from B to B''. The resulting intercepts on the abscissa following the increase in G are equal to:

$$(y - ks)/(R[s] + w[s]). \qquad (13.5)$$

The capitalization of the public good into land rent by the amount $w[s]$ is sufficient compensation to offset the increase in the provision of G and thereby maintain the initial spatial equilibrium level of welfare. The resulting land rent $R*[s]$ can then be referred to as the compensated land rent.

Definition 13.7 The *compensated land rent* is the spatial equilibrium land rent that includes a change or subsidy at least sufficient to offset the change in utility attributable to changes in the provision of a public good or externality, specifically:

$$R*[s] = R[s] + w[s]. \qquad (13.6)$$

Substituting equation (13.6) into (13.5) results in:

$$(y - ks)/R*[s]. \qquad (13.7)$$

Because the price of land increases from $R[s]$ to $R*[s]$, the welfare that the household receives from the consumption of private goods is reduced. Welfare attributable to private good consumption decreases at s_1 by $u'[s_1] - U$, and at s_x decreases by $u'[s_x] - U$.

Spatial equilibrium welfare at s is partitioned into welfare attributable to private goods:

$$U_{\text{private goods}} = U^*[Z^*[s], Q^*[s]]. \quad (13.8)$$

Consumption identified by function U^* can be referred to as the compensated demand. $Z^*[s]$ and $Q^*[s]$ are respectively the composite demand for composite goods and land. Welfare attributable to public goods:

$$U_{\text{public goods}} = U[G, s]. \quad (13.9)$$

Because the resulting welfare must be remain at U in the open city, then the summation of welfare received from private and public good consumption must equal the spatial equilibrium welfare, namely:

$$U^*[Z^*[s], Q^*[s]] + U[G, s] = U. \quad (13.10)$$

The welfare that the household receives from the consumption of public goods can be derived by rearranging equation (13.10):

$$U[G, s] = U - U^*[Z^*[s], Q^*[s]]. \quad (13.11)$$

The increase in land rent from $R[s]$ to compensated land rent $R^*[s]$ results in land rent being greater than the cost of conversion between h and h'; the city then expands over this range (Figure 13.1(b)). Households decrease their consumption of land by $Q[s] - Q^*[s]$. In Figure 13.1(a), $Q[s] > Q^*[s]$. The effect of the decrease in land consumption results in an increase in population density. Spatial equilibrium size of population, therefore, increases as a result of radius and density effects (Figure 13.1(c)).

Consider what would happen if the marginal utility of public good were to be a strongly increasing function of distance. Say, $u'[s_1]$ were to remain as in Figure 13.1(a), but $u'[s_x]$ were to be placed further from the origin, say at $u''[s_x]$. The resulting budget line with land rent sufficient to compensate for this large increase in welfare at s_x could lie to the left or be on A''. In other words, if the MUPG is a strongly increasing function of distance:

$$(y - ks_x)/R^*[s_x] < = (y - ks_1)/R^*[s_1]. \quad (13.12)$$

Rearranging inequality (13.12) and using equation (2.7):

$$1 > (y - ks_x)/(y - ks_1) < = R^*[s_x]/R^*[s_1]. \quad (13.13)$$

We can write:

$$R^*[s_x] < = > R^*[s_1]. \quad (13.14)$$

If public good complements are provided because when the MUPG is a mildly increasing function of distance $R^*[s_x] < R^*[s_1]$, and also because from inequality (13.13) when MUPG is a strongly increasing function of distance $R^*[s_1] < = R^*[s_x]$. Therefore, if the MUPG is a strongly increasing function of distance, then because of the provision of public goods land rents can be an increasing, constant, or decreasing function of distance. This is a truly remarkable result, especially considering that actually in practice public goods do contribute significantly to the welfare of most households.

The following principle sums up the results of a ubiquitous public good with the MUPG increasing over space in an open city:

Principle 13.3 On the indirect effect of introducing a ubiquitous public good complement to land in an open city:

(i) The change in land rents is proportional to the marginal utility of public good.

(ii) If the MUPG is a mildly increasing function of distance, then land rents and population density will everywhere increase, but remain decreasing functions of distance. The urban radius will expand.

(iii) If the MUPG is a strongly increasing function of distance, then land rents and population density can become constant or increasing functions of distance.

Consider case 2 in Table 13.1, where the MUPG decreases with distance from the CBD, that is the public good is a substitute for land. Say, in Figure 13.1(a), welfare from the introduction of the public good increases at s_1 to $u''[s_1]$ and at s_x to $u'[s_x]$. The resulting budget line with land rent sufficient to compensate for the relatively large increase in welfare at s_1 would lie to the left of A''. The resulting budget line with land rent sufficient to compensate for the increase in welfare at s_x can lie on B''. If the MUPG is a steeply declining function of distance the intercept will lie to the right of B'' on the abscissa. Consequently, if the MUPG is a decreasing function of distance:

$$(y - ks_1)/R^*[s_1] < = (y - ks_x)/R^*[s_x]. \tag{13.15}$$

Rearranging inequality (13.15) and using equation (2.7):

$$1 < (y - ks_1)/(y - ks_x) < = R^*[s_1]/R^*[s_x]. \tag{13.16}$$

Inequality (13.16) implies:

$$R^*[s_x] < = R^*[s_1]. \tag{13.17}$$

If the MUPG is a decreasing function of distance, then with the provision of public goods, land rents can range from being a constant to a sharply decreasing function of distance. This also is an intriguing result. If public goods that substitute for land are provided in sufficient quantity, then households will live in higher density. A corollary of this result can be stated: that if public good substitutes for land are not provided, then households will consume more land. This may be a significant contributing factor to the decades old trend of suburbanization: cities that do not provide adequate public park space lead households there to provide the desired open space privately by purchasing larger house lots.

The following principle can be used to sum up the results of a ubiquitous public good with the MUPG decreasing over space in an open city:

> *Principle 13.4*   On the indirect effect of introducing a ubiquitous public good substitute for land in an open city: if the MUPG is a mildly or strongly decreasing function of distance, then:
>
> (i) Land rents and population density will everywhere increase. The urban radius can expand outward if household welfare at the urban margins increases because of the public good.
>
> (ii) Land rents can be a constant or sharply decreasing function of distance.
>
> (iii) When public good substitutes for land are not provided in sufficient quantities, households will compensate by consuming more land.

It is worth emphasizing an intriguing corollary of principles 13.3 and 13.4: the greater the provision of public goods (either substitute for or complement to private goods), the greater will be the population of the city.

13.4   Closed city with spatially uniform public goods

Consider case 1 in Table 13.1, where public good and land are complements. Identify that annulus s_x about the CBD of a closed city, where the change in provision of public goods in turn changes the level of household welfare by an amount that conforms to conditions of spatial equilibrium (see principle 4.9, p. 48). At s_x no indirect adjustment in land rent is necessary for the system to comply with conditions of spatial equilibrium.

On annuli s_1 and s_x about the CBD, where $s_1 < s_x$ following the change in the provision of the local public good, welfare increases respectively to $u'[s_1]$ and $u'[s_x]$. By principle 4.9, we can write $u'[s_x] = U'$; also using Table 13.1 $u'[s_1] < U'$ (Figure 13.2).

Households at s_1 have budget line AA and households at s_x have budget line BB. The direct effect of an increase in welfare from an increase in G has been noted in section 13.2, above, to be equivalent to a decrease in land rents by the amount $w[s]$. Budget lines shift obliquely from AA and BB respectively to the positions AA' and BB'.

Because the "shadow budget line" BB' is tangent to U', households on annulus s_x obtain aggregate welfare U', partitioned into U from the consumption of private goods and $U'-U$ from the consumption of public goods. The consumption of private goods is still identified by tangency between budget line BB and utility curve U for households at s_x. Therefore, land rent and the consumption of land remains at $R[s_x]$ and $Q[s_x]$.

Shadow budget constraint AA' is tangent to a level of welfare $u'[s_1]$ which

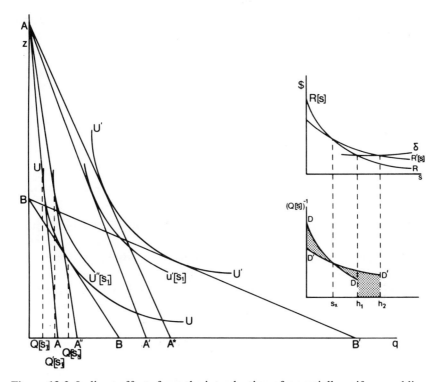

Figure 13.2 Indirect effects from the introduction of a spatially uniform public good in a closed-interactive city (after Thrall, 1982a)

lies below U'. Draw $AA*$ to be tangent to U'. The difference $A*-A'$ identifies the proportional decrease in land rent at location s_1 that is necessary to increase welfare from the consumption of private goods; this is the required compensation for households that remain at s_1 since they did not obtain as great an increase in welfare as households more distant from the CBD by the increase in public good provision. Households outmigrate from s_1, bidding down land rent in proportion to the difference $A*-A'$.

Land rents at location s_1 decrease, the budget constraint obliquely shifts from the original AA to the final AA'', where $|A-A''| = |A'-A*|$. With budget line AA'', households can obtain the compensated welfare curve for private goods $U''[s_1]$, where:

$$U''[s_1] - U = U' - u'[s_1]. \qquad (13.18)$$

Tangency between budget line AA'' and $U''[s_1]$ identifies the consumption of private goods (compensated demand) necessary for households at s_1 to be just as well off as their counterparts at more remote locations.

The mix of the composition of private good consumption will change because of the change in the price of land. Land consumption will increase at those locations closer to the CBD than s_x.

Welfare from the consumption of private goods is equal to:

$$U''[s_1] = U + (U' - u'[s_1]). \tag{13.19}$$

Welfare from the consumption of public goods is equal to:

$$U[G,s_1] = U' - U''[s_1] = u'[s_1] - U. \tag{13.20}$$

The aggregate household welfare at s_1 is the sum of equations (13.19) and (13.20):

$$\begin{aligned} U' &= U''[s_1] + U[G,s_1] \\ &= U + (U' - u'[s_1]) + u'[s_1] - U. \end{aligned} \tag{13.21}$$

Population density decreases (remains the same) interior to (on) annulus s_x. Since the population of a closed city is constant, the region exterior to s_x must accommodate the influx of people from the region interior to s_x. This result will be confirmed in the following analysis.

Let households initially have budget constraints BB and CC respectively on annuli s_x and s_2, for $s_2 > s_x$ (Figure 13.3). Using case 1, Table 13.1,

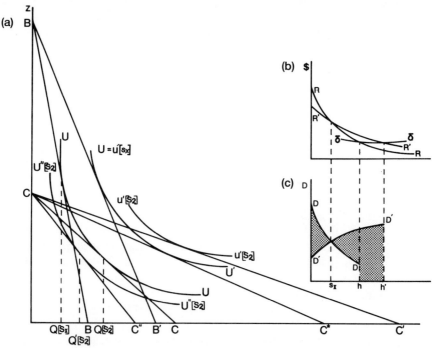

Figure 13.3 Indirect effects at the urban margins of a closed-interactive city from the introduction of a spatially uniform public good (after Thrall, 1982a)

household welfare at s_x increases to $u'[s_x]$, and at s_2 increases to $u'[s_2]$, where:

$$u'[s_2] > u'[s_x] = U'. \tag{13.22}$$

An equivalent increase in welfare as indicated in inequality (13.22) could have resulted from decreasing land rent so budget constraints shift obliquely from BB to BB' and CC to CC'. Budget line BB' is tangent to U', while CC' is tangent to the higher $u'[s_2]$.

Households inmigrate to s_2 until land rents increase in proportion to $C'-C^*$, thereby decreasing the level of welfare from consumption of private goods by $u'[s_2] - U'$. By this process, the aggregate change in welfare at s_2 is limited only to the spatial equilibrium increase of $U' - U$.

On annulus s_2 the compensated spatial equilibrium level of welfare attributable to the consumption of private goods is now:

$$U''[s_2] = U - (u'[s_2] - U'). \tag{13.23}$$

The greater marginal utility of public good received by households from the increased provision of G at distances further than s_x from the CBD is compensated for by decreases in the welfare obtainable from the consumption of private goods.

If the MUPG is a steeply rising function of distance, and if the increase in public good directly increases welfare at s_2 by an amount greater than $u'[s_2] - U$, then the compensating decrease in welfare from consumption of private goods must also be greater than $U - U''[s_2]$. In this scenario, the consumption of land must then decrease by more than $Q[s_2] - Q'[s_2]$. The resulting quantity of land consumed at s_2 can then be less than land consumption at s_x.

This is an intriguing counterintuitive twist: when public goods are provided that are complements to land consumption, population density can increase with increasing distance from the CBD (Figure 13.3(c)):

Principle 13.5   On the indirect effect of introducing a ubiquitous public good complement to land in a closed city:

(i) Land rents decline at the urban core and increase toward the urban margins; the radius of the city increases.

(ii) The population density gradient can become lower and flatter than the initial density gradient, or may become inverted and increase with increasing distance from the CBD.

13.5   Open city with externalities

The principles developed in the above analysis are used here, and in the following section of this chapter, to determine the effect upon the internal structure of a city because of a change in the presence of externality X.

In this section, the case of an open city is developed using an example of an increase in a negative externality. A contrasting illustration, the case of a positive externality, is developed for a closed city. Also it is assumed that the MUPG increases with increasing distance from the CBD (case 1, Table 13.1). Hence, the externality is a "negative complement" to land, that is it detracts from the consumption of land. The more land one consumes, the greater the additive detraction. Unlike the ubiquitous public good, the externality has a specific source where its density is greatest, and whose density declines with distance from the source. An example of such an externality is an earthquake fault, where the damage may be greatest at the fault and declines with distance from the fault. Other examples include: odor from nearby industry; noxious seepages from waste-disposal sites (Love Canal) or nuclear power plants (Three Mile Island); noise from a local transportation node or artery; and the presence of a racial or ethnic population that is prejudiced against by the surrounding population.

Let the intensity at location s of the negative externality density function centered at s^* be represented by $X[-, s]$ (Figure 13.4(b)). The externality

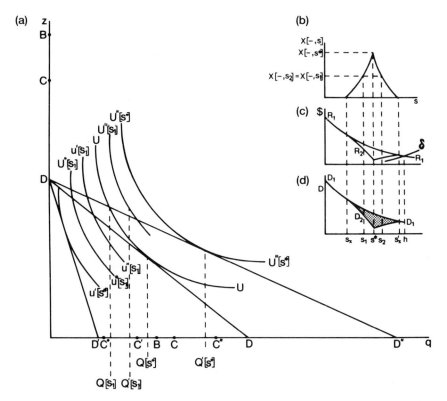

Figure 13.4 Indirect effects at the urban core from the introduction of a negative externality in an open-interactive city (after Thrall, 1982a)

density function descends about s^*, diminishing to zero at an inner annulus s_x and outer annulus s'_x. Let the externality density function be smooth and uniform thereby making annuli s_x and s'_x equal distances from the source of the externality.

Let budget lines *BB*, *CC*, *DD*, *EE*, and *FF* be those for households at locations respectively $s_x < s_1 < s^* < s_2 < s'_x$. Following the introduction of the negative externality X, welfare at s^* decreases to $u'[s^*]$ (Figure 13.4(a)). The decrease in welfare attributable to the increase in $X[-, s^*]$ is $U - u'[s^*]$; this difference is equivalent to a decrease in welfare attributable to an increase in land rents that obliquely shifts *DD* to *DD'*.

By definition, welfare in the open city must remain at U. But the externality has reduced welfare of households by the amount $u'[s^*] - U$. An increase in the consumption of private goods by the amount $U - u'[s^*]$ will as compensation counterbalance $X[-, s^*]$, resulting in no net change in welfare. Denote the new welfare at s^* attributable to the consumption of private goods as $U''[s^*]$, where:

$$U''[s^*] - U = U - u'[s^*]. \tag{13.24}$$

Equilibrium is regained as a result of households' outmigrating from s^* in response to the negative externality; land rents decrease by the amount necessary to obliquely shift *DD* to *DD''* tangent to $U''[s^*]$.

The compensated population density can be derived for location s^*. On the abscissa $D'' > D$, and $Q'[s^*] > Q[s^*]$; land rents and population density, therefore, decrease in response to the introduction of the negative externality $X[-, s^*]$.

Suppose the density of externality at locations s_1 and s^* were the same, namely $X[-, s_1] = X[-, s^*]$; welfare then at s_1 would decrease to $u^*[s_1]$. Under the circumstances that the MUPG increases over distance, it must be true that:

$$(U - u'[s_x]) > (U - u_1[s_1]) \text{ for } s_1 < s_x. \tag{13.25}$$

However, spillovers follow a distance decay pattern about s^* (Figure 13.5(b)), and:

$$X[-, s_1] < X[-, s^*]. \tag{13.26}$$

The combined effects of the MUPG at s_1 being less than that at s_x (equation 13.25), and lower externality density at s_1 than at s^* (equation 13.26), results in a decrease in welfare at s_1 only to $u'[s_1]$, where $u'[s_1] > u'[s^*]$ (Figure 13.4(a)). This decrease in welfare is equivalent to an increase in land rent at s_1 necessary to shift the intercept of the budget line on the abscissa by $C-C'$; if drawn, budget line *CC'* would be tangent to $u'[s_1]$. A decrease in land rent can compensate for the deleterious effect of the negative externality. Note that it is not only the lower land rent that compensates, but also compensation comes from lower land rents allowing the household to increase consumption of private goods; the compensated demand curves are integral to the maintenance of spatial equilibrium. Consumption increases to the level identified by tangency of CC'' and $U''[s_1]$. The welfare compensation is therefore:

$$U''[s_1] - U = U - u'[s_1]. \tag{13.27}$$

By inspection of Figure 13.4, it can be seen that $D'' - D > C'' - C$ on the abscissa, land rents then can decrease proportionally more at s^* than at s_1 (Figure 13.4(c)). Because $Q'[s^*] - Q[s^*] > Q'[s_1] - Q[s_1]$, then population density will decrease more at s^* than at s_1 (Figure 13.4(d)).

At location s_2, on the opposite side of s^* than s_1, let:

$$X[-, s_2] = X[-, s_1] < X[-, s^*] \text{ for } s_1 < s^* < s_2. \tag{13.28}$$

Equation (13.28) merely places in symbolic form what was drawn in Figure 13.4(b). In Figure 13.5(a), budget lines DD, DD', and DD'' are as in Figure 13.4(a). Because it has been assumed that the MUPG increases with increasing distance from the CBD, then the introduction of the negative externality (equation 13.28) creates a change in welfare by the amount $U - u'[s_2] > U - u'[s_1]$. It must, then, be true that $u'[s_2] < u'[s_1]$.

Because $u'[s_2] < u'[s_1]$, and $u'[s_1] > u'[s^*]$, it is possible that $u'[s_2] = u'[s^*]$; this is indeed a fascinating result. Even though the density of externality is less at s_2 as compared to its source at s^*, households at both locations can suffer the same decrease in welfare. Furthermore, even though the density of externality is the same at s_1 and s_2, households – because of their relative spatial location – suffer a greater reduction in welfare at s_2 than at s_1.

An increase in rent proportional to $E - E'$ on the abscissa (Figure 13.5(a)) will decrease welfare by an amount necessary to equal the effect of the negative externality $X[-, s_2]$. The necessary compensatory reduction in land rent at s_2 will shift intercepts on the abscissa from E to E''; EE'' is tangent to $U''[s_2]$ and the increase in welfare from private good consumption $U''[s_2] - U$ is equal to the decrease in welfare from the externality $U - u'[s_2]$.

Since on the abscissa $E'' - E > D'' - D > C'' - C$ (Figures 13.4(a) and 13.5(a)), the proportional decrease in land rents at s_2 may be greater than that at s_1 and s^*. Had the difference $U''[s_2] - U$ been smaller, then it would have been possible that $E'' - E < D'' - D$.

By inspection of Figures 13.4(a) and 13.5(a), $Q'[s_1] - Q[s_1] < Q'[s_2] - Q[s_2]$. This is a very intriguing result: even though both locations received the same density of negative externality, there is a greater reduction in population density at s_2 than at s_1 (Figure 13.4(d)).

The difference between density gradients (Figure 13.4(d)) represents the decrease in total spatial equilibrium population because of the externality. There is a population density crater centered about the source of the externality, with edges of the crater more steeply ascending toward the city center and more gradually ascending toward the urban margins.

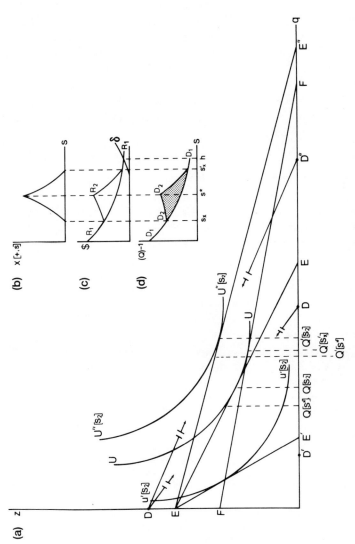

Figure 13.5 Indirect effects at the urban margins from the introduction of a negative externality in an open-interactive city (after Thrall, 1982a)

These fascinating results can be summarized in the following principle:

Principle 13.6   On the indirect effect of introducing an externality in an open city:
  (i) If the externality is negative, then land rents and population density are inversely proportional to the externality. If the externality is a complement to (substitute for) land, the reduction will appear as a crater, with sides steeply ascending toward (away from) the CBD from the source and shallow ascent from the source away from (toward) the CBD.
  (ii) If the externality is positive, land rents and population density are directly proportional to the externality (Figure 13.5(b), (c), and (d)). If the positive externality is a complement to (substitute for) land, the increase will appear as a peak, with sides steeply descending toward (away from) the CBD from the source and slowly descending from the source away from (toward) the CBD.

13.6   Closed city with externalities

Let budget lines *AA*, *BB*, *CC*, *DD*, *EE*, and *FF* be those for households respectively on annuli $s_1 < s_x < s^* < s_2 < s'_x < s_3$ (Figures 13.6(a) and 13.7). Let there be introduced a positive externality emanating from site s^*: $X[+, s]$ (Figure 13.6).

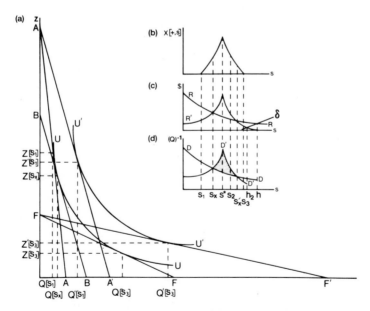

Figure 13.6 Indirect effects at the urban core from the introduction of a positive externality in a closed-interactive city (after Thrall, 1982a)

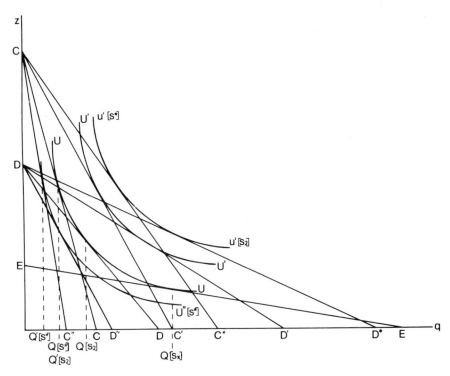

Figure 13.7 Indirect effects at the urban margins from the introduction of a positive externality in a closed-interactive city (after Thrall, 1982a)

Let household welfare at s_x and s'_x increase to U' such that no indirect adjustments in land rent are required to satisfy conditions of spatial equilibrium. The new spatial equilibrium level of welfare is represented by U' (Figure 13.6(a)). Note that, depending upon the behavior of the MUPG over space, $s^* - s_x < = > s'_x - s^*$.

Let an increase in the nonubiquitous public good at s^* increase welfare to $u'[s^*]$. Because $s^* > s_x$ and $X[+, s^*] > X[+, s_x]$, and assuming that the MUPG increases with distance from the CBD, then it must be true that $u'[s^*] > U'[s_x]$. To counter this greater than spatial equilibrium increase in welfare from the externality, private good consumption at s^* will decrease by the difference:

$$u'[s^*] - U' = U - U''[s^*]. \tag{13.29}$$

Land rent increases thereby shifting the budget line from CC to CC'' to become tangent to $U''[s^*]$. By inspection of Figure 13.7, consumption of land decreases from $Q[s^*]$ to $Q'[s^*]$. Population density then increases at the source of the positive externality.

When the MUPG increases with increasing distance from the CBD, it is possible for the increase in welfare at s_2 to be greater than that at s^*, even though $X[+, s^*] > X[+, s_2]$. Because of this, in our example following an increase in the positive externality, let $u'[s_2] = u'[s^*]$. An increase in welfare attributable to the externality at s_2 could also have resulted from a decrease in land rent in proportion to D^*-D on the abscissa. This increase in welfare attracts households to inmigrate to s_2 in an attempt to capture the relatively higher level of welfare. The inmigration of households will limit the increase in welfare to $U'-U$.

A land rent increase at s_2 proportional to $D-D''$ translates into decreased private good consumption; this limits the increase in welfare following the introduction of the externality to the differential $U' - U$. It is indeed intriguing that because $D - D'' > C - C''$, then the proportional increase in land rent can possibly be greater at s_2 than that at the origin of the externality s^*. Also the resulting increase in population density can be greater at s_2 than that at s^*.

Say that the direct effect of the externality is zero at s_1 and s_3 (Figure 13.6(b)). The indirect effect of the introduction of the externality is to move welfare everywhere in the closed city up to $U' = u'[s_x]$. Households outmigrate from those locations whose direct increase in welfare was less than $U' - U$ into those locations where the direct effect was to increase welfare by more than $U' - U$. Therefore, households outmigrate from locations interior to s_1 and exterior to s_3. In those resulting inner and outer zones, land rent and population density decrease as budget lines shift to become tangent to U' (Figures 13.6 and 13.7). Utility from private good consumption at s_1 and s_3 becomes:

$$U'[Z'[s_1], Q'[s_1]] = U'[Z'[s_3], Q'[s_3]] = U'. \qquad (13.30)$$

By definition, land rents have not changed at s_x or s'_x, and therefore budget lines from private good consumption do not change at s_x and s'_x, leaving land consumption and consequently population density unaffected. Because population is constrained to remain constant in the closed city, the difference in population density functions to the left of s_x and the right of s'_x, must equal the shaded area between s_x and s'_x, representing the number of households that have inmigrated (Figure 13.6(d)).

It is intriguing to note that land rent and population density decline in the zones between s_1 and s_x, and between s'_x and s_3, even though those zones have received positive spillovers from the externality. The amount of spillover there, however, was insufficient compensation for the relatively greater increase in welfare that could be obtained in the zone between s_x and s'_x.

These results can be summarized in the following principle:

Principle 13.7   On the indirect effect of introducing an externality in a closed city:
    (i) If the MUPG is spatially uniform, then the site of the externality will

be the location of the maximum change in land rent and population density. If the MUPG is an increasing (decreasing) function of distance, then the site of maximum change can occur at locations of less (more) proximity to the CBD.

(ii) If the externality is positive (negative), then land rents and population density at the site of emissions will be directly (inversely) related to the density of externality.

(iii) The change in land rent and population density will become smaller with increasing distance from the place of maximum change. As distance to the place of maximum change increases, then even though spillovers can still be measured, the change in land rent and population density can become zero, or even opposite that of the change at the site of the externality.

Principle 13.7 sheds some light upon the correct interpretation and formulation of empirical analyses. Regardless of the fact that an externality can be measured, it is not necessary that the externality be capitalized into land rents and land consumption; moreover, a negative externality is consistent with an increase in land rents in some regions, and an increase in positive externalities is consistent with a decrease in land rents over some regions!

13.7 Conclusion

In this chapter, the change in the geography of the city from public goods either distributed uniformly in space or distributed as externalities has been derived. The direct effect from the increased provision of a positive public good was to increase household welfare, while a negative public good can decrease household welfare. The public goods were defined to fall within two categories as to their effect upon welfare from the consumption of land. If they are complements to land, then consumption of the public good increases the utility received from the consumption of land. Substitutes, on the other hand, allow local public goods and land to be exchanged for one another with no resulting change in aggregate welfare.

The key to deriving the effect from the provision of the public good in the spatial setting was in the definition of the marginal utility of public good (MUPG). When the public good is a complement to private land consumption, then the MUPG of households that reside at the urban margins where land consumption is greater was argued to be greater than the MUPG of households who reside in the urban core. If the public good substitutes for private land consumption, then the MUPG of households that reside at the urban core will be greater than the MUPG of households who reside at the urban margins.

In an open city, if a ubiquitous and positive public good were introduced that was a complement to land, then the change in land rents was shown to be proportional to the marginal utility of public good. If the MUPG is a mildly increasing function of distance, then land rents and population density would everywhere increase. The urban radius expands. If the MUPG is a strongly increasing function of distance, then land rents and population density can become constant or even increasing functions of distance.

Introducing a ubiquitous public good substitute to land in an open city, where the MUPG is a mildly or strongly decreasing function of distance, results in land rents and population density everywhere increasing. Land rents can become a constant or sharply decreasing function of distance. An intriguing implication for city planners is that when public good susbstitutes for land are not provided in sufficient quantities, then households will compensate by consuming more land thereby lowering the population density.

The effect of introducing an externality in an open city depends upon the distance decay of the good, as well as whether the good is positive or negative, a complement, or a substitute. If the externality is negative, land rents and population density are inversely proportional to the externality. If the externality is positive, land rents and population density are directly proportional to the externality; if the positive externality is a complement (substitute) to land, the increase will appear as a peak, with sides steeply descending toward (away from) the CBD from the source, and slowly descending from the source away from (toward) the CBD.

In a closed city, introducing a ubiquitous public good complement to land results in a decline in land rents at the urban core and increase toward the urban margins. The population density gradient can become lower and flatter than the initial density gradient, or may become inverted and increase with increasing distance from the CBD.

The effect of introducing an externality into a closed city also depends upon the distance decay of the good, as well as upon whether the good is positive or negative, a complement, or a substitute. If the MUPG is spatially uniform, then the site of the externality will be the location of the maximum change in land rent and population density. If the MUPG is an increasing (decreasing) function of distance, then the site of maximum change can occur at locations with less (more) proximity to the CBD. If the externality is positive (negative), then land rents and population density at the site of emissions will be directly (inversely) related to the magnitude of externality. The change in land rent and population density will become smaller with increasing distance from the place of maximum change; as proximity to this place diminishes, then even though spillovers can still be measured, the change in land rent and population density can become zero, or opposite to the change at the site of the externality.

Note

The analysis of Chapter 7 assumed that the transportation node served only as a possible "budget constraint shifter." However, the node may also save time in commuting and hence be a "utility shifter." The analysis of a transportation node that saved time in commuting and thereby increased leisure time would be analogous to the analysis of positive externality in this chapter.

References

Barr (1972)
Berry and Neils (1969)
Bradford (1971)
Fisch (1980)
Holterman (1972)
James (1979)
Lea (1979)
Musgrave (1969)
Polinksy and Shavell (1976)
Samuelson (1954, 1955, 1969)
Sandler (1975)
Schular and Holahan (1977)
Thrall (1979a, 1979b, 1982a)
Tiebout (1961)
Wright (1977)
Yellin (1974)

PART V

Multilevel Decision-making

14

Housing

14.1 Introduction

In previous chapters, the household has been restricted to choosing only between amount of composite good and land to consume, in addition to relative spatial location. In those instances where multiple sector models have been discussed, such as in the discussion of the public sector in Chapters 7–13, and in the discussion of the interaction of the consumption with production sectors in Chapter 4, the household was not able individually to choose how much public good or externality was to be consumed, how much was to be taxed, how to be zoned, what proportion of the city should be devoted to the production sector, or where low-cost transportation nodes should be located. Such complexities can be added to the Consumption Theory of Land Rent, resulting in insights that include the contrast of maximizing social welfare versus maximizing individual welfare, and the effect of various voting and citizen participation in government formulae.

In this chapter, a geometry will be presented that outlines how the CTLR can be extended to examine settings where the household has an ability to choose between more than two kinds of good; the household will choose between composite good, land, and housing capital. Land and housing capital in combination form the aggregate good, housing.

The procedure that will be used to include the choice of three goods will be reminiscent of the microeconomics literature on stepwise decision-making (Brown and Hein, 1972; Phlips, 1974, p. 67).[1] Specifically, in the first branch of the utility tree, the household chooses between how much composite good and how much housing to consume; then in the second branch in the utility tree, the household chooses how much land and capital are to compose housing.[2]

This extension of the CTLR is particularly valuable because people generally purchase the aggregate good housing, not land alone. Housing has vintage, requires maintenance, and decays at varying rates depending upon maintenance and the initial quality of construction. All the analyses of the previous thirteen chapters of this book, including the discussion of malleability in Chapter 9 (see also Thrall, 1982b), can be extended to the following setting to evaluate the respective effects upon housing capital, in addition to the other usual endogenous variables of the system.

14.2   The housing model

14.2.1   The first branch of the utility tree

Housing is composed of land and capital that rests upon that land. In the United States, larger cities often have relatively large amounts of capital per unit of land at the inner core of the city perhaps with many dwellings stacked one upon another to form a high-rise building; at the urban margins there may be only one dwelling per several acres of land. The capital to land ratio in these cities generally decreases with increasing distance from the central business district (CBD). In contrast, the larger cities in Canada, the United Kingdom, and Europe generally have relatively uniform capital to land ratios.

The household when making a decision to purchase housing will consider how much money is to be allocated to housing versus other goods including the composite good and transportation. Once the proportion of income that housing will receive has been decided upon, then this expenditure can be further decomposed into how much is to be spent on land and how much is to be used for housing capital. That is, the decisions of the households are assumed to conform to the following proposition:

Proposition 14.1   Households' decisions about the composition of goods to consume conform to a multilevel decision process. At the first level, total group expenditures are determined; at the second level, a more disaggregated individual commodity is selected.

Household income y is partitioned into expenditures on housing $x[s]$ with price $v[s]$, composite good $z[s]$ with price p, and transportation cost $T[s]$ at distance s from the CBD:

$$y = pz[s] + v[s]x[s] + T[s]. \tag{14.1}$$

Analogous to the budget line in equation (2.5), the budget line based upon the income–consumption relationship of equation (14.1) can be expressed:

$$z[s] = (y - T[s])/p - (v[s]/p)x[s]. \tag{14.2}$$

Equation (14.2) has intercept on the ordinate:

$$z[s] = (y - T[s])/p \quad (x = 0) \tag{14.3}$$

and intercept on the abscissa:

$$x[s] = (y - T[s])/v[s] \quad (z = 0). \tag{14.4}$$

Analogous to equations (2.2) and (2.3), equations (14.3) and (14.4) are the maximum possible consumption by a household of either composite good or housing; the right-hand terms in these equations on any given annulus s are all exogenous with the exception of the endogenous spatial equilibrium housing price $v[s]$. Linear budget lines, characterized by the intercepts on ordinate and abscissa, are drawn in Figure 14.1(a), with AA, BB, and CC for annuli respectively s_1, s_x, and s_2, where $s_1 < s_x < s_2$.

Let the households have utility function:

$$u[z,x] = u[z,f,q]. \qquad (14.5)$$

This utility function is referred to as direct because its value depends upon the goods such as z and x; it is also referred to as weakly separable because the contribution to total welfare from each individual good is assumed to be able to be separated out and identified. In equation (14.5), the aggregate good housing can be separated out and then disaggregated into two goods, land q and housing capital f.

The principles developed in the previous chapters for land can be restated for housing. The spatial equilibrium price of housing is $V[s]$, where $V[s_1] > V[s_2] > V[s_3]$. A market value of housing at s greater than (less than) spatial equilibrium $V[s]$ will have associated with it a budget constraint tangent to a level of welfare that is less than (greater than) the spatial equilibrium level of welfare.

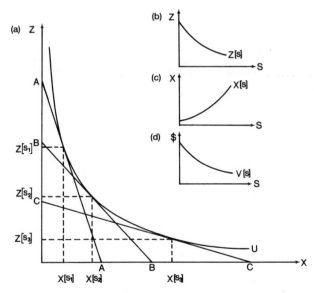

Figure 14.1 Derivation of spatial equilibrium housing expenditures, and spatial equilibrium consumption of housing and composite good: the first branch of the utility tree

Budget constraints *AA*, *BB*, and *CC* satisfy spatial equilibrium conditions since they are tangent to the spatial equilibrium level of welfare *U*. The budget constraints, following principle 2.6 (p. 24), become lower and flatter with decreasing proximity to the CBD. Composite good consumption decreases at a decreasing rate (Figure 14.1(b)), while housing consumption increases at an increasing rate (Figure 14.1(c)) with increasing distance from the CBD.

Reading from Figure 14.1(a), the spatial equilibrium quantity of housing consumed is $X[s]$; hence, the spatial equilibrium expenditure on housing is the product $V[s]X[s]$. As would be expected from principle 2.3 (p. 23), the consumption of housing is inversely related to central city access. Housing price decreases at a decreasing rate with increasing distance from the city center.

14.2.2   The second branch of the utility tree

The household's utility function can be decomposed into the contribution to total welfare from the consumption of composite good $u_1[Z[s]]$, and the contribution to total welfare from the consumption of housing $u_2[X[s]]$. In turn, housing can be further decomposed into the household's selection of housing capital f and land q, that is:

$$U[Z[s], X[s]] = U = U[u_1[Z[s]], u_2[F[s], Q[s]]]. \qquad (14.6)$$

Spatial equilibrium requires aggregate utility to remain constant across space. But by principle 2.8 (p. 25), $Z[s]$ declines with increasing distance from the CBD; hence, $u_1[Z[s]]$ also declines. In compensation, $u_2[X[s]]$ must increase with increasing distance from the CBD; application of principle 2.7 (p. 25) to this setting would confirm this to be true. Therefore, since:

$$u_1[Z[s_1]] > u_1[Z[s_2]] \qquad (14.7)$$

then it must be true that:

$$u_2[F[s_1], Q[s_1]] < u_2[F[s_2], Q[s_2]] \qquad (14.8)$$

in order to satisfy conditions of spatial equilibrium that:

$$U[u_1[Z[s_1]], u_2[X[s_1]]] = U[u_1[Z[s_2]], u_2[X[s_2]]]. \qquad (14.9)$$

As the utility function can be decomposed into its constituent parts, so too can the household's budget constraint be further disaggregated into its constituent parts. The household first determines the proportion of budget to spend upon housing $V[s]X[s]$, following the same procedure used throughout this book. Then the household further disaggregates these expenditures into land and capital:

$$V[s]X[s] = Wf[s] + r[s]q[s]. \qquad (14.10)$$

Equation (14.10) introduces the endogenous consumption of capital $f[s]$ with exogenously given price W.

Substituting equation (14.10) into equation (14.1) and rearranging, the intercepts for the housing budget constraint can be expressed as:

$$f[s] = y^*[s]/W = V[s]X[s]/W \quad (q = 0) \qquad (14.11)$$

and:

$$q[s] = y^*[s]/r[s] = V[s]X[s]/r[s] \quad (f = 0) \qquad (14.12)$$

where:

$$y^*[s] = y - pZ[s] - T[s] = V[s]X[s]. \qquad (14.13)$$

The linear housing budget line, the intercepts of which are identified in equations (14.11) and (14.12), places bounds on the combinations of land and capital that the household can select given the allocation of y^* for housing.

In order to determine spatial equilibrium $R[s]$, $Q[s]$, and $F[s]$, the spatial behavior must first be derived of y^*, rather $V[s]X[s]$, from the numerator of the intercepts in equations (14.11) and (14.12). It must first, then, be determined whether with increasing distance from the CBD, the household's allocation of income to housing, and the resulting housing budget constraint, shifts upwards, remains the same, or decreases. Holding $r[s]$ constant, and given W, determine from equation (14.13) the direction of inequality $y^*[s_1]$ $<?> y^*[s_2]$, namely:

$$y - pZ[s_1] - T[s_1] <?> y - pZ[s_2] - T[s_2]. \qquad (14.14)$$

Inequality (14.14) can be reduced to:

$$(T[s_2] - T[s_1]) - (pZ[s_1] - pZ[s_2]) <?> 0 \qquad (14.15)$$

which can be interpreted as $|\Delta T| - |\Delta pZ| <?> 0$ since usually $T[s_2] > T[s_1]$ and $pZ[s_1] > pZ[s_2]$.

The direction of the sign of inequality (14.15) then depends upon the relative magnitude of the change (increase) in expenditure on transportation $\Delta T[s]$ over space versus the change (decrease) in expenditure on composite good over space $\Delta pZ[s]$. There are four possible cases; the important component of the argument is to determine the direction of inequality $|\Delta T[s]| <?> |\Delta pZ[s]|$ for the particular environment and, if equal, whether there are one or more places where the terms are equal.

14.3 Cases of the second branch of the utility tree

14.3.1 Case I: $|\Delta T[s]| > |\Delta pZ[s]|$

In case I, the increase in transportation expenditure is greater than the

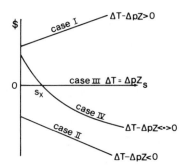

Figure 14.2 The four cases for the second
branch of the utility three depend
upon whether the increase in
transportation expenditure is offset
by a decrease in composite good
expenditures

decrease in expenditure on composite good; hence, the sign of inequality (14.14) is > meaning that $y*[s_1] > y*[s_2]$. The scenario of case I requires that spatial equilibrium housing expenditure decreases with increasing distance from the CBD. The intercepts on the ordinate of households' budget constraints shift downward with increasing distance from the CBD; the shift in the housing budget line is parallel.

The behavior over space of $R[s]$, $F[s]$, and $Q[s]$ is evaluated for case I (Figure 14.2) in the following manner: refer to Figure 14.3; between a pair of locations, say, s_1 and s_2, initially hold land rent constant at $R[s_1]$. The household at s_1 receives welfare $u_2[X[s_1]]$ from the consumption of housing. With movement outward from s_1 to s_2, the budget constraint shifts from AA downward and parallel to the left to BB. Budget line BB allows the household at s_2 to receive a level of welfare from housing less than households at s_1, when in fact by equation 14.8 the household at s_2 should be receiving greater welfare from the consumption of housing than households at s_1. Land rents decrease from $R[s_1]$ to $R[s_2]$ thereby swinging BB to BB' to become tangent to $u_2 = u_2[F[s_2], Q[s_2]]$.

As depicted in Figure 14.3, the consumption of capital is lower at s_2 than at s_1. However, if the difference $u_2[X[s_2]] - u_2[X[s_1]]$ is sufficiently great, or if taste preferences are such that the slope of u_2 is sufficiently flat, or if the slope of the budget line is such that BB is sufficiently flat, then it is possible that $F[s_1] < = > F[s_2]$ (Figure 14.3(b)). Like earlier analyses, land consumption increases with increasing distance from the CBD; thus population density decreases with increasing distance from the CBD.

Housing capital intensivity is the ratio $F[s]/Q[s]$. Since the market allows $F[s]$ to increase, decrease, or be constant with increasing distance from the

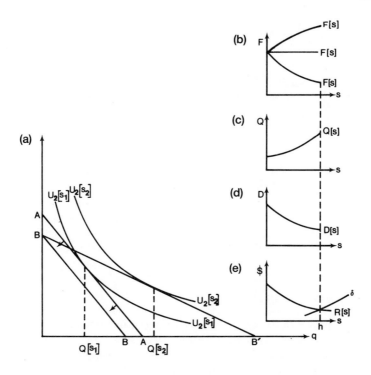

Figure 14.3 Evaluation of case I of the second branch of the utility
tree

city center, while $Q[s]$ increases, case I then generates a setting with the
greatest intensive capital development at the city center, urban margins, or
capital intensivity being everywhere the same. The implications of case I can
be summarized in the following principle:

Principle 14.1 When increasing distance from the city center is accompanied by an increase in transportation expenditure that is greater than the
decrease in expenditure on composite good, then:
 (i) Intercepts on the ordinate of households' budget constraints shift
downward and to the left with increasing distance from the CBD.
 (ii) The ideal city will be characterized by increasing, constant or
decreasing housing capital consumption and increasing land consumption, with increasing distance from the CBD, all other things being equal.
 (iii) The capital to land ratio describes an ideal city with the greatest
intensive development at the city center, urban margins, or the capital to
land ratio being everywhere the same.
 (iv) Land rent decreases with increasing distance to the CBD.

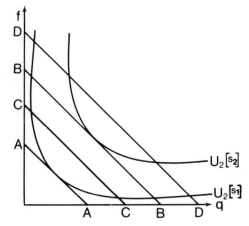

Figure 14.4 Evaluation of case II of the second
branch of the utility tree

14.3.2 Case II: $|\Delta T[s]| < |\Delta p Z[s]|$

In case II (Figure 14.2), as proximity to the CBD decreases, the change
(increase) in transportation expenditures is less than the change (decrease) in
composite good expenditures thereby leaving an increasing pool of funds to
be allocated to housing expenditures. As shown in inequalities (14.14) and
(14.15), the housing budget constraint will shift upward and to the right with
increasing distance from the CBD.

For illustration, let AA represent the household's budget constraint for
housing in spatial equilibrium at location s_1 (Figure 14.4). Holding land rent
equal to $R[s_1]$ as distance to the CBD is increased from s_1 to s_2 the budget
constraint moves parallel *upward and to the right*.

If the resulting housing budget constraint were CC (Figure 14.4), then land
rent at s_2 must be less than that at s_1, so that CC can shift to become tangent to
$u_2[X[s_2]]$. Further implications of housing budget line CC are the same as for
case I (Figure 14.3).

If the resulting housing budget constraint were BB (Figure 14.4), then no
adjustment in land rent between s_1 and s_2 would be necessary to satisfy
conditions of spatial equilibrium. So long as for all s, $u_2[s]$ are smooth and
parallel, then both $F[s]$ and $Q[s]$ will increase with increasing distance from
the CBD; depending upon their relative rates of increase, the capital to land
ratio can again increase, remain constant, or decrease with increasing
distance from the CBD. An intriguing implication of this case (and like that
of case I) is that if the ratio of $F[s]$ and $Q[s]$ were to ascend across space, then
a market solution would describe capital intensity being greater at the urban
margins than at the city core.

Continuing with case II, if the resulting budget constraint were DD, then it would be necessary for land rents to increase with increasing distance from the CBD, that is DD would have to shift obliquely to the left to become tangent to $u_2[s_2]$. In this instance, land rents will be highest at the urban margins. Whether land consumption will increase, remain constant, or decrease over space is indeterminate. The consumption of capital will, barring extremes of taste preferences, increase. The capital to land ratio can then be greatest at the urban margins, greatest at the urban core, or everywhere the same.

To sum up case II, land rent and land consumption may either increase, remain the same, or decrease with increasing distance from the CBD. Housing capital and the capital to land ratio may increase, remain constant, or decrease with increasing distance from the CBD. The free market solution is indeed intriguing where the urban margins may harbor the greatest capital to land ratios in the city. These results can be summarized in the following principle:

Principle 14.2   If the increase in transportation expenditures is less than the decrease in composite good consumption across space, then:
   (i) Intercepts on the ordinate of the budget constraint for housing will shift upward and to the right with increasing distance from the CBD.
   (ii) Land consumption can increase, remain constant, or decrease with increasing distance from the CBD.
   (iii) The consumption of capital will increase with increasing distance from the CBD.
   (iv) The capital to land ratio can be greatest at the urban margins, greatest at the urban core, or everywhere the same.
   (v) Land rent may increase, remain the same, or decrease with increasing distance from the CBD.

14.3.3   Case III: $|\Delta T[s]| = |\Delta pZ[s]|$

In case III (Figure 14.2), the change (increase) in transportation expenditure is exactly counterbalanced by the change (decrease) in composite good expenditures, as distance from the CBD increases. Therefore, initially holding land rent equal to the same value, say, $R[s_1]$, the housing budget constraints will be coincident between all locations. As shown in inequality (14.8), utility from housing consumption must increase with increasing distance from the CBD all other things being equal, namely $u_2[X[s_2]] > u_2[X[s_1]]$. Therefore, to maintain spatial equilibrium, land rent must decrease with increasing distance from the CBD.

For illustration, let AA represent the household's budget constraint in spatial equilibrium at location s_1 (Figure 14.5). Holding land rent equal to $R[s_1]$ as distance to the CBD is increased from s_1 to s_2, no movement of the budget constraint will be observed.

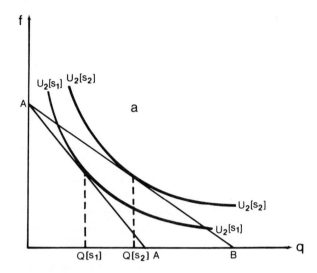

Figure 14.5 Evaluation of case III of the second branch of the utility tree

In order for the housing budget line at s_2 to be tangent to $u_2[s_2]$, land rents must decrease, resulting in a shift from AA to AB (Figure 14.5). Land rent at s_2 must then be less than that at s_1. By inspection of Figure 14.5, it is seen that quantity of land consumed increases with increasing distance from the CBD; however, the point of tangency between AB and $u_2[s_2]$ depends upon the difference between $u_2[s_1] - u_2[s_2]$, leaving the behavior of $F[s]$ over space as indeterminate. The capital to land ratio is then also indeterminate.

To sum up case III, land rent will decrease and land consumption will increase with increasing distance from the CBD. Since the behavior of capital consumption is indeterminate, the capital to land ratio may increase, remain constant, or decrease with increasing distance from the CBD. The urban margins in this scenario may then harbor the greatest capital to land ratios in the city, or the lowest capital to land ratios. Furthermore, this case is also compatible with a capital to land ratio being everywhere the same. The results of case III can be summarized in the following principle:

Principle 14.3 If the increase in transportation expenditures is exactly counterbalanced by a decrease in composite good consumption across space, then:

(i) All intercepts on the ordinate of the housing budget constraint will be the same, regardless of location of the household.

(ii) Land consumption will increase with increasing distance from the CBD.

(iii) Capital consumption can increase, decrease, or remain constant with increasing distance from the CBD.

(iv) The capital to land ratio can be greatest at the urban margins, greatest at the urban core, or everywhere the same.

(v) Land rent will decrease with increasing distance from the CBD.

14.3.4 Case IV: $|\Delta T[s]| < = > |\Delta p Z[s]|$

Case IV combines the implications of cases I, II, and III; in the example (Figure 14.2), case I prevails for $0 < = s < s_x$, and case II prevails for $s > s_x$; case III prevails at $s = s_x$. An intriguing implication of case IV is that the conditions for local agglomeration and multiple nucleation of cities are sufficiently defined when $|\Delta T[s]| - |\Delta Z[s]|$ intersects the zero axis several times leaving $D[s]$, $R[s]$, and $F[s]/Q[s]$ possibly to unfold over space in an undulating manner. This can be caused by the introduction of low-cost transportation nodes as discussed in Chapter 7; this implication of case IV can be summarized in the following principle:

> *Principle 14.4* If the change in transportation expenditures is alternately greater or less than the change in composite good expenditures with increasing distance from the CBD, then an oscillation of the population density and capital intensity gradients can occur, suggesting the spatial form of a multinodal (many centered) city.

See King (1984) for a further discussion of the spatial distribution of such centers.

Households spend a total of $V[s]X[s]$ on housing, which translates into $V[s]X[s]/Q[s]$ housing expenditure per unit of land. Since housing expenditure can be decomposed into expenditures on capital and expenditures on land, then so too can housing expenditures per unit of land be decomposed:

$$V[s]X[s]/Q[s] = y^*/Q = R[s] + W(F[s]/Q[s]). \qquad (14.16)$$

The urban margins are identified by equality of urban land rent $R[s]$ and cost of converting nonurban land to urban land δ; since urban land rent is only one component of urban housing rent, then there is expected to be a significant differential between agricultural land rent and the cost of housing per unit of land at the urban fringe.

14.4 Conclusion

In this chapter a method has been outlined by which the CTLR can be extended to settings where the household chooses between more than two kinds of good. Here the household chooses between three illustrative goods: composite good, land, and housing capital. However, the setting is more general and can be adapted to many of the problems outlined in the previous chapters of this book, including malleability and neighborhood decay.

The illustration of the stepwise decision process for housing capital is particularly valuable because in the city households inhabit housing, not land. And housing has associated with it many problems not associated with land, namely vintage, maintenance, and style.

Housing is composed of land and capital that rests upon that land. It was shown that the market solution for the ideal city is consistent with housing capital increasing, remaining constant, or declining with increasing distance from the CBD. The capital to land ratio can be most intensive at the city center, be everywhere uniform, be most intensive at the urban margins, or in some instances even oscillate across space.

Notes

1 I should like to thank Murray Brown, Department of Economics, State University of New York, for his comments in 1981 concerning my work on this branching utility problem.
2 I first worked on a related housing problem using branching utility functions in 1972 as part of my M.A. thesis in Economics at Ohio State University. Comments at that time by John Weicher were appreciated.

References

Brown and Hein (1972)
Dendrinos, with Mullally (1985)
Phlips (1974) p. 67
Thrall (1982b) p. 149

15

Postscript

15.1 Introduction: the personal experience

Personal experiences can be the most important driving force in motivating one to become knowledgeable in the mechanisms behind the creation of urban landscapes. In this context, the dedication to this book is important: my own motivation for the study of urban form has come from the chance of living in one of the world's great metropolitan areas during its transformation from what was largely a scatter of small centers to that of a true megalopolis. Hence, my own motivation is a product of the chance of time and location of birth placing me at the leading edge of the post World War II Californian population explosion.

Like that of other scientists, my personal experiences contribute in a noninsignificant manner to the research agenda. More important, urban scientists must rely upon their personal experiences to build their research agenda and to build their intuition. So, in the inquiry of urban form, each of our own unique and personal experiences come first.

When I was a child in southern California, my family were new arrivals from the Midwest; they took great pleasure in exploring the landscape on the Sunday drive, trying out each new freeway which like fingers poked the agricultural and desert hinterlands, shortly to be followed by the growing palm of the city. This landscape of seemingly limitless expansion was for me the way cities were supposed to be; it was the "normal" landscape.

This was, for me, the norm until I left Los Angeles in 1963 to spend my junior year of high school in the United Kingdom; no person could miss the observation that the spatial form of Los Angeles was different from that of London. But why? What characteristics were important in contrasting these places? What was most important to me at the time was that I was too young to drive in Los Angeles, therefore I was spatially limited to my immediate neighborhood, or dependent upon those older than myself for transportation, yet when I was in London, the entire city was only a tube ticket away. At the same time, these places shared many features in common, otherwise they would not be recognizable as urban places.

My continuing urban experiences included: summers in Santa Barbara; a $99-for-99-days Greyhound Bus pass taking me to the lowest-income neighborhood of every major city in the United States; and living in the Midwest while I was completing requirements for graduate degrees in economics and geography. And subsequently living in Hamilton, Canada; Buffalo, New York; and Gainesville, Florida.

Each of us has our own unique urban experiences, and these experiences shape our emotions about and expectations of the urban environment. They shape the kind of questions we ask. For example, my own motivation for writing the article (Thrall, 1982b) upon which Chapter 9 was based was because, while living on the Canadian border with the United States, I watched the Canadian national news; on TV real estate brokers were marching on Parliament in Ottawa demanding that Canadian income tax laws be changed to be like that of the United States, to allow mortgage interest deductions. The same evening I watched the American national news where the lead story was a very serious proposal to abolish mortgage interest deductions. Urban analysts should be providing answers to real urban questions.

Regardless of the depth of personal urban experiences, by themselves they are limited to being a hodge-podge of events and a clutter of facts until tied together with some unifying idea, a theory however elementary. Perhaps the most basic idea, certainly one of the earliest ideas that came to me as a child, was that the pattern of land use was not random. Once one has gleaned such elementary ideas, or theories, the ideas themselves become part of the personal experience; moreover, such ideas influence the way in which one observes the landscape and hence collects further data or experiences of that landscape.

15.2   Heuristics, experience with CTLR theory and landscapes

Personal experiences cannot now be separated from our interpretation of an urban landscape. The following three examples of Guadalajara, Vienna, and Hamilton illustrate how knowing a general theory can aid our intuition in explaining particular landscapes.

First, consider the residential map of Guadalajara, Mexico (Figure 15.1). Guadalajara has been divided into zones according to the social-economic class of the resident (Buttner, 1986; Caviedes, 1986). The belief that cities have some regular spatial order to them is reinforced by the apparently smooth gradation from the higher class in the west who, in turn, are surrounded by persons of successively lower social-economic status.

An understanding of the Consumption Theory of Land Rent (CTLR) also becomes part of the personal experience which, in turn, leads us to make certain inquiries to explain why Guadalajara has the particular pattern as

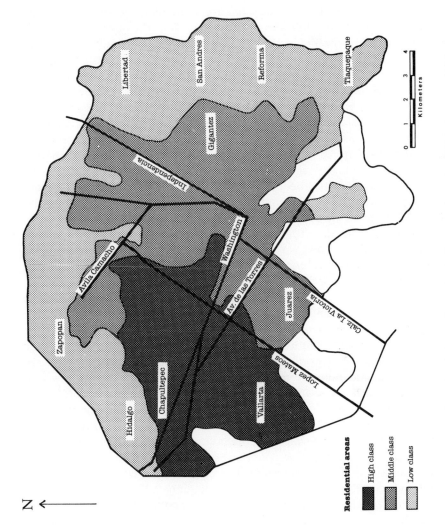

Figure 15.1 Neighborhoods of Guadalajara, Mexico, by class of resident (Buttner 1986)

shown in Figure 15.1 vs one typical of cities in the United States where persons of higher social-economic status invariably reside at the urban margins.

Guadalajara is situated in a steep valley, ascending from west to east. Because of the lack of public infrastructure, particularly roads, it is difficult to travel along the steep hillsides of the valley. Thus the positive externality (see Chapter 13) of the highlands with their pleasant views and being situated above the air pollution is outweighed by the negative environment with mudslides and at times impassable roads, hence lower land values.

Also in Guadalajara there is a high ratio of persons of lower social-economic status to persons with higher social-economic status; moreover, there is a great difference in welfare and income between persons of higher vs lower social-economic status. Therefore, as seen in Chapter 4, we would expect such a state of affairs to create a general landscape like that of Guadalajara: the higher-class persons inhabit the central core flatlands on the west side of the city, the middle-class inhabit the land with next greater proximity to the city center, and the poor inhabit the least accessible and difficult terrain of the hillsides.

Second, consider the urban landscape of Vienna, Austria (Figure 15.2; based upon Sauberer and Cserjan, 1972; see also White, 1984). In Vienna the difference in welfare and income between high- and low-income persons is not as extreme as it is in the Latin American example of Guadalajara. Nevertheless, Vienna retains vintage housing capital reflecting an era when there were extreme welfare and income differentials. Much of the older part of the city dates from when Vienna was the capital of the Hapsburg Empire. In the mid- to late nineteenth century, Vienna was a wealthy and liberal city, with a large middle class. A product of this era was the Ringstrasse, a boulevard with monumental public buildings. The CTLR analysis from Chapter 4 suggests that such circumstances will lead to higher-income households living near the city center and lower-income persons at the urban periphery. Indeed in Vienna, like those of Guadalajara, the higher-income groups dominate the inner core while the lower-income population has a greater average distance to commute to the city center.

In Vienna, a middle-class district has recently emerged at the (northern) periphery as would be expected in the CTLR analysis for a city experiencing both an increase in numbers of households and an increase in income.

The Danube has for thousands of years been a major commercial transportation artery, thus that is where urban industry is expected to be found. Heavy industry is noisy and polluting, thereby generating negative externalities (Chapter 13) for nearby residential areas and decreasing residential land values. But at the same time, centers of industry become the central node for workers of that industry; hence workers congregate about the Danube industrial corridor.

Third and last, consider the urban landscape of Hamilton, Ontario,

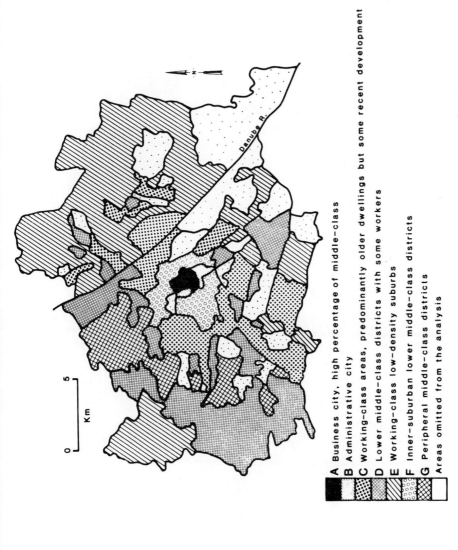

A Business city, high percentage of middle-class

B Administrative city

C Working-class areas, predominantly older dwellings but some recent development

D Lower middle-class districts with some workers

E Working-class low-density suburbs

F Inner-suburban lower middle-class districts

G Peripheral middle-class districts

Areas omitted from the analysis

Danube R.

Km

0   5

Figure 15.2 Neighborhoods of Vienna, Austria, by class of resident, 1961

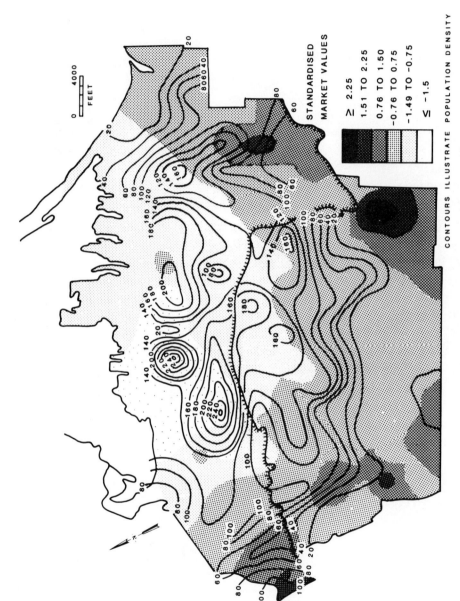

Figure 15.3 Relation between market values and population density in Hamilton, Canada

Canada. In Figure 15.3, isolines of population density are overlaid upon a contour map of market values for housing in standard deviation units. (Data for this map was from the same study as Thrall, 1979 c and d, and published in Webber, 1979; see also Webber, 1979, figure 1.2). Our intuition leads us to expect that land rent and population density are directly related. But in Figure 15.3, the region of greatest population density has the lowest housing values for single family dwellings; other factors, then, dominate over the simple rent–density relationship.

Our experience with the CTLR guides us to look on the landscape for the presence of externalities, for example, and housing of varying vintages and quality. Examination of Hamilton reveals that central-core neighborhoods with the highest population density typically also are the oldest, and contain housing that requires greater maintenance than newer housing at the urban periphery in the south and west. Much of the inner core housing dates from the same era as late-nineteenth-century Vienna, but the Hamilton housing was built for persons of much lower income. The urban fringe of Hamilton expanded very quickly during the 1970s because of better automobile and bus transportation access to the area south of the Niagara Escarpment (indicated on the figure by the cross-hatched line). The discussion centered on Figure 9.4 (see p. 127) indicates that such rapid expansion can contribute to declining values of the inner-core neighborhoods. Land values may have fallen even further had it not been for the high rate of laboring-class inmigration from Quebec, Europe, and Asia.

In Hamilton, the zones of the highest housing values are generally tangential to parklands and regions of particularly attractive environmental interest. The zones of lowest housing values occur in those regions where there is the greatest employment – see Figure 15.4 (drawn using data published in Webber, 1979, figure 1.1); transportation is sufficiently good that persons are not willing to pay a high premium to live in close proximity to the workplace, and moreover the Hamilton heavy industrial workplace can often be characterized as a significant generator of negative externalities by way of noise and atmospheric pollution. Hamilton, then, does have similarities with the American city where wealthier households reside at the urban periphery and the poor reside in the older inner-core neighborhoods.

The corporate offices of the nearby heavy manufacturing industry have remained in the Hamilton central core (as has occurred in Pittsburgh, Pennsylvania). This along with city planners limiting the peripheral expansion of commercial floorspace when the vacancy rate is considered to be excessive (see Chapter 12 and the discussion centered on Figure 9.4) has kept Hamilton from following the course of central city decay as has often been the case in the United States.

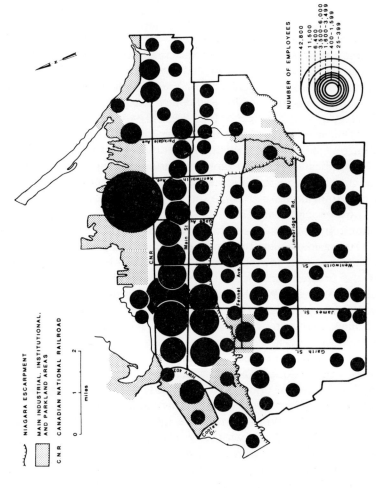

Figure 15.4 Location of employment in Hamilton, Canada, 1971

15.3 Theory before formal empirical inquiry

Why not, then, proceed directly from one's personal experiences and intuition to empirical-statistical analysis? In section 1.1 (pp. 3–4) are listed four points as support for the argument that a solid foundation in theory should precede the formal empirical inquiry. Briefly, these four points were:

(1) Whose environment should be examined?
(2) What should be the focus of the inquiry?
(3) What processes that create urban form are common between places?
(4) Can past urban forms be explained and future urban forms predicted?

Now with the CTLR analysis of the previous fourteen chapters behind us, I will proceed to sketch briefly a response to each of these questions.

First, any urban environment should be able to be examined by one fluent in the language of urban theory; and one criterion for whether an urban theory is of practical use is whether it is sufficiently robust to be able to be applied in almost any setting. Whether the particular case is of interest to a specific person is another issue and depends upon their own personal experiences.

Particular case studies become of interest to a wide audience because of evidence that the case study provides for varifying a general theory that can, in turn, be put to some practical use elsewhere. One place as an illustrative landscape is not, a priori, more important than any other. For example, I have found the book by historian William Utter (1956), *Granville: The Story of an Ohio Village*, to be of personal interest because the lives of several of my ancestors are documented; but the book is unlikely to be of interest to those without personal ties to Granville, Ohio. Also unless one's personal experiences provide the motivation, there is no reason to expect the spatial structure of Vienna to be of interest to a person only familiar with the Los Angeles urban environment, and conversely. The personal experience that can contribute to such studies being of interest and practical value is in their linkage to the theory.

Second, among the myriad events occurring around us laws that governments enact, values that prevail, institutions that come and go, personal interactions that take place, and so on, I have argued that a small subset of all possible things are most important to an explanation as to why a place has come to be as it is. Each chapter of this book has focused upon how a specific element affects urban spatial structure. These particular elements have been chosen for examination because I believe them to be the most important in the determination of the spatial structure of cities; at the same time, the CTLR model is sufficiently robust to be extended to accommodate most other elements that others may believe to be important contributing factors to urban spatial structure.

Third, these elements or parameters I have discussed in point 2, above, contribute to making a place unique by the individual weight they have at each location. Furthermore, it is important *when* during the evolution of the city the elements receive the particular weights they do. For illustration, do low transportation costs, high rates of inmigration, and relatively high income prevail during the housing capital accumulation phase of the city as in the case of Los Angeles during the post World War II era, or does the introduction of low transportation cost occur after housing capital is in place and population is outmigrating as was the case in Buffalo, New York, in the middle 1980s? The importance of the element of low transportation cost is expected to be different in each case depending upon the weight of the other important elements. Yet even in these polar cases, the CTLR provides a mechanism to analyze and compare; if one of the major parameters of these or other places changes, the CTLR can be used to anticipate what will be the likely impact that this parameter change will have upon the landscape.

Fourth, the CTLR is an attempt to explain why cities have come to be as they are; it is not a method limited to describing an idea of a landscape. Rather, if for whatever reason a particular urban spatial structure has been defined as one that is considered best for a place to evolve into, then other than directly constructing that landscape the CTLR is one of the few available guides as to how the sought-after urban form can be achieved.

15.4   Empirical verification of the principles

Heuristics and formal empirical inquiry are related, but not the same thing. Specifically, heuristics is a method whereby one is pointed toward an association between various ideas. In section 15.2, the discussion pointed the principles of the CTLR toward an interpretation of real cities; but there was no formal statistical demonstration that any particular principle of the CTLR had indeed been prevalent in Guadalajara, Vienna, or Hamilton.

In this book, I have identified a set of parameters hypothesized to contribute to changing land values. Moreover, all the principles and propositions of the CTLR should be candidates for formal statistical-empirical examination and indeed have intriguing real-world implications.

Consider, for example, Table 15.1 which includes a list of average market values of housing for a sample of cities in the United States during 1985, and the percentage change in those market values from the previous year. The CTLR can contribute to both a formal and an intuitive understanding of what processes bring about the urban landscape. Why is it that Boston led the United States at that time in increasing market values of housing, while market values of housing declined in Oklahoma City, Orlando, and Portland? Why is it that in this sample of cities, New York City and Hartford, Connecticut, are above average in market value, while Detroit and Buffalo are below average? It is beyond the scope of this book to detail

Table 15.1 Median sales prices and price increases of existing homes in selected metropolitan areas of the United States, 1984–5

Metropolitan area	Median price in fourth quarter, 1985 ($)	Percentage change from fourth quarter, 1985 (%)
Albany, Schenectady, N.Y.	61,500	+ 14.3
Anaheim, Santa Ana, Calif.	51,600	+ 6.8
Baltimore, Md.	72,800	+ 9.3
Birmingham, Ala.	64,600	+ 4.7
Boston, Mass.	144,800	+ 38.2
Buffalo, Niagara Falls, NY	45,600	+ 6.3
Chicago, Ill.	81,500	+ 4.8
Cincinnati, Ohio	58,500	+ 2.3
Cleveland, Ohio	62,200	+ 1.3
Columbus, Ohio	88,200	+ 9.2
Dallas–Fort Worth, Tex.	88,200	+ 10.2
Denver, Colo.	84,500	+ 2.2
Detroit, Mich.	51,700	+ 7.9
Fort Lauderdale, Fla.	75,500	+ 2.7
Hartford, Conn.	103,900	+ 13.3
Houston, Tex.	86,100	+ 15.1
Indianapolis, Ind.	55,100	+ 7
Jacksonville, Fla.	58,600	+ 3.9
Kansas City, Mo.	59,500	+ 1
Louisville, Ky.	49,100	+ 1.7
Memphis, Tenn.	62,400	− 3.3
Miami, Fla.	79,200	+ 1.8
Milwaukee, Wis.	68,100	+ 6.2
Minneapolis–St Paul, Min.	75,400	+ 2.4
Nashville, Tenn.	66,600	+ 6.1
New York, Long Island, NY	139,800	+ 29.8
Oklahoma City, Okla.	63,300	− 1.7
Orlando, Fla.	69,000	− 1
Philadelphia, Penn.	69,300	+ 7.8
Phoenix, Ariz.	75,700	+ 1.9
Portland, Ore.	59,500	− 5.1
Providence, R.I.	70,200	+ 18.4
Rochester, N.Y.	63,700	+ 5.5
Tampa, Clearwater, Fla.	58,900	+ 0.5

Source: National Association of Realtors.

empirically the existing and changing conditions of the urban form of each center in the sample; yet the major parameters that lead to market values of housing have been identified in this book, and the CTLR can be used to evaluate the direction likely to be taken in market values because of changes in those parameters. Hence, the foundations are in place for a detailed and formal empirical analysis of why housing values behaved as they did in this sample of cities.

Also the theoretical analysis should be followed by empirical examinations of the principles and propositions derived from the theory. For illustration, consider a short list of implications taken only from Chapter 4:

Hypothesis from principle 4.6 Persons of the same occupation will receive greater income the larger the city size they work in. If so, is the income sufficiently great to offset the greater expenditures necessary to live in the larger city?

Hypothesis from principle 4.7 The spatial distribution of households by income in countries whose social systems lead to a high degree of welfare or income inequality will be characterized with the highest-income persons at the inner core, and the lowest-income inhabitants at the urban periphery.

Hypothesis from proposition 4.1 Where the ratio of numbers of wealthy people to poor people is low, the wealthy people will reside at the city center.

Hypothesis from principle 4.11 As the general income of the population increases, land rent at the urban margins increases and that at the city center has a relative decrease.

Hypothesis from principle 4.13 The wealthier the population, the flatter will be their rent gradient.

Regrettably one of the weaker aspects of the science of urban analysis has been linking the formal theory with formal empirical-statistical analysis. The audience for urban theory has been largely limited to other theorists. Empiricists are all too often unfamiliar with the theory; their research agenda has been based largely upon their personal experiences without the benefit of the theory. The burden for this weakness does not fall only upon the empiricist; too often theorists have made little attempt to communicate their findings to empiricists. More important, there have been too few urban analysts who have made the effort to contribute to both theoretical and empirical analysis. It is my hope that this book, and the CTLR methodology presented here, will serve to attract the greater attention of empiricists to examine hypotheses based upon this type of formal reasoning rather than only intuition or statistical correlations.

15.5 Concluding statement: toward a science of urban analysis

The Consumption Theory of Land Rent is a theory of why the urban landscape has the general makeup that it has. The CTLR is a geometric solution of the urban land use and land rent problem. The geometry can be used to derive the trend and long-term consequence upon urban spatial structure resulting from policy decisions by government such as introducing light rail rapid transit systems, or a parameter change in the economy such as a general rise in real income. Like the paradigm of the supply and demand curve geometry in classical aspatial economics that enables one to analyze the relationships between price and quantity, the CTLR is an accessible geometry for analyzing the effect of changes in institutional constraints and various exogenous parameters upon the geography of the city.

The figures and tables in this chapter are not sufficient to verify that the Consumption Theory of Land Rent conforms to the real world. Rather what I have attempted to do in this chapter is to place into proper perspective the role of the CTLR theory versus that of intuition and formal empirical-statistical analysis. I believe that in the development of urban science, empirical-statistical analyses should be based upon the hypotheses of the formal theory.

References

Buttner (1986)
Caviedes (1986)
Sauberer and Cserjan (1972)
Thrall (1979c, 1979d, 1982b)
Utter (1956)
Webber (1979)
White (1984)

Glossary

Standard symbolic notation

Note: capitalization of symbols that are endogenous generally means that the term satisfies conditions for spatial equilibrium. Lower case symbols of endogenous terms generally indicate that conditions for spatial equilibrium are not satisfied.

$ATLV$	assessed total land value, or the summation of the product of market values for all households' properties and the assessment rate.
c	the transportation cost per unit distance overland "across the grain" to a low-cost transportation node. The households' cost of access to the node is cd (used only in Chapter 7).
d	distance between the low-cost transportation node and the location of the household (used only in Chapter 7).
δ	cost of converting nonurban land to urban utilization.
$D[s]$	population density on annulus s.
E	transportation effort, the percentage of income allocated to transportation expenditures.
$F[s]$	household consumption of housing capital.
G	public good.
h	radial extent of the urban area.
k	transportation cost per unit distance.
ks	total transportation cost for household located on annulus s.
$L[s]$	land rent whose determinants are from the production sector.
m	the degree to which mortgage interest payments can be deducted

from gross income and thereby have a lower taxable net income (used only in Chapters 8 and 9).

M net income, the difference between gross income y and income taxes (used with this definition only in Chapters 8 and 9).

n exogenously specified number of persons per household. Usually this is set to be equal to one person.

Ω household property tax (refer to equations 8.15–8.20)

p price of composite good, may be exogenously set to equal one as a numeraire.

ρ nonurban land rent.

P total population of the city. If P is endogenous and U is exogenous, the city is said to be open. If U is endogenous and P is exogenous, the city is said to be closed.

π 3.14159 . . .

$Q[s]$ household quantity of land consumed.

$R[s]$ rent per unit of land on annulus s.

s distance from the city center or central business district (CBD).

t tax rate. t_1 is the sales tax. t_2 is an *ad valorem* property tax. t_3 is the income tax.

$T[s]$ a household's total transportation expenditures whose residence is on annulus s about the CBD. This transportation cost function is not restricted to being increasing and linear with increasing distance from the CBD, as is the product ks. In Chapter 7 it is a flat rate fee, while in Chapter 14 $T[s]$ can increase at an increasing, constant or decreasing rate with increasing distance from the CBD.

U welfare of the individual household. When the system is in spatial equilibrium, then households cannot obtain a level of welfare sufficiently higher elsewhere to induce them to relocate.

$V[s]X[s]$ Endogenously derived total housing expenditure.

$V[s]$ endogenous spatial equilibrium price of housing (used with this definition only in Chapters 1 and 14).

W the exogenously given price of housing capital (used only in Chapter 14).

W_H The upper range of a welfare band that can exist and still have households without the incentive to relocate in order to obtain greater levels of welfare. If welfare levels greater than W_H can be obtained elsewhere, then households will relocate in order to achieve this. Generally, for brevity, W_H is set equal to U. See also U and W_L. (Used only in Chapter 2; see Figure 2.2.)

W_L the greatest deviation below average welfare available elsewhere that households will tolerate. Levels of welfare less than W_L will lead to a decision by the household to relocate. For brevity, W_L is generally equated to the welfare surface U. See also U and W_H. (Used only in Chapter 2; see Figure 2.2.)

$w[s]$ the capitalization of public good into land rent. Capitalization of the public good into land rent by the amount $w[s]$ is sufficient compensation to offset the increase in the provision of externality or public good (used only in Chapter 13).

$X[s]$ endogenously derived spatial equilibrium quantity of housing consumed (used only in Chapter 14).

$X[-, s]$ externality density function. $X[-, s]$ registers the spillin or
or density of negative externalities at s, while $X[+, s]$ registers the
$X[+, s)$ spillin or density of positive externalities at s (used only in Chapter 13).

y household income.

y^* household's disposable income after transportation expenditures have been accounted for; $y^* = y - ks$.

$y^*[s]$ endogenously derived income allocated for housing.

$Z[s]$ consumption of composite good.

ζ millage rate, generally the ratio of the total cost of the local public sector, $C[G]$, and the total assessed land value, $ATLV$, of a city, namely $\zeta = C[G]/(ATLV)$ (used with this definition only in equations (8.15)–(8.17)).

χ the assessment rate, or assessed value to market value ratio.

Terminology and definitions

Abscissa. In general the horizontal or x-axis. Here the term is often used interchangeably with the quantity of land axis, in contrast to the composite good axis which is known as the *ordinate* (*q.v.*).

Absolute spatial location. A location in space defined by x–y or longitude and latitude coordinates versus *relative spatial location*, where location is defined in terms of other places.

Aggregate social welfare. For households with identical income and taste preferences, their aggregate welfare is the summation of each of their individual levels of welfare. The aggregate social welfare may be maximized in a *planned city* by providing greater levels of welfare for some individuals and lesser for others, depending upon their relative spatial location; the aggregate social welfare in this manner may become greater than that where all households have the same level of welfare. Maximization of aggregate social welfare is considered an optimum solution since a social welfare criterion has been introduced.

Assessed value. Unless property has recently been sold, the value of land or housing must be guessed at for purposes of tax assessment; this guess is referred to as the assessed value. The assessed value in North America is usually required by law to be the amount that the property is expected to realize if sold in the open market by a willing seller to a willing buyer.

CBD. Acronym for central business district.

Closed city. One of three general classifications of cities, open, closed, or planned. The closed city assumes an exogenous population and endogenous household welfare.

Compensated land rent. Land rent whose value is dependent in part upon compensation necessary to offset the change in utility attributable to changes in the provision of *public good* or *externality*.

Consumption Theory of Land Rent (CTLR). A comprehensive theory developed by Grant Ian Thrall of why the urban landscape has the general makeup that it does. The CTLR is a geometric solution of the urban land use and land rent problem. The geometry can be used to derive the trend and long-term consequences upon urban spatial structure resulting from policy decisions by government such as introducing light rail rapid transit systems, or a parameter change in the economy such as a general rise in real income. Like the paradigm of the supply and demand curve geometry in classical aspatial economics that enables one to analyze the relationships between price and quantity, the CTLR is an accessible geometry for analyzing the effect of changes in institutional constraints and various exogenous parameters upon the geography of the city.

Cost of conversion. The cost of transferring land from use in the nonurban sector to use in the urban sector. This includes, for example, the cost of necessary infrastructure as well as payments for the opportunity cost of the land.

CTLR. See *Consumption Theory of Land Rent*.

Density effect. The *revealed effect*, or change in population attributable to a shift in the population density gradient.

Direct effects. The impact upon the system resulting from the change in some external component of the model while holding land rent constant. They are the consequence of a change in an exogenous parameter while holding spatial equilibrium land rent equal to its initial value. Direct effects are common between open and closed cities.

Direct utility function. see *Indirect utility function.*

Endogenous.   A term whose origin comes from the biological sciences and meaning originating from within, or due to internal causes. Endogenous variables obtain their particular values because of the manner in which they interact with other endogenous and exogenous variables and constants in the system. Examples include R and Z, but also P in the open city and U in the closed city.

Excludable.   State of affairs when one's consumption of the good can be restricted or limited. If a good is nonexcludable, then technology does not exist that can prohibit a person from receiving benefit from the good if it is provided.

Exogenous.   A term whose origin comes from the biological sciences and meaning originating from without, or due to external causes. Exogenous constants or variables obtain their particular values in an unspecified manner. Examples include p and W, but also U in the open city and P in the closed city.

Externalities.   These are treated as a special class of *public goods* whose density of availability is not everywhere the same. The presence of the externality often is most intense at the source of the externality and decreases with increasing distance from the source. The manner in which the externality unfolds across space can be thought of as a distance decay function centered on the site of emission or source of the good; the site or source can be either fixed as a point or ray in space, or mobile through space. The direct effect of a positive externality can increase household welfare, while a negative externality can decrease household welfare. See also *public good* for a discussion of substitutes and complements.

Higher-order cities.   A term from central place theory (see King, 1984) that differentiates cities on the basis of the kind of goods available in the city. The important distinguishing characteristic of the goods here is the number of persons in the city and surrounding hinterland that are required to sustain enough sales of the goods to ensure that entrepreneurs offer the goods in business. Higher-order goods have a greater threshold number of persons than lower-order goods. Since a city is classifiable as to the type of goods available in that city, then higher-order cities offer higher-order goods. There is a positive correlation between order of a city and size of population, but this correlation is not 1:1.

Indifference curve.   A locus of points mapping combinations of goods to which the household is indifferent. Each combination of goods on an indifference curve yields the same level of total utility.

Indirect effects.   Isolation of the effects that are attributable to adjustments in land rent necessary to drive the system back into spatial equilibrium. They are the endogenous changes that are the result of the system regaining spatial equilibrium once it has been propelled into a state of spatial dis-equilibrium, and are mainly the result of adjustments in spatial equili-brium land rents. The indirect effects are specific to the definitions of open and closed cities.

Indirect utility function. A utility function that is expressed in terms of prices as opposed to the *direct* counterpart of being expressed in terms of goods. For example, consider a two-good world where households receive utility only from composite good z with price p, and land q with price r. The household's income y is exhausted with expenditures on land and composite good. Given prices and income, the demand for each good can be derived, say, $z°[p,y]$ and $q°[r,y]$. The direct utility function will be expressed $u°[z°,q°]$, thereby indicating the utility level for the household with the particular consumption of $z°$ and $q°$. One can then also write the utility function as $u°[z°[y,p],q°[y,r]]$ or without loss of information simply as $u°[y,p,r]$, which is the indirect utility function.

Interactive city. Classification of an ideal city whose urban boundary is derived by the condition that urban land rent is equal to the cost of converting nonurban land to urban land utilization.

Isotropic surface. A featureless plain extending in all directions without limit.

Land use. The observed and dominant activity that occurs at a particular location. For the most part, this book defines three classes of land use according to whether it is used for production, consumption, or nonurban activities.

Large city. This has greater population density and land rent, larger total population, and generally greater radial extent than a small city.

Malleability. An ideal city that is assumed to be perfectly malleable can be characterized, following a parameter change or perturbation to the system, by all endogenous variables instantaneously adjusting to new equilibrium positions; most important, this necessitates immediate and perfect adjustments in population density, household location, and capital to land ratios. When one or more important endogenous variables are sticky in not easily being changed from their inherited population density or capital to land ratios, they are referred to as nonmalleable. In the nonmalleable city, instead of the household obtaining the population density conditional only upon the present market, the household may for example only have the choice of (a) living in an inherited population density, (b) relocating else-where, or (c) with additional expense converting the inherited population density.

Marginal utility of public goods (MUPG). The direct change in household welfare attributable to a change in the provision of the public good.

Mortgage interest deductions. The reduction in taxable income by the amount of interest payments that the household makes; this becomes the taxable income. Where income taxes are progressive, the percentage of income that one pays in tax will increase as income increases. Hence, a lower taxable income may also lower the tax rate.

MUPG. see *Marginal utility of public good*.

Open city. One of three general classifications of city (open, closed, or planned). In the open city, it is assumed that population is endogenous while household welfare is exogenous.

Openness. A city between the polar extremes of being an *open city* or a *closed city* has degrees of "openness" or "closedness".

Opportunity cost. Alternative that must be given up. The highest valued alternative that is sacrificed.

Option demand. The present *opportunity cost* may be low, however in time it may become the highest use. Once the choice to develop has been made, the option is forever lost. Option demand for land then is a transaction across generations to withhold land from current development so that it is available in an undeveloped state to future generations.

Ordinate. In general, the vertical or *y*-axis. Here the term is often used interchangeably with the quantity of composite good axis, in contrast to the land axis which is known as the *abscissa*.

Planned city. One of three general forms of city, in addition to *open* and *closed*. A planned city has one or several of the important set of variables which instead of being endogenous are specified by some external agency. Such exogenous specification may under some circumstances prohibit the use of *spatial equilibrium* terminology because the usual spatial equilibrium mechanisms cannot operate. For example, in an open or closed city land rent is considered an endogenous variable; however, in a planned city it is one of the variables that may be specified exogenously by way of rent controls. Another example is imposing zoning that restricts population density to be some exogenously determined amount versus some endogenously derived value. Any variable may be specified exogenously in a planned city.

Private goods. Contrasts with a *public good*, a pure private good possesses both *rivalry* and *excludability*. In this book, composite good, land, and housing capital are considered private goods. It should be noted, however, that the activity which occurs on a parcel of land may posess publicness, and the utility that the household receives from private goods may in part be dependent upon the provision of public goods.

Production Theory of Land Rent (PTLR). The theory that land rent obtains the value it does because of the productive capacity of the land. The productive capacity translates into a monitary return for the landowner or landuser, and hence decisions concerning the land are based upon the returns that can be obtained from the parcel of land. Spatial production theories of land rent generally are based upon the nineteenth-century work of Johann Von Thünen. See, in contrast, *Consumption Theory of Land Rent*.

PTLR. See *Production Theory of Land Rent*.

Public good. Contrasts with a *private good*, a pure public good does not possess *rivalry* or *excludability* – while a pure private good is characterized by both *rivalry* and *excludability*. A public good is considered a complement to land if consumption of the good increases the utility received from the consumption of land. A public good is considered a substitute to land if the consumption of land can be replaced by a public good, with no resulting change in aggregate welfare.

Radially constrained city. The radial extent of the city is determined exogenously by a central planning authority or by a collusion of monopolistic landowners.

Radius effect. The *revealed effect* or change in population attributable to a change in the radial extent of the city.

Relative spatial location. Location in space defined in terms relative to some other important location. For example, a household's residential location is generally defined as being so many kilometers from the city center, hence, the residence is situated relative to the CBD. In contrast, the *absolute spatial location* of the residence is defined by *x–y* or longitude and latitude coordinates.

Revealed effects. The difference between the *indirect* and *direct* effects that are attributable to some change in system definition or parameter.

Rivalry. If an individual's consumption of a particular good prohibits another individual from receiving benefit (utility) from that good, the good is considered to be rival. Nonrivalry is that state of affairs when one person's consumption of a good does not compete with (affect the welfare of) another's consumption of the good.

Shadow budget line. The budget line that would allow the household to obtain the same level of welfare as that commensurate with the additional provision of *public goods* or *externalities*. The shadow budget line is used to derive the *compensated land rent*.

Solitary city. A city whose radial extent is limited to that region where population density exceeds a specified number of persons per square mile.

Spatial equilibrium. Households at any particular location can achieve a certain level of utility because of the environment of that place (including land values) and the accessibility that the place has relative to other places. When people relocate, they affect the environment and therefore change the level of welfare at the particular location from that which prevailed to some new level. Households continue to relocate as long as the system is in disequilibrium, that is until the households cannot obtain higher levels of utility by an additional move. The system is said to be in spatial equilibrium when the household is indifferent between all other locations, or equivalently when there is insufficient incentive for the household to make an additional move and thereby obtain a higher level of welfare.

Spatially biased. The direct effect (incidence) of a parameter change is spatially biased when that parameter change affects welfare of households (who have the same income and taste preferences) to an extent that is not everywhere the same, and the manner in which their welfare is affected by the parameter change depends upon the households' location. This is in contrast to a parameter change that is *spatially netural.*

Spatially neutral.   The direct effect (incidence) of a parameter change is spatially neutral when that parameter change affects welfare of households (who have the same income and taste preferences) in exactly the same manner, irrespective of the households' location. This is in contrast to a parameter change that is *spatially biased.*

Spillover.   When the benefits of a good (either positive or negative) are not exclusive to the location where the good is consumed, then the benefits are said to spill over onto neighboring locations. The good thereby acts as an *externality*, and generally these terms are interchangeable.

Transportation effort.   The percentage of income required to obtain transportation; it is calculated as the ratio of transportation expenditures to income. Say that total gasoline consumption for households at s is 1000 gallons; say also that the price of gasoline is p_g; transportation effort then can be written as $E = 1000(p_g/y)$.

Urban form.   The general trend in land use of an urban area. In addition to describing the activity of production, consumption, or nonurban sectors, descriptions of urban form generally center upon the shape of the city in terms of radial extent, population density, and housing capital to land ratios.

Utility curve.   See *Indifference curve.*

Bibliography

The original purpose of writing this book was to provide a comprehensive and unified research monograph on the CTLR paradigm. It was not my purpose to provide an introductory survey of the literature on mathematical land rent, urban geography, planning or regional science. It is rather the comprehensiveness of the topics covered in this book, and moreover the generality, utility, and ease of understanding the CTLR paradigm, that allows the present book to serve the dual purpose of documentation for this research and as a resource for classroom use.

This bibliography is, with few exceptions, composed of citations from my articles on land use and land rent published in geography and regional science journals, upon which this book was based.

Alonso, W. (1964) *Location and Land Use: Toward a General Theory of Land Rent*, Cambridge, Mass., Harvard University Press.

Anas, A., and Dendrinos, D.S. (1976) "The New Urban Economics: A Brief Survey," in Papapeorgiou, G.J. (ed.), *Essays in Mathematical Land Use Theory*, Lexington, Mass., Lexington Books.

Barr, J. (1972) "City Size, Land Rent, and the Supply of Public Goods," *Regional and Urban Economics*, 2, 67–103.

Berry, B.J.L. and Neils, E. (1969) "Location, Size and Shape of Cities as Influenced by Environmental Factors," in Perloff, H.S. (ed.), *The Quality of the Urban Environment*, Baltimore, Md., Resources for the Future, 257–302.

Berry, B.J.L., Simmons, J.W., and Tennant, R.J. (1963) "Urban Population Densities: Structure and Change," *Geographical Review*, 53, 389–405.

Black, D.E. (1972) "The Nature and Extent of Effective Property Tax Rate Variation within the City of Boston," *National Tax Journal*, 25, 203–10.

Bourne, L.S. (ed.) (1971) *Internal Structure of the City*, Toronto, Oxford University Press.

Bourne, L.S. (1981) *The Geography of Housing*, New York, Wiley.

Bradford, D.F. (1971) "Joint Products, Collective Goods and External Effects; Comment," *Journal of Political Economy*, 79, 119–28.

Brown, M. and Hein, D. (1972) "The S-branch Utility Tree: A Generalization of the Linear Expenditure System," *Econometrica*, 40, 737–47.

Bruce–Briggs, B. (1974) "Gasoline Prices and the Suburban Way of Life," *Public Interest*, 37 (Fall), 131–6.

Brunn, S.D. and Williams, J.F. (1983) *Cities of the World: World Regional Urban Development*, New York, Harper & Row.

Buttner, E. (1986) "Social Geography of Mexico," in Caviedes, C. (ed.), *A Social Geography of Latin America*, New York, Westview Press.

Carlton, D.W. (1981) "The Spatial Effects of a Tax on Housing and Land," *Regional Science and Urban Economics*, 11, 509–27.

Casetti, E. (1971) "Equilibrium Land Values and Population Densities in an Ideal Setting," *Economic Geography*, 47, 16–20.

Caviedes, C. (ed.) (1986) *A Social Geography of Latin America*, Boulder, CO, Westview Press.

Clark, C. (1982) *Regional and Urban Location*, St. Lucia, Queensland, University of Queensland Press.

Clark, W.A.V. (1986) "Human Migration," in Thrall, G.I. (ed.) *Scientific Geography Series*, 7, Beverly Hills, CA, Sage.

Dendrinos, D., with Mullally, H. (1985) *Urban Evolution: Studies in the Mathematical Ecology of Cities*, Oxford, Oxford University Press.

Fisch, O. (1980) "Spatial Equilibrium with Locational Interdependencies, the Case of Environmental Spillovers," *Regional Science and Urban Economics*, 10, 201–9.

Fischler, S. (1976) *Uptown, Downtown: A Trip through Time on New York's Subway*, New York, Hawthorne Books.

Gordon, P., Richardson, H.W. and Wong, H.L. (1986) "The Distribution of Population and Employment in a Polycentric City: the case of Los Angeles," *Environment and Planning A*, 18, 161–73.

Henderson, J.V. (1977) *Economic Theory and the Cities*, New York, Academic Press.

Holterman, S.E. (1972) "Externalities and Public Goods," *Economica*, 39, 78–87.

Isard, W. (1956) *Location and Space Economy*, New York, Wiley.

Isard, W. (1975) *Introduction to Regional Science*, Englewood Cliffs, N.J., Prentice-Hall.

James, E. (1979) "Joint Goods, Collective Goods, and External Effects; Comment," *Journal of Political Economy*, 79, 1129–35.

King, L.J. (1984) "Central Place Theory," in Thrall, G.I. (ed.), *Scientific Geography Series*, Vol. 1, Beverley Hills, Calif., Sage.

King, L.J., and Golledge, R.G. (1978) *Cities, Space, and Behavior: The Elements of Urban Geography*, Englewood Cliffs, N.J., Prentice-Hall, 213–37.

Lea, A.C. (1979) "Welfare Theory, Public Goods, and Public Facility Location," *Geographical Analysis*, 2, 217–39.

Lounsbury, J.F., Sommers, L.M., and Fernald, E.A. (1981) *Land Use: A Spatial Approach*, Dubuque, Iowa, Kendall/Hunt.

Mayer, H.M. and Hayes, C.R. (1983) *Land Uses in American Cities*, Champaign, Ill., Park Press.

Mills, E. (1972) *Studies in the Structure of the Urban Economy*, Washington, D.C., Resources for the Future.

Mills, E. and MacKinnon, J. (1973) "Notes on the New Urban Economics," *Bell Journal of Economics and Management Science*, 4, 593–601.

Mumford, L. (1961) *The City in History: Its Origins, its Transformations, and its Prospects*, New York, Harcourt Brace Jovanovitch.

Musgrave, R.A. (1969) "The Provision for Social Goods," in Margolis, J. and Guitton, H. (eds.), *Public Economics*, New York, St. Martin's Press.

Muth, R.F. (1969) *Cities and Housing: The Spatial Pattern of Urban Residential Land Use*, Chicago, University of Chicago Press.

Netzer, D. (1966) *Economics of the Property Tax*, Washington, D.C. Brookings institution.

Newling, B.E. (1966) "Urban Growth and Spatial Structure: Mathematical Models and Empirical Evidence," *Geographical Review*, 56, 213–25.

Oldman, O., and Aaron, H. (1965) "Assessment–Sales Ratios under the Boston Property Tax," *National Tax Journal*, 18, 36–49.

Paglin, M., and Fogarty, M. (1972) "Equity and the Property Tax: A New Conceptual Focus," *National Tax Journal*, 25, 557–65.

Peterson, G. (1973) *Property Tax Reform*, Washington, D.C., The Urban Institute.

Phlips, L. (1974) *Applied Consumption Analysis*, Amsterdam, North–Holland.

Pines, D. (1975) "On the Spatial Distribution of Households According to Income," *Economic Geography*, 51, 142–9.

Pirenne, H. (1925) *Medieval Cities*, Princeton, N.J., Princeton University Press.

Polinksy, A.M., and Shavell, S. (1976) "Amenities and Property Values in a Model of an Urban Area," *Journal of Public Economics*, 5, 119–29.

Puryear, D.L., Ross, J., and Shapiro, P. (eds.) (1979) "Proceedings of a Conference of Tax and Expenditure limitations," in *National Tax Journal* (supplement), 32, June.

Richardson, H.W. (1977) *The New Urban Economics and Alternatives*, London, Pion.

Rogers, A. (1985) "Regional Population Projection Models", in Thrall, G.I. (ed.) *Scientific Geography Series*, 4, Beverly Hills, CA, Sage.

Samuelson, P.A. (1954) "The Pure Theory of Public Expenditure," *Review of Economics and Statistics*, 36, 387–9.

Samuelson, P.A. (1955) "Diagrammatic Exposition of a Theory of Public Expenditures," *Review of Economics and Statistics*, 37, 350–6.

Samuelson, P.A. (1969) "The Pure Theory of Public Expenditure and Taxation." in Margolis, J., and Guitton, H. (eds.), *Public Economics*, New York, St. Martin's Press.

Sandler, T. (1975) "Pareto Optimality, Pure Public Goods, Impure Public Goods and Multiregional Spillovers," *Scottish Journal of Political Economy*, 22, 25–38.

Sauberer, M. and Cserjan, K. (1972) "Sozialräumliche Gliederung Wien 1961: Ergebnisse einer Faktorensnalyse'," *Der Aufbau*, 27, 284–306, as quoted in White, P., *The West European City*, New York, Longman, 1984.

Schuler, R., and Holahan, W. (1977) "Optimal Size and Spacing of Public Facilities in Metropolitan Areas: The Maximum Covering Location Problem Revisited," *Papers of the Regional Science Association*, 39, 137–56.

Smith, T.R. (1972) "Sales Ratios and Property Tax Regressivity," *Assessors' Journal*, 7, 25–43.

Solow, R.M. (1972) "Congestion, Density Costs and the Use of Land in Transportation," *Swedish Journal of Economics*, 74, 161–73.

Thrall, G.I. (1979a) "States of Urban Spatial Structure," *Environment and Planning A*, 11, 23–35.

Thrall, G.I. (1979b) "Public Goods and the Derivation of Land Value Assessment Schedules within a Spatial Equilibrium Setting," *Geographical Analysis*, 11, 23–35.

Thrall, G.I. (1979c) "Spatial Inequities in Tax Assessment: A Case Study of Hamilton, Ontario," *Economic Geography*, 55, 123–34.

Thrall, G.I. (1979d) "A Geographic Criterion for Identifying Property Tax Assessment Inequity," *Professional Geographer*, 31, 278–83.

Thrall, G.I. (1980a) "The Consumption Theory of Land Rent," *Urban Geography*, 1, 350–70.

Thrall, G.I. (1980b) "Property, Sales, Income Taxes and Urban Spatial Structure," *Environment and Planning A*, 12, 1287–96.

Thrall, G.I. (1981a) "Taxation and the Consumption Theory of Land Rent," *Professional Geographer*, 33, 197–207.

Thrall, G.I. (1981b) "Dynamics in the Structural Form of Property Taxes," *Professional Geographer*, 33, 450–6.

Thrall, G.I. (1982a) "Public Goods, Externalities, and the Consumption Theory of Land Rent," *Papers, Regional Science Association* (Montreal Conference), 50, 132–49.

Thrall, G.I. (1982b) "Mortgage Interest Rate Deductions and the Consumption Theory of Land Rent," *Canadian Geographer*, 26, 142–52.

Thrall, G.I. (1982c) "The Effect of Rising Transportation Cost upon Urban Spatial Structure: An Analysis Using the Graphical Consumption Theory of Land Rent," *Urban Geography*, 3, 121–41.

Thrall, G.I. (1983a) "The Proportion of Household Income Devoted to Mortgage Payments: A Model with Supporting Evidence," *Annals of the Association of American Geographers*, 73 (June), 220–30.

Thrall, G.I. (1983b) "Three Pure Planning Scenarios, and the Consumption Theory of Land Rent," *Political Geography Quarterly*, 2 (July), 219–31.

Thrall, G.I. (1985) "Derivation of Income Necessary for Prospective Movers to Be Indifferent between Two Locations: A Simulation Using a Dynamic-Menu Display with a Program in BASIC," in *Modeling and Simulation* (Proceedings of the Sixteenth Annual Pittsburgh Conference, Department of Electrical Engineering, School of Engineering, University of Pittsburgh), pt. 1, 16, 81–6.

Tiebout, C.M. (1961) "An Economic Theory of Fiscal Decentralization," in Margolis, J. (ed.), *Public Finances: Needs, Sources and Utilization*, Princeton, N.J. Princeton University Press, 79–96.

Utter, W.T. (1956) *Granville: The Story of an Ohio Village*, Granville, Ohio, Granville Historical Society/Denison University.

Von Thünen, J.H. (1821) *Der isolierte Staat in Beziehung auf Landwirstschaft und Nationalekonomie*, Hamburg.

Webber, M.J. (1979) *Information Theory and Urban Spatial Structure*, London, Croom Helm.

Werner, C. (1985) "Spatial Transportation modeling," in Thrall, G.I. (ed.), *Scientific Geography Series*, Vol. 5, Beverly Hills, Calif., Sage.

Wheaton, W.C. (1974) "A Comparative Static Analysis of Urban Spatial Structure," *Journal of Economic Theory*, 9, 223–37.

White, P. (1984) *The West European City*, New York, Longman.

Wilson, A.G. (1974) *Urban and Regional Models in Geography and Planning*, New York, Wiley.

Wright, C. (1977) "Financing Public Goods and Residential Location," *Urban Studies*, 14, 51–8.

Yellin, J. (1974) "Urban Population Distribution, Family Income, and Social Prejudice: I, The Long Narrow City," *Journal of Urban Economics*, 1, 21–47.

Index